Allegorizing History

DISTINGUISHED DISSERTATIONS IN CHRISTIAN THEOLOGY

Series Foreword

We are living in a vibrant season for academic Christian theology. After a hiatus of some decades, a real flowering of excellent systematic and moral theology has emerged. This situation calls for a series that showcases the contributions of newcomers to this ongoing and lively conversation. The journal *Word & World: Theology for Christian Ministry* and the academic society Christian Theological Research Fellowship (CTRF) are happy to cosponsor this series together with our publisher Pickwick Publications (an imprint of Wipf and Stock Publishers). Both the CTRF and *Word & World* are interested in excellence in academics but also in scholarship oriented toward Christ and the Church. The volumes in this series are distinguished for their combination of academic excellence with sensitivity to the primary context of Christian learning. We are happy to present the work of these young scholars to the wider world and are grateful to Luther Seminary for the support that helped make it possible.

Alan G. Padgett
Professor of Systematic Theology
Luther Seminary

Beth Felker Jones
Assistant Professor of Theology
Wheaton College

www.ctrf.info
www.luthersem.edu/word&world

Allegorizing History

The Venerable Bede, Figural Exegesis, and Historical Theory

TIMOTHY J. FURRY

☙PICKWICK *Publications* • Eugene, Oregon

ALLEGORIZING HISTORY
The Venerable Bede, Figural Exegesis, and Historical Theory

Distinguished Dissertations in Christian Theology 10

Copyright © 2013 Timothy J. Furry. All rights reserved. Except for brief quotations in critical publications or reviews, no part of this book may be reproduced in any manner without prior written permission from the publisher. Write: Permissions, Wipf and Stock Publishers, 199 W. 8th Ave., Suite 3, Eugene, OR 97401.

Image of Ezra from the Codex Amiatinus used with permission of National Central Library of Florence, Italy.

Pickwick Publications
An Imprint of Wipf and Stock Publishers
199 W. 8th Ave., Suite 3
Eugene, OR 97401

www.wipfandstock.com

ISBN 13: 978-1-62032-656-5

Cataloguing-in-Publication data:

Furry, Timothy J.

   Allegorizing history : the Venerable Bede, figural exegesis, and historical theory / Timothy J. Furry.

   Distinguished Dissertations in Christian Theology 10

   xii + 162 pp. ; 23 cm. Includes bibliographical references and index(es).

   ISBN 13: 978-1-62032-656-5

   1. Historiography. 2. Bede, the Venerable, Saint, 673–735—Historiography. 3. History—Religious aspects—Christianity. 3. Bible—Criticism, interpretation, etc. 4. History—Philosophy. I. Title. II. Series.

BS511.3 .F98 2013

Manufactured in the U.S.A.

For Corrie

Contents

List of Images | viii

Acknowledgments | ix

Introduction | 1

1 (Re)Framing History: A Contemporary Historiography of Bede's *Historia* | 12

2 Can History Be Figural? A Study of Bede's *Historia Ecclesiastica* and *De Templo* | 44

3 Interpreting Genesis: Creation and the Relationship between the Literal and Figural Senses | 64

4 Anachronism and the Status of the Past in Bede's *Historia* and Figural Exegesis | 92

5 Bede and Frank Ankersmit: The Inevitability of Figural History | 112

Conclusion | 135

Bibliography | 147

Index | 159

Images

Image 1: Ezra in the Codex Amiatinus | 99

Acknowledgments

THIS BOOK CAN BE blamed on many people. Probably most important, at least in terms of its genesis, was Robert Orsi. Professor Orsi came for a graduate seminar at the University of Dayton where we discussed his fascinating reflections in *Between Heaven and Earth*.[1] At the time, I was wrestling with questions about the relationship between scholarly descriptions of religious practices and how those practicing them would self describe.[2] The conversation turned to the complexities in descriptive statements in the writing of history and anthropology, and with utmost seriousness and a hint of cynicism I asked, "What is history?" Many in the room furrowed their eyebrows at me indicating misunderstanding, disapproval, confusion, or a combination thereof. Not even slightly fazed by my query, Orsi responded: "Great question." That exchange resulted in several brief conversations with Bob during seminar breaks where he introduced me to contemporary historical theory, specifically Constantin Fasolt and Frank Ankersmit. He only somewhat jokingly admonished me not to tell anyone that he gave me these names to study. At the time, I did not understand why, but I heeded the advice from such an accomplished scholar and thinker. The proverbial cat is now out of the bag. While I doubt he will ever read this, please accept my sincere apologies Professor Orsi. What follows in my argument owes an immense debt to the thinkers Orsi recommended.

1. Orsi, *Between Heaven and Earth: Religious Worlds People Make and the Scholars Who Study Them*.
2. Thanks to Orsi's recommendation of Constantin Fasolt, I would later realize that I am actually wrestling with the difference in grammar or logic between first and third person statements. Ludwig Wittgenstein summarizes it nicely: "One can mistrust one's own senses, but not one's own belief. If there were a verb meaning 'to believe falsely,' it would not have any significant first person present indicative." *Philosophical Investigations*, 190.

There are many others to whom I owe a debt as well; while perhaps painfully obvious, my dissertation committee who trusted me enough to make the argument I have made deserve praise: William Portier, Dennis Doyle, Silviu Bunta, Ephraim Radner, and John Inglis. They have been extremely gracious and generous. I want to especially thank John and Ephraim. As my director, John worked with me constantly, offered critical remarks, and encouraged my work every step of the way. I think Radner's work is some of the most important theology being done in North America right now. He deserves more credit and a wider readership than he currently enjoys. Ephraim has been involved more with my work for years, and his help, encouragement, and insight have been invaluable. Moreover, I am forever grateful for the advice in other personal matters even more important than this work that Ephraim has provided me. Frank Ankersmit, whose work also deserves a wider audience, read parts of this manuscript and offered wonderful feedback. His consistent and incisive correspondence with a strange, American graduate student who emailed him out of the blue one day is a testament to his character and love of teaching and scholarship. Ethan Smith and Wes Arblaster also functioned as critical sounding boards as I worked through my argument. Their comments and feedback have made this book better, but more importantly their friendship helped sustain me through my years of study.

Beth Felker Jones and Alan Padgett, the editors of the *Distinguished Dissertations in Christian Theology Series* in which this volume appears, also deserve my gratitude. Their helpful suggestions improved the final manuscript, as did the editors, Charlie Collier and Dave Belcher, at Cascade Books. Christian Amondson, also from Wipf and Stock, made the publishing process much easier as well. Mary Peterson, librarian at Cranbrook Kingswood where I currently teach, formatted the manuscript and assembled the index. Mary's attention to detail and love of all things book related made my life much easier and better.

Finally, and most crucially, I thank my family. My parents instilled in me an inquisitive mind that should not shirk hard questions and have been an unfailing support and encouragement. My children, Ezekiel and Samuel, without conscious knowledge of doing so, made sacrifices for me as well. There were many times I could have been playing or tending to them that I was not because of this book—not to mention the times when I was "with" them though absent in mind because of this project. Most of all, thanks to my wife, Corrie. To allow me to reach this point, she has endured three moves (two within a couple weeks of each other) and more uncertainty than she probably expected. She even ended up teaching junior high, which was not in her plans. Her ability to adapt and be open to God's movement and work in her life inspires me. It demonstrates the openness we humans should have before God's providential work in history. Only she knows what it could possibly mean for this work to be dedicated to her.

—T. J. F.
Feast of St. Benedict
Anno Domini Nostri Jesu Christi

Introduction

WHAT IS HISTORY? THIS question can be taken in many ways, including radically skeptical ones, but I ask it not with that axe to grind. Instead, I ask it because it has become clear to me, through my study of Bede and other ancient Christians, that history is not so simple. To be sure, many, if not all scholars, know that thanks to the work of postmodern philosophers and twentieth-century historical theorists like R. G. Collingwood, Hans-Georg Gadamer, and Hayden White. In what follows, I will show that there are competing notions and purposes of historical practice, more specifically between Bede and the scholars who have recently studied him. Moreover, I seek to shed light on why this difference matters and what implications result in such competing notions and practices of history, especially in the exegesis of Scripture as well as how exegesis also influences conceptions of history. My work here is an extension of historians and theologians who have sought to blur the lines between theology and other disciplines, like social theory and politics, in both historical and contemporary arguments.[1] In other words, if biblical exegesis was not an isolated discipline for ancient and medieval Christians, then its effects should be seen in other arenas. My argument here is that one of these arenas or disciplines is history.

There have been many recent attempts to understand ancient and medieval Christian exegesis[2] and even attempts to retrieve some kind of

---

1. Some examples of such works appear in the next footnote, but I will mention two others here: Milbank, *Theology and Social Theory* and Caspary, *Politics and Exegesis*.

2. For a sampling of such work see, for example, de Lubac, *Exégèse medieval*. For the English translation, see de Lubac, *Medieval Exegesis*; idem, *History and Spirit*; Smalley, *The Study of the Bible in the Middle Ages*; Auerbach, "Figura;" Whitman, *Allegory*; Dawson, *Allegorical Readers and Cultural Revision in Ancient Alexandria*; idem, *Christian Figural Reading and the Fashioning of Identity*; Simonetti, *Biblical Interpretation in the Early Church*; Turner, *Eros and Allegory*; idem, "Allegory in Christian Late Antiquity;" Young, *Biblical Exegesis and the Formation of Christian Culture*; Ayres, *Nicea and Its Legacy*; O'Keefe and Reno, *Sanctified Vision*; DiTommaso and Turcescu, *Reception and Interpretation of the Bible in Late Antiquity*; Spijker, *Multiple Meanings of Scripture*;

theological exegesis of Scripture from biblical scholars.[3] However, few, if any, have attempted to figurally exegete Scripture in a patristic or medieval mode.[4] I find this lacuna interesting and wish to begin to understand why allegorical/figural readings no longer appear persuasive to modern minds. This book is the start of that inquiry. My initial conclusions are found in what follows and have to do with how theological and philosophical conceptions of history and its practice impact the writing of history and reading of Scripture.

I explore the relationship of the exegetical and historical works of the Venerable Bede to show how conceptions of the past determine the writing of history. I argue that while Bede undoubtedly had a theological conception of the past, his lack of attention to important issues in philosophy and exegesis resulted in ambiguity and problematic readings of the literal sense of Scripture. The contemporary lesson to be learned from Bede is that trenchant philosophical and theological issues matter in the writing of history, since they are part of its inevitable representational structure. Bede is treated, not as object in the past, but as an historian worthy of a place at the table alongside contemporary historians, despite the issues I find in his work. In fact, despite his own separation of exegesis and history, it is shown that Bede did, just like his contemporary interpreters, represent the past in empirically ambiguous ways that includes theology.

On the surface, Bede may appear to be a perfect match for my study, but once one begins reading his work it will be discovered that Bede was not interested in the theoretical questions that animate my work in what follows. Indeed, as Arthur Holder has said, the "non-speculative quality of all Bede's writing is inescapable."[5] From his English upbringing[6] to a void in

---

Kannengiesser, *Handbook of Patristic Exegesis*; Reventhlow, *History of Biblical Interpretation, Volume 1*; idem, *History of Biblical Interpretation, Volume 2*; McAuliffe, Walfish, and Goering, *With Reverence for the Word*.

3. This literature is also vast and includes entire commentary series, like *Brazos Theological Commentary on the Bible* and Eerdmans' *Two Horizons New Testament Commentary*. Some notable works and authors: Childs, *Biblical Theology in Crisis*; Hays, *Echoes of Scripture in the Letters of Paul*; idem, *Conversion of the Imagination*; Watson, *Text, Church and World*; Fowl, *Engaging Scripture*; Green and Turner, *Between Two Horizons*; Minear, *Bible and the Historian*.

4. Ephraim Radner might be the sole exception, though he does not address theoretical concerns in the historical task in an explicit manner. See Radner, *The End of the Church*; idem, *Hope Among the Fragments*; idem, *Leviticus*, and most recently, idem, *A Brutal Unity*.

5. Holder, "Bede and the Tradition of Patristic Exegesis," 406.

6. Capelle, "Le rôle théologique de Bède le Vénérable," 1–40.

his library[7] and also his own historical and pastoral situation,[8] scholars have provided differing rationales for why Bede did not undertake "systematic" or speculative theology like Augustine. While these historical speculations are not mutually exclusive, I tend to think that Bede's own circumstances, which included a fledgling church and priests in need of basic training, are what kept him focused on the practical and concrete.

Part of the reason I have worked with Bede is precisely due to his less speculative focus, because I am convinced that philosophical and theological issues matter even in more concrete disciplines like history. I also selected Bede because the relationship between his exegetical and historical works has drawn the attention of many scholars. In what follows, I will show that Bede's narrow, if historically necessary, focus on practical matters actually gets him into unnecessary conundrums, especially in his literal commenting on Genesis. In short, Bede's lack of attention to philosophical issues often impacts his historical writing and literal exegesis, giving him problems that someone like Augustine was able to avoid because of his philosophical and theological "speculations." More specifically, I intend to argue that while Bede did attempt to sharply distinguish the literal and figural senses, thereby prompting him to not figurally exegete non-biblical history, he did it anyway insofar as all historical inquiry is intrinsically constituted by representation; the necessity of representation in history, and what I mean by it, occupies the subject of my final chapter. Ultimately, I will suggest that Augustine and Bede differ in their theologies of nature and grace and that these frame and shape their reading of Scripture and writing of history.

In order to prevent misunderstanding, I think it appropriate to say what I am not arguing or doing at the outset, even before I summarize each chapter and clarify how I am using terms. I am decidedly not advocating merely propositional understandings of texts. Far from it; Bede did not read texts exclusively in this way, but he also did not have our unquestioned impulse to place all texts and events in their historical context; that is, it did not occur to him that there is just *one* proper historical context by which events, persons, and objects *must* be understood. The polarization between such conceptions, either propositional truths or mere historically embodied and contingent claims, is precisely what I want to challenge. I am also not advocating a disavowal of historical inquiry or its usefulness. I use contemporary historical practices and historians to make my argument, and I do not think it inconsistent with the case I am making. More specifically,

---

7. Bonner, "Bede and Medieval Civilization," 71–90.
8. Davidse, "Sense of History in the Works of the Venerable Bede," 647–95.

I want to demonstrate the limits of history so they can be transcended.[9] I think that can happen, and to invoke Wittgenstein, to think otherwise is to be held captive by a picture. Hence, I am seeking more to disabuse us of certain attitudes and beliefs regarding history than to do away with history itself, whatever that could even mean. If one believes I am doing away with history, then this only reveals that one cannot think of history in a different way—much like a blind person saying there cannot be a chair in the room because she cannot see it.

I beg the reader's patience as I muddle through this difficult terrain hoping to clear a path for subsequent work that will make this argument clearer and more persuasive. Many of the issues I have raised in this introduction so far do not receive direct treatment here. However, I think it important to mention them because it helps properly locate and frame my work both conceptually and even historically. Before proceeding to the body of my argument, I should clarify how I am and will use certain important terms and give a brief summary of Bede's life to offer some historical context to Bede's own writings and theology.

Brief Summary of Bede's Life

The specifics of Bede's life, including his monastic discipline, remain fuzzy. There are no extant English monastic rules from Bede's time, and we possess only one rule prior to the Carolingian reforms. Unfortunately, this rule dates well past Bede's time. There have been attempts to reconstruct and understand Bede's life in some general fashion from Northumbrian culture, but these usually begin by noting the lack of evidence and texts that undergird the necessary confidence to speak with any historical authority specifically about Bede.[10] The best primary source evidence and description we have comes from Bede himself.

> I, Bede, servant of Christ and priest of the monastery of St. Peter and St. Paul which is at Wearmouth and Jarrow, have, with the help of God and to the best of my ability, put together this account of the history of the Church of Britain and of the English

---

9. On this I am indebted to Fasolt, *Limits of History*.

10. Thompson, *Bede: His Life, Times and Writings*; Blair, *Northumbria in the Days of Bede*; idem, *World of Bede*; Fairless, *Northumbria's Golden Age*; Farrell, *Bede and Anglo-Saxon England*; Higham, *English Empire*; Meyvaert, "Bede and the Church Paintings of Wearmouth-Jarrow," 63–77; Brown, *Bede, The Venerable*; Wormald with Bullough and Collins, *Ideal and Reality in Frankish and Anglo-Saxon Society*; Goffart, *Narrators of Barbarian History (A.D. 550–800)*; Ward, *Venerable Bede*; DeGregorio, "Nostrorum socordiam temporum," 107–22.

people in particular, gleaned either from ancient documents or from tradition or from my own knowledge. I was born in the territory of this monastery. When I was seven years of age I was, by the care of my kinsmen, put into the charge of the reverend Abbot Benedict and then of Ceolfrith, to be educated. From then on I have spent all my life in this monastery, applying myself entirely to the study of the Scriptures; and, amid the observance of the discipline of the Rule and the daily task of singing in the church, it has always been my delight to learn or to teach or to write. At the age nineteen I was ordained deacon and at the age of thirty, priest, both times through the ministration of the reverend Bishop John on the direction of Abbot Ceolfrith. From the time I became a priest until the fifty-ninth year of my life I have made it my business, for my own benefit and that of my brothers, to make brief extracts from the works of the venerable fathers on the holy Scriptures, or to add notes of my own to clarify their sense and interpretation.[11]

Immediately following this quotation, Bede lists the works he has produced up to that point in his life. There has also been an attempt to reconstruct the books he had available in Wearmouth-Jarrow libraries.[12]

Despite the copious scholarship on later monasticism in England,[13] Sarah Foot has provided the only English account of Anglo-Saxon monasticism in Bede's day.[14] It is reasonable to believe that more general studies on Benedictine monastic life in the late patristic or early medieval time periods would shed light on Bede's life.[15] However, his life at the edges of the civilization at that time might have caused important differences in how monasticism functioned; this is partly what Foot is driving at in her argument that most monastic rules were mixed—that is they contained both

---

11. Bede, *Ecclesiastical History of the Anglo-Saxon People*, 5.24.

12. Laistner, "Library of the Venerable Bede."

13. David Knowles is the prime representative of this scholarship. See, for example, Knowles, *Monastic Order in England*; idem, *Medieval Religious Houses, England and Wales*; idem, *Heads of Religious Houses, England and Wales, 940–1216*.

14. Foot, *Monastic Life in Anglo-Saxon England, c. 600–900*.

15. For example, Dalye, *Benedictine Monasticism*; Leclerq, *Love of Learning and the Desire for God*; Clark, *Benedictines in the Middle Ages*. The debate between Francis Clark and Adalbert de Vogüé on the origins of Benedictine monasticism are only ancillary to my concerns, since my focus is on monastic culture in Bede's day. See Clark, *"Gregorian" Dialogues and the Origins of Benedictine Monasticism*; Gregory the Great *Dialogues* and *Commentaire sur le premier livre des Rois*. For more specifics on how Bede's monastic life impacted his exegesis, see DeGregorio, "Bede, the Monk, as Exegete: Evidence from the Commentary on Ezra-Nehemiah," 343–69.

contemplative and secular components making the boundaries between cloisters and the world more porous than most monasteries.

In summary of this literature, we can say about Bede, however tentatively, that his focus was on devotion and obedience to God through learning, teaching, and writing. Moreover, he also sought to reform the monasteries that he thought were becoming lax and unfaithful, and this can be seen in his later exegesis.[16] It is difficult to tell if Bede favored the mixed rule that Foot's scholarship is describing or if it is, in fact, the object of his criticism. Nonetheless, his concern for the education and faithfulness of the English church shines forth on every page of his work. What shaped Bede the most was perhaps liturgical singing and the Office. Cuthbert records that near the time of Bede's death the antiphons of the office came most readily to Bede.[17] In my view, it would be hard to overestimate the importance of the daily office, monastic discipline, and liturgical life on Bede's work and writing. However, the dearth of specifics on Bede's practices makes it difficult to address these with any authority in my subsequent analysis.

Terminological Clarification

I will begin with the easiest, history. The vast majority of times I use the word "history" I do not mean the past or what happened in the past. Instead, I follow Constantin Fasolt's definition: "By history I mean knowledge of the past, as well as the technique by which such knowledge is produced and the activity required to that end, especially in the forms developed by professionally trained historians."[18] Distinguishing the past and how it is known is of utmost importance in my argument because our knowledge of the past impacts what counts as relevant history or *as* historical. Thus, my primary concern is with the discipline that produces knowledge of the past, though I do use history to mean the past at times. Context will clarify.

More slippery and difficult to define is "figural." I will give a brief definition and then provide an argument for it, though I do not take my use of it to be highly contested in current scholarship. Basically, I follow Erich Auerbach, "Figural interpretation establishes a connection between two events or persons, the first of which signifies not only itself but also the second, while the second encompasses or fulfills the first. The two poles of the figures, are within time, but both, being real events or figures are within

---

16. For more specifically on Bede's later works and his attempt at reform, see DeGregorio, "*Nostrorum socordiam temporum;*" idem, "Bede's *In Ezram et Neemiam* and the Reform of the Northumbrian Church," 1–25.

17. Cuthbert, "Letter on the Death of Bede," 300–301.

18. Fasolt, *Limits of History*, xiii.

time, within the stream of historical life."[19] This definition could use further elaboration, so perhaps what I take figural to not mean will be helpful to sketch. Figural reading does not proceed by recourse to the category of meaning, if we take meaning to be logically independent from the words or events to which it is related. If meaning is logically independent, then the meaning can then substitute completely for the word or event in question. Once one "gets" the meaning, the original event or language can now be superseded by its meaning. Engaging Auerbach and regarding logical independence of meaning, David Dawson says, "one can state meaning apart from the representation without loss; the representation is, at best, a useful but dispensable illustration."[20] Hence, figural reading decidedly does not imply the loss of the historical event or literal sense of a text.

I use Auerbach cautiously and with some modification, however. While my argument will show where and how I depart from Auerbach, I will give some preliminary details regarding my reservations with his definition. I first want to note that I do not object to the language quoted above in and of itself. I think it adequate as a formal definition. However, Auerbach inflects this definition in potentially problematic ways. Auerbach's very conception of history is what I find problematic and Dawson once again helpfully teases out the issue at hand. Comparing Auerbach to Origen Dawson explains:

> For Auerbach, what is historical is what is real, and what is real is what is material or bodily. Real, material things are what they are, and they do not exist merely to signify other things. So when Auerbach says that figural reading does not undermine the physical or bodily reality, he means that figural reading does not undermine the physical or bodily reality of what the text represents. Origen also has an interest in preserving the historical character of biblical figures, but to him, their historical character consists in their act of occurring in the real world and their continuing capacity to affect individuals. Origen is no less concerned than Auerbach with the historical as the real, but for Origen, reality is a quality first of all of events that engage the spiritual lives of individuals in the present.[21]

My concern is not with Origen, but Dawson's words here show that what one takes to be historical makes all the difference. History is not simply given.

---

19. Auerbach, "Figura," 53.

20. See Dawson, *Christian Figural Reading and the Fashioning of Identity*, 86; for more see ibid., 84–91.

21. Dawson, *Christian Figural Reading and the Fashioning of Identity*, 115. For Dawson's detailed analysis of Auerbach, see *ibid*, 83–113.

There are not facts just "out there," including so-called empirical reality. As a result, I do not adhere to idealism, but I do find problematic philosophical versions of empiricism that have not reckoned with contemporary philosophy of language. I need not give such an explicit philosophical account for my argument here, though I do presume it throughout. Suffice it to say that I find the work of Wittgenstein, Sellars, and Quine congenial.[22]

Figural and allegorical exegesis can but do not have to be distinguished. Sometimes allegorical reading uses historical events and texts as a means to discuss something logically independent from the event or text. The likes of Henri de Lubac have shown why allegory is a complex term and frequently used equivocally in the hands of Christian thinkers through the ages.[23] Aside from my summary of others who use such language, I sometimes avoid the term allegory because of its status as a literary device that can be deployed without reference to historical matters as an intra-textual or extra-textual reference without grounding in physical reality. Again, it has not always been used this way and certainly nothing intrinsic to it, as far as I can discern, requires such an ahistorical deployment. When I do use allegorical, I use it as synonymous with figural as sketched above.

Finally, the literal or historical sense needs clarification. I have yet to find a more concise and accurate description of the literal sense in early church exegesis than Lewis Ayers. Though he prefers "plain sense" on account of modern connotations of "literal," I will use his summary that he borrowed from Eugene Rogers' work on Aquinas. The literal sense "is the way the words run."[24] While seemingly simple, the literal sense itself can be multivalent. Since Christian authors believed that God and humans were both the authors of Scripture, a text can be read literally or plainly by discerning who the speaker is at any given point, along with discerning which, if any, rhetorical device might be at work (i.e. genre).[25] As I will show, what one takes the literal sense to be makes an enormous difference for

---

22. I am indebted to the following works of each philosopher just mentioned: Wittgenstein, *Philosophical Investigations*; idem, *On Certainty*; Quine, "Two Dogmas of Empiricism," 20–43; Sellars, "Empiricism and the Philosophy of Mind," 253–329.

23 de Lubac, *Exégèse medieval*; in English *Medieval Exegesis*.

24. Ayers, *Nicea and Its Legacy*, 32–33. Cf. Rogers, "How the Virtues of an Interpreter Presuppose and Perfect Hermeneutics," 64–81. For more on the literal or plain sense, see Frei, "The 'Literal' Reading of Biblical Narrative in the Christian Tradition," 36–77; Tanner, "Theology and the Plain Sense," 59–78. Specifically on Aquinas, see Johnson, "Another Look at the Plurality of the Literal Sense," 117–41. For an overview of early- and mid-twentieth century views of the literal sense, see Scheidners, "Faith, Hermeneutics, and the Literal Sense of Scripture," 719–36.

25. See Ayers, *Nicea and Its Legacy*, 33–40. See also Rogers, "How the Virtues of an Interpreter Presuppose and Perfect Hermeneutics," 64–68.

subsequent figural readings (or what counts as a figural reading), since the literal is constitutive of the figural. However, the figural also impacts literal due to the representational structure of historical writing.

Summary

My argument is intended to be a contribution to theology today. However, I do make advances in Bedan scholarship, as well as the understanding of *figura* and the figural sense, especially in how they have been conceived in the twentieth century. Regarding scholarship on Bede, my account is probably the most explicitly theological reading of Bede insofar as I seek to understand the theological relationships between his texts, as well as his own theological insights as a Christian thinker. I will highlight both aspects of my contributions in the following summary.

Chapter 1 attempts to focus my argument through a historiography of recent scholarship on Bede's *Ecclesiastical History* and how it is conceived in relationship to his exegesis and theology. I begin with Plummer's introduction to his 1896 critical edition of Bede's famous text, which set the stage for most twentieth century Bedan scholarship. Early twentieth-century work on Bede has dogmatic overtones in its evaluation, either positive or negative, of Bede's historical work. Scholars either read Bede as a precursor to modern historical methods and criteria, or they hold him subject to such standards both explicitly and implicitly. Nearly all these early scholars have trouble making sense of Bede's figural exegesis and integrating his obvious theological purposes for the *Historia*, especially the miracles Bede recounts. Bede frequently ends up looking like a schizophrenic scholar lapsing in and out of "true" historical inquiry and theology.

As the century marches onward, scholars become more sensitive to Bede's theological concerns and the difference between the eighth and twentieth centuries. Through attention to Bede's "*uera lex historia*," scholars come to more precise understandings of what Bede thought he was doing. Thus, mid- and late-twentieth-century scholars often level a criticism of anachronism on their predecessors for not reading Bede in his patristic and Augustinian heritage. For the first time, Bede seeks to be understood within a larger theological and even metaphysical framework. Tensions in understanding Bede come to a head in the work of Jan Davidse, who rightly notes that modern conceptions of history, and even fallacies like anachronism, are foreign to Bede. This leaves one asking: How can contemporary understandings of history make sense of Bede's histories when the differences between them seem so great? This question haunts my argument through the final chapters.

The second chapter offers a focused analysis of Bede's *Historia* by comparing it to his commentary on the temple (*De templo*) because Bede was writing both simultaneously. There has been some attention to the relationship between *De templo* and the *Historia*, but my analysis offers an in-depth study of their theological relationship that has only been previously outlined or suggested. While maintaining his broader theology of history, which will be summarized in chapter 4, Bede surprisingly does not figurally exegete historical events. In other words, Bede does not make direct connections between events in the English church and Scripture even when connections seem to be obvious. For example, Bede's insistence about the importance of kings for the building of Christianity in England is not explicitly connected to Solomon's use of gentile leaders in building the temple. To be sure, Scripture makes appearances in the *Historia*, but Bede chooses not to make figural connections between the bible and the history he recounts, despite having examples of such in the preceding tradition. The reason why Bede may not make such connections is the subject of the next chapter.

I argue in chapter 3 that Bede's literal exegesis of Genesis 1 provides a theological rationale for why he does not figurally exegete history. By comparing Bede and Augustine, I show how each read the literal sense of Genesis 1 quite differently. In fact, Bede takes Augustine's reading to be allegorical at places, despite these being in Augustine's literal commentary. A prime example of this is Bede's taking "In the beginning" to refer to the actual start of time in conscious difference to Augustine's reading that understands it as a reference to the Word/*Logos*. Moreover, Bede frequently understands a tension to exist between the literal and figural senses to the point where it becomes hard to see how the literal sense is internal to the figural or how the figural is an extension of the literal. The tension manifested in Bede's exegesis comes from his implicit belief that literal language should describe or refer to empirical events. Though the influence of Augustine on Bede has been noted by scholars, no one has provided a comparison of their commentary on Genesis that highlights their different readings of Genesis 1, nor does anyone highlight their different philosophical and theological perspectives that animate their readings. The upshot for my overarching argument demonstrates that theological and philosophical notions and arguments matter for literal and historical reading and writing.

Contemporary historical theory makes its appearance in chapter 4 regarding how the past has been conceived by Bede and how contemporary historians frequently conceive of it. Beginning with defining and summarizing the rise of anachronism in history, I show that concerns to avoid anachronism arose in a particular setting, the early Renaissance, in the thought of Petrarch. In short, anachronism was born from a sense of loss; that the present was no longer like the past and understood to be fundamentally different from it. In comparison, I summarize Bede's conception of the past that did not have concerns about anachronism and how this impacted his history writing and exegesis. Furthermore, I argue that Bede's ignorance of anachronism helped enable Bede to write the *Historia* as an intentional piece of theology, though carrying with it the perplexities and tensions mentioned in the previous chapters.

Building on and extending the work of Jan Davidse who has taken a similar approach in using contemporary historical theory to investigate Bede, chapter 5 continues the use of historical theory by using the work of Frank Ankersmit to distinguish between description and representation in historical writing. I summarize my previous work on Bede to show that he thought historical language or the literal sense only described, language about God being the only exception. Using contemporary philosophy of language, Ankersmit's distinction shows that history cannot be reduced to empirical claims about reality or the past. I compare Ankersmit and Bede to suggest that all history, ancient and contemporary, can be called figural or allegorical insofar as it remains about the past but not reducible to description or reference. I also apply the logic of representation that Ankersmit articulates to Bede's figural exegesis. Ultimately, I conclude that Bede was right to do history theologically, but his specific practice runs into problems. More specifically, Bede's understanding of the presence of the past is helpful for theological conceptions of history, but Bede did not take the next steps in his historical work insofar as he refused to figurally exegete history by not distinguishing description and representation and thereby not clearly understanding that the figural/allegorical sense intrinsically constitutes literal/historical language. Because of the representational constitution of history, Bede and contemporary historians can both be understood to be historians, not merely separated by a temporal gap with their own historical circumstances being the only deciding difference.

I conclude by wrapping up some loose ends and discussing in more detail one specific and theological representational frame, nature and grace, as well as offering more conceptual clarification between Ankersmit's representation in the writing of history and the figural reading of Scripture. The final result of my overall work is an interdisciplinary argument around the work of the Venerable Bede about how different conceptions of the past and the function of historical language impact the writing of history and exegesis in both the past and the present.

I

(Re)Framing History
A Contemporary Historiography of Bede's Historia

"To attempt to judge of Bede merely as an historian is inevitably to misjudge him. In history and in science, as well as in theology, he is before all things the Christian thinker and student."

—CAROLUS PLUMMER
EDITOR'S PREFACE TO THE 1896 *OPERA HISTORICA*

Introduction

AS WITH SCHOLARSHIP ON any historical figure, much has changed in how the Venerable Bede has been understood, specifically as an historian and with respect to what he was trying to accomplish in his *Historia ecclesiastica gentis anglorum*. This chapter will explore historiographical issues beginning with Plummer's introduction to the 1896 edition of the *Historia* and ending with more recent publications on Bede and his histories. I will show how scholars wrestled with integrating Bede's theological, exegetical, and historical works into even a quasi-coherent account throughout the twentieth century, while highlighting theoretical obstacles that caused them difficulties. Due to the extensive writing on this topic, I will have to be selective in my more detailed analysis by studying the more substantive and influential scholarship on Bede and history.

A definite trajectory can be seen in the work on Bede and history in the twentieth century, and it often mirrors developments in historical theory itself as the century progressed; for instance, earlier scholarship frequently addressed questions of miracles and their place in a historical work. In short, authors often see Bede moving in and out of the proper practice of history because of his theological or hagiographical interests. This results in a picture of Bede in constant tension with himself and presumes history to be a simple and objective reporting of facts that can be corroborated through critical study of sources. These scholars tend to be more overtly dogmatic about the superiority of modern historical methods and assumptions in comparison to Bede. In the middle and latter parts of the century, the influence of Bede's exegesis and theological interests on Bede's *Historia* began to be investigated and discussed. A conversation ensued that continued to become more complex as the century moved forward; not only were the influences of Bede's exegetical works and theology seen as important for understanding the *Historia*, larger theoretical concerns about the discipline of history as such began to be addressed.

Setting the Stage: Carolus Plummer's 1896 Edition of the *Historia*

Plummer's English introduction to Bede's *Ecclesiastical History* set the English scholarly agenda on Bede for the twentieth century.[1] Not all scholars agreed with Plummer, but his insightful summary, introduction, and scholarship on manuscripts began the major conversations regarding Bede and his works that took place over the subsequent century. While some of Plummer's work has been rightly criticized and corrected, much of Plummer's scholarship has stood the test of time. For example, his dating of Bede's birth (672/673) has become the presumed date.[2] Plummer understood that Bede primarily thought of himself as a biblical exegete and Christian theologian and that one must understand Bede's exegetical and theological works in order to understand Bede's histories. In this regard, Plummer is like many of the scholars who will follow him and who struggle to integrate Bede's exegesis and theology with the *Historia*.

Mostly sympathetic to Bede and his accomplishments, Plummer takes Bede and other authors from the eighth century at their word. To be sure, Plummer addresses modern concerns, like Bede's allegorical approach to Scripture and the miracles in the *Historia*, but I will say more about that below. The strength of Plummer's work is that he recognizes the importance

---

1. Bede, *Opera Historica*, ix–lxxix. See also Wallace-Hadrill's praise in "Bede and Plummer," 366–85.
2. Bede, *Opera Historica*, xi.

of Bede's monastic way of life for Bede's own scholarship,[3] and he also shows how political concerns and a declining Northumbrian culture (both monastic and secular) influence Bede's narration in the *Historia* and his commentary on Luke.[4] Plummer even takes the time to cite at length Cuthbert's description of Bede's last days that details the kind of monastic and pious life that Bede led.[5]

Plummer describes Bede's "mode of exposition" as "allegorical" and rightly notes the influence of Scripture and preceding patristic, exegetical tradition.[6] Again, showing his sympathy, Plummer states that Bede's allegorical exegesis "rests upon the belief, in itself, surely, no ignoble one, that nothing in Scripture can be devoid of significance."[7] Plummer also astutely describes Bede's use of *sacramentum* in his exegesis as "the inner and spiritual meaning of an external fact, or narrative, or name."[8] Plummer recognizes that Bede's allegorical and figural interpretation does not eclipse the literal or plain sense but seeks to transform it, exempting perhaps Bede's commentary on the Song of Songs.[9] Using Bede's own texts, Plummer rightly attempts to show that Bede's spiritual exegesis is not as arbitrary or subjective as moderns sometimes think. Bede often employed rules and standards in his allegorical method, and Plummer cites many relevant examples.[10] However, Plummer's description does not attempt to understand the theo-logic that underlies Bede's approach to allegorical exegesis in any sufficient detail. Thus, while Plummer can offer an accurate description and summary of what Bede said and how he read Scripture, Plummer does not venture to explicate the logic of what makes allegorical exegesis "work" and explain that to modern readers.

Following his treatment of Bede's allegorical approach to Scripture, Plummer addresses "another point which may strike the modern reader unfavourably . . ."[11] This potentially unfavorable point is the miraculous ele-

---

3. Ibid., xxx–xxxiii.
4. Ibid., xxxiii–xxxv.
5. Ibid., lxxii–lxxviii.
6. Ibid., lvi.
7. Ibid.
8. Ibid., lvii.
9. Ibid., lvii–lix.
10. Ibid., lix *nn.* 6–8.
11. Ibid., lxiv. "Another," in this context, may refer either to Bede's strict orthodoxy or allegorical interpretation. It is unclear. Nonetheless, my point and argument will remain intact regardless of which one Plummer might have had in mind. Of course, it is entirely conceivable that "another" simply means "in addition to" both Bede's allegorical exegesis and adherence to orthodox theology.

ment found in Bede's histories. Plummer somewhat subtly voices suspicion regarding Bede's narration of miracles. For example, he says it was "natural" for Bede and his "religious spirit" to find the supernatural everywhere.[12] A footnote on that sentence states, "There are ages when belief is so utterly uncritical that it does seem as if they could not under any circumstances afford us satisfactory evidence of miraculous occurrences."[13] Moreover, Plummer says that "the large majority of them [medieval miracles] may be set aside at once, as being quite deficient in anything like contemporary evidence."[14] Thus, Plummer dismisses the miracles for numerous reasons. First, they can be condemned on internal evidence (e.g., "being silly" or even immoral).[15] Second, many of the recounted miracles mirror biblical miracles thereby showing their derivative nature. Third, some are classical myths or folklore disguised in Christian garb. And finally, some can be explained simply as coincidences that could have taken place naturally.[16] Plummer does allow, however, for a "residuum" of truth that cannot be so easily explained, albeit rather indecisively: "But, after all these deductions have been made, the question remains, whether there is not a residuum which cannot be explained away."[17] Plummer leaves the topic of miracles at this point and goes on to describe Bede's piety and good sense when it came to monastic discipline (e.g., if one were sick, one could break one's fast for the sake of health) before summarizing Cuthbert's recounting of Bede's death.[18]

After the sympathetic interpretation of Bede's allegorical exegesis, Plummer curiously moves to a more skeptical position with regard to miracles. I find this interesting, but most importantly it reveals how Plummer treated his historical task. It is worth noting that Plummer takes the time to assure his reader that Bede was not a subjective reader of texts, especially Scripture, even though Bede favored figural interpretation. Plummer provides examples or evidence of Bede's interpretive method. This actually fits well with Plummer's later description of Bede's good sense that includes how Bede reads some of Scripture's more difficult exhortations.[19] However, Plummer then quickly

12. Ibid.
13. Ibid., n2. Plummer approvingly cites Charles Gore's 1891 Bampton Lectures at Oxford.
14. Ibid., lxiv.
15. Ibid.
16. Ibid., lxiv–lxv.
17. Ibid., lxv.
18. Ibid., lxv–lxxviii.
19. For example, Plummer notes that Bede read 1 Thess 5:17 and Eph 6:18, which encourages Christians to pray always or without ceasing, does not mean that Christians should always be literally on their knees in explicit prayer. See Bede, *Opera Historica*, lxix..

sets aside miracles for lack of evidence. I find this curious because in one paragraph Plummer uses Bede's texts as evidence (and even defense) for the spiritual interpretation of Scripture based upon the noble belief in Scripture's inspired significance, then a few paragraphs later textual evidence is suddenly insufficient, despite Bede's professed care to check sources.[20] If Plummer wants to hold the belief in the fecund status of Scripture, which is certainly a physical object in the natural world, at least in some sense, then why are miracles not given the same sympathetic treatment?

The answer to the question lies in why Plummer shows more sympathy to allegorical exegesis than to miracles in history, and the answer reveals not only epistemological issues but also ontological ones. While Plummer attempts to read Bede with sympathy and charity, their different philosophical and theological commitments are quickly made manifest. Plummer defends the non-arbitrary nature of allegorical exegesis based on its *method*; it has "fixed laws and rules."[21] Plummer then approvingly cites many examples of Bede's exegesis that demonstrate Bede's insight into the spiritual realm or fair harmony of things.[22] In other words, the application of fixed methodological laws and principles guards against arbitrary human subjectivity thereby preventing figural exegesis from lapsing into arbitrary moments. It is hard to find a more nineteenth-century philosophical view than the one Plummer finds in Bede in order to keep Bede's figural exegesis intelligible and somewhat persuasive for modern readers.

When it comes to miracles in Bede, similar types of epistemological criteria cannot be found to Plummer's (and many others') satisfaction because the laws of nature are just that, immutable laws.[23] Hence, miracles are easier to dismiss, since they would be clear violations of what we know with near certainty does not happen. Plummer might object that words used for figural exegesis and historical events are quite different—true enough. However, they are both "things" (*res*), in that they exist, giving them some shared natural and ontological status, and both are certainly involved in causal and natural relationships; unless, of course, one holds to a Cartesian or Kantian anthropology where the self doing the figural exegesis is

---

20. See, for example, the preface to the *Life of Cuthbert* where Bede discusses giving his text to the local priest who knew Cuthbert to check for accuracy and similarly the preface to the *Historia* submitted to King Ceolwulf prior to its publication.

21. Ibid., lix.

22. Ibid., lxi; see *Historia* 4.23 (214).

23. In fairness, Plummer wrote before Einstein and operated with a more determinist and Newtonian view of nature and reality. Thus, what passed for scientific knowledge for Plummer is quite different than what does for us in light of relativity theory and quantum mechanics.

cordoned off from the causal and natural world into the noumenal realm, which would be far from Bede's theological and Augustinian anthropology and semiotics.[24] Plummer's sympathy with figural exegesis and skepticism toward miracles are therefore in tension, at least as far as Bede would see it. To which side of the scale sympathy for Bede tips depends on many factors, and my point here is not to argue that the miracles in the *Historia* actually happened. Instead, I am showing how Bede's exegesis and history get framed in light of philosophical and theological commitments. This tension will continue throughout the twentieth century as scholars reflect and study Bede's exegesis and history.

Scholarship on Bede's *Historia* in the First Half of the Twentieth Century

The next major works to treat Bede shared similar titles: George F. Browne's *The Venerable Bede: His Life and Writings*[25] and a collection of essays entitled, *Bede: His Life, Times, and Writings: Essays in Commemoration of the Twelfth Centenary of His Death*.[26] Browne calls the *Historia* "Bede's greatest work," though he never explicitly says why or offers the criteria by which he has made such a judgment.[27] The closest Browne comes to offering a rationale for the *Historia* being Bede's greatest work is his calculation of the amount of time it must have taken Bede to write the *Historia* (over 1,800 hours). The fact that Browne structures his entire book around Bede's historical writings is more telling. He begins to treat Bede's oeuvre not in chronological order but with the *Historia*. He gives separate and entire chapters to the *History of the Abbots*, the *Life of St. Cuthbert*, and *Letter to Egbert*, while combining all of Bede's exegesis and homilies into a single chapter of twenty-four pages.[28] Since Bede saw his primary vocation as commenting on the sacred page of Scripture, it is doubtful that he would have thought of the *Historia* as his "greatest" work, and he certainly would not appreciate how little time Browne spends on his biblical exegesis.[29]

---

24. I am not saying that Plummer is necessarily presuming a Kantian or Cartesian anthropology. My point is simply that exegeting a text is not categorically different from the occurrence of miracles insofar as both occur in the "natural" realm without any obvious and salient differences, thereby making Plummer's hypothetical objection problematic.

25. Browne, *Venerable Bede*.

26. Thompson, *Bede*.

27. Browne, *Venerable Bede*, 96.

28. Ibid., 231ff.

29. See Bede, *Histoire Ecclésiastique du Peuple Anglais*, 5.24 where Bede says he applied all of himself and his work to the study of Scripture ("omnem meditandis

The *Historia* is magnificent and worthy of adulation, but Browne goes too far in his evaluation showing his modern preferences for brute facts over theology and the bible.[30] When specifically addressing the *Historia ecclesiastica*, Browne continues to reveal his perspective spending most of his time deciphering Bede's sources and simply summarizing the *Historia*, a necessary and worthwhile task, to be sure. However, he fails to see the connections between the *Historia* and Scripture that Bede intended, making Browne's summary read like a modern history book neglecting faith elements that pervade Bede's own text. Even when Browne does summarize something Bede would have understood to be theological, Browne responds condescendingly and with sarcasm: "There were mines of copper, iron, lead, and silver, with plenty of jet, bright and sparkling, of which Bede remarks that when rubbed it holds fast anything to which it is applied as amber does. He [Bede] adds that when heated it drives away serpents. Probably it does, when it is hot enough."[31] Furthermore, Browne later characterizes Bede's figural interpretations as "somewhat far-fetched" indulgences of his imagination.[32] Through his neglect of biblical elements and themes throughout the *Historia*, his misunderstanding of figural exegesis, and his snide remark regarding the miraculous power of jet, Browne makes clear that his primary interest in Bede is not so much to understand him but to read him as a small step forward in the progress toward the modern discipline of history that Browne practices and holds in high esteem. The teleological rendering of Bede's practice of history that finds its consummation in contemporary historical practice is common in the early twentieth century, as I will continue to show.

Wilhelm Levison's "Bede as Historian" shares many characteristics with Browne's analysis.[33] In fact, the compilation of essays in which Levison's piece appears has a chapter that immediately follows Levison's entitled, "Bede as Exegete and Theologian" by Claude Jenkins, implying that Bede's works should be read in separate disciplinary ways or perhaps dividing his more explicitly religious works from his historical ones.[34] Moreover, the

---

scripturis operam dedi"). All subsequent Latin citations of the *Historia* will be from *Histoire Ecclésiastique du Peuple Anglais* and will be abbreviated, *HE*. Unless otherwise noted, all English translations are from *Ecclesiastica History of the English People* and will be abbreviated, *EH*.

30. Browne, *Venerable Bede*, 98–111.
31. Ibid., 108.
32. Ibid., 251.
33. Levison, "Bede as Historian," 111–51.
34. While I do not want to make too much out of this, even Brown's recent book, *Companion to Bede*, organizes his introduction to Bede with such disciplinary distinctions.

chapter after Jenkins's by Colgrave has the specific task of dealing with the miracles in Bede's works, presuming some level of unfittingness for miracles to be in a history, properly speaking.[35] Too much can be read into the separation of the disciplines in these titles, but I will show that these discussions of Bede frame his work in problematic ways.

Levison makes a valiant attempt at offering a sympathetic treatment of Bede's historical works, but, despite these efforts, he cannot help but compare and evaluate Bede in light of modern historical practices. Levison rightly notes that any reader who neglects the last five chapters of *De tempore ratione*, which discuss the world ages, "gets only an imperfect knowledge of Bede's mind."[36] Likewise, Levison understands that eschatology is a "constituent part of his [Bede's] historical conception."[37] While properly observing the importance that theology plays in Bede's understanding, Levison states that eschatology "does not belong to history in the modern sense."[38] This seemingly innocuous and obviously true statement about modern history, however, must be understood in light of other descriptions that Levison makes about Bede's historical work.

From his early chronologies through his hagiographies and *History of the Abbots*, Levison traces Bede's progress toward "the province of real history" that finds its culmination in the *Ecclesiastical History*.[39] Levison calls the *Historia* "Bede's masterpiece, to which he owes his glorious name of historian . . ."[40] Bede's attention to detail and particularity helps him earn the title of a real historian, according to Levison. Unlike his predecessors (e.g., Eusebius and Rufinus), Bede was concerned both with the universal church and a particular church, the British and Anglo-Saxon people. "It was Bede's intention to add [to Eusebius and Rufinus] a British and Anglo-Saxon supplement to the older work, and he thus produced the first special ecclesiastical history of an occidental people . . . So Bede, in spite of his consciousness of the universality of the Church and his desire for unity with Rome, manifests a kind of national feeling."[41] Furthermore, Bede also "endeavored to obtain documentary evidence, that is, letters and synodical proceedings," which make appearances in their entirety inside the pages of

---

35. Colgrave, "Bede's Miracle Stories," 201–29. See also Colgrave's introduction to his translation, *Bede's Ecclesiastical History of the English People*.
36. Levison, "Bede as Historian," 122.
37. Ibid.
38. Ibid.
39. Ibid., 131.
40. Ibid., 132.
41. Ibid., 133.

the *Historia*.[42] Beyond collecting written sources, Bede "sought also to learn the oral traditions of the different parts of England."[43]

Bede's historical sense is made apparent when he took "the history of the English Church as a united whole and, with regard for synchronism, did not separate simultaneous happenings."[44] According to Levison, "only in this way could he [Bede] present a *real* picture of the progress of the Christian mission, its vicissitudes and dependence on political events, ending with a survey of the contemporary English bishops."[45] In other words, by taking care to keep events in mostly chronological order and indicating contemporaneously occurring events, Bede shows himself to be a true historian. When Bede occasionally deviates from this synchronization it is the fault of Bede the theologian. In book 5 of the *Historia* Bede discusses Abbot Adamnan, his acceptance of the true dating and celebration of Easter, and Adamnan's own work on the Holy Places, which Bede adapts and includes lengthy quotations. Levison calls Bede's insertion of these quotes "really out of place" because it takes away from the chronology and synchronization. Thus, when Bede explains he included the quotes for the edification of the readers, Levison implies that Bede loses his historical sense because, in the quotations and his reasons for including them, "Bede the theologian is therein manifested."[46]

Finally, "[t]he principle of sincerity and [v]eracity thus marks [Bede] as a real historian, within the limits of his times."[47] Real historians write sentences that correspond to or describe reality according to chronology, in other words. Moreover, "he is a child of his times . . . in his predilection for the miraculous, and the importance he attaches to the paschal question."[48] The interesting phrase here is "within the limits of his times." Every human is limited to and influenced by a specific time in history, but Levison exceeds his task when he implicitly assumes that contemporary historians are better historians as such when compared to Bede. In this, he begs the question and fails to actually attend to the fact that perhaps what is in question is the discipline of history itself. While Levison certainly understands that there are differences between modern and medieval conceptions of history, he continuously assumes the superiority of the modern discipline without argument. The fore-

---

42. Ibid., 138.
43. Ibid., 140.
44. Ibid., 143.
45. Ibid., emphasis added.
46. Ibid., 144.
47. Ibid., 147.
48. Ibid., 146.

going analysis demonstrates that for Levison any time theology enters into Bede's history, Bede's historical works automatically become less history and more theology. While Levison recognizes Bede had no problem with history being theological, it is obviously true that we moderns are better historians, according to the proper practice of history, when theology is kept out of history. This, of course, is a perfectly legitimate position, but it is one that needs arguing, not presumption. Until one engages Bede at the theological level of history, that argument is not being had, and one will not fully understand how Bede conceives of history and its task. In this regard, Levison fails at his task to describe and understand Bede as an historian.

While Claude Jenkins's treatment of Bede as an exegete and theologian offers some salient descriptions of Bede for my purposes,[49] the more germane article addresses the miracle stories in Bede's works.[50] I want to reiterate that my attention to miracles in Bede's historical works and modern Bedean scholarship is not concerned with the ontological question of the possibility of miracles; instead, it is largely historiographical. I am simply drawing attention to how Bede's historical works get framed by modern interpreters and how this impacts their ability, or lack thereof, to understand Bede's theological conception of history.

Colgrave quickly sets up the problem in the opening sentences:

> It probably comes as a shock to the reader unacquainted with medieval literature who approaches Bede's *Ecclesiastical History* for the first time, to find that a miracle occurs on almost every page. What reliance can be placed on the historian who tells us in his very first chapter that "scrapings of leaves of books that had been brought out of Ireland being put into water have cured persons bitten by serpents," who goes on to deal with the life of Alban and to describe how the river dries up to allow the holy man the more rapidly to receive his martyr's crown, while the executioner's eyes drop out at the same moment as the martyr's head drops off[?][51]

Acknowledging Bede's own belief in the occurrence of these miracles, Colgrave points out that when compared to other contemporary literature Bede's *Historia* is surprising insofar as Bede does not recount *more* miracles.[52] Quickly, however, Colgrave shows his modern condescension, albeit with a putative historical sympathy. After commenting that moderns cannot

49. Jenkins, "Bede as Exegete and Theologian," 152–200.
50. Colgrave, "Bede's Miracle Stories," 201–29.
51. Ibid., 201.
52. Ibid.

expect Bede to know about the eighteenth- and nineteenth-century advances in science that show how the universe is "ruled by unchanging laws,"[53] he describes Bede's age as "primitive in its outlook, it was naturally credulous, and the nature of evidence was but vaguely understood. All around them men saw inexplicable phenomena, and the most marvelous explanation was always the easiest and the most readily accepted."[54] Interestingly, Colgrave even goes on to describe the sources of this primitive outlook in the paganism that preceded Christianity.[55] Colgrave eventually states his purposes for his essay where he will "endeavor to see how he [Bede] is influenced by the hagiographical interests of his age."[56] In short, Colgrave rightly wants to place Bede's miracle stories in the wider context of the Latin hagiographical tradition that begins with Evagrius of Antioch's translation of Athanasius's *Life of St. Antony*, and Bede makes Colgrave's analysis relatively easy, since Bede almost always named his sources. For my purposes, the important part of Colgrave's study centers on how he handles these miracle stories and how he thinks the hagiographical context impinges on Bede's narratives.

First, Colgrave observes the similarity of many of Bede's miracle stories from the *Historia* to Scripture:[57] a river drying up,[58] blind people being healed,[59] a mute's healing,[60] storms being calmed,[61] and water springing from a rock.[62] One example will suffice to show the striking similarity between Bede's stories and Scripture that Colgrave rightly notices: the calming of the sea by Germanus in book one of the *Historia*.[63] In the midst of the Pelagian heresy being spread by Agricola, the English called on the bishops from Gaul, Germanus and Lupus, for doctrinal help in refuting the subtleties of the heretics. The bishops quickly agreed to come to the aid of the Britons and their fledgling faith. However, they encountered a storm crossing the channel. Germanus, the leading bishop and champion of the group, had gone below deck to rest. The storm became so violent that all

53. Ibid.
54. Ibid., 202.
55. Ibid., 202–4.
56. Ibid., 205.
57. Ibid., 207–8.
58. See Colgrave, *Ecclesiastical History of the English People*, 1.7.
59. Ibid., 1.18, 2.2.
60. Ibid., 5.2.
61. Ibid., 1.17, 3.15, 5.1.
62. Ibid., 1.7.
63. Ibid., 1.17. Colgrave misreads the story saying Lupus calmed the storm when it was actually Germanus who sprinkled holy water on the sea and invoked the name of Christ and the Trinity. However, all were actively praying when the storm calmed.

(Re)Framing History 23

onboard believed they were going to sink, so they woke up Germanus who subsequently invoked the name of Christ and the Trinity while sprinkling water on the raging sea. Then, as a group, they all prayed and God answered by calming the waters allowing them safe passage to England to refute the Pelagian heresy. The resemblance between this story and Jesus' calming of the sea in Matthew 8 and Mark 4, where a sleeping Jesus is awakened by his panicking disciples to a raging storm, is obvious. Jesus commands the turbulent waters to be still, and they obey.

Colgrave then relates Bede's miracle stories to the "legends" of the saints in preceding hagiographical traditions. "These scriptural miracles found in the legends naturally become standardized and usually preserved certain features of the biblical miracles on which they are based."[64] While he never explicitly mentions it, Colgrave assumes that these "imitations" of miracles in the hagiographical tradition and in Bede are fraudulent because of the fact that they are imitations and could have been influenced by other classical sources. In other words, since the miracle stories lack originality and have precedence, they must be constructions based on the Scriptural text and therefore are not accurate or true.[65]

Colgrave tips his hand, relaying a narrative from book II of the *Historia* where Edwin renounces his pagan religion, receives baptism, and becomes a Christian, along with his followers. Colgrave remarks, "All this seems natural and has the appearance of strict history. But meanwhile Bede interpolates somewhat awkwardly a long account of a vision which Edwin had had when he was in exile . . . and in great danger."[66] Bede adds this story, Colgrave speculates, because "[p]erhaps he felt that the conversion of his own land to Christianity was an event of such importance that it could hardly have happened without an accompanying sign from heaven: more probably it was a piece of popular tradition which was well known in Northrumbria . . ."[67] Thus, Bede repeats these stories in his *Historia* because he was using his authorities and sources. Colgrave thinks that Bede probably thought them to be true because he believed these sources to be trustworthy and most likely eyewitness accounts or based on such accounts: "It is clear then that when Bede produces his witnesses, he is acting in accordance with the hagiographical tradition of his times. [. . .] The stories had been written

---

64. Colgrave, "Bede's Miracle Stories," 208.
65. Ibid., 208–10, 213, 215–16.
66. Ibid., 216.
67. Ibid.

down and it is too much to expect of a historian of his age that he should have refused to give them credence."[68]

Colgrave does try to hear Bede on his own terms by quoting Bede's preface to the *Historia*: "Bede has in fact done no less than he claimed to do, namely to 'labour to commit to writing with sincerity such things as we have gathered from common report, which is the true law of history.'"[69] Ultimately, therefore, Colgrave condescends less than his predecessors but nonetheless finds himself distinguishing different Bedes to make sense of what Bede was doing. "Perhaps we ought to recognize three men in Bede, the theologian, the hagiographer, and the historian . . . in writing the writing of the *Ecclesiastical History* both Bede the hagiographer and Bede the historian took part . . . Bede the hagiographer was only a little in advance of his times. Bede the historian was far in advance of them."[70]

To summarize up to this point, some sensitivity to Bede's own views and what he even purported to be doing has been shown by Colgrave (and to a lesser extent Levison), despite his clear empiricist philosophical perspective, foreign to Bede.[71] However, Plummer's point and analysis that stated that Bede remained above all a Christian thinker are now fading into the background in favor of a more putatively complex reading of Bede that sees conflicting disciplines weighing on the saint's mind, or at least in tension, throughout his writings. Once Bede is shown to be in such conflicted tension, his insights as a real historian can come to the surface and be shown to be "far in advance" of his own time, thereby reading Bede as a precursor to modern historical methods and their emphasis on source criticism and accurate and descriptive renderings of the past. However, "accurate" can now be understood in a sense different from what Bede himself would have likely thought since it has been separated from his theology and exegesis. An investigation into how Bede understood his historical task will have to wait until a later chapter, but for now it suffices to say that it differs from the aforementioned scholars.

While many of his scholarly predecessors wrestled with Bede's *Historia*, Charles Jones provides the first erudite and detailed discussion of what Bede meant by *historia* and its differences from modern conceptions of history.[72] Jones's analysis is focused in one chapter, but the rest of his

68. Ibid., 224–25; quote from 225.
69. Ibid., 226.
70. Ibid., 228–29.
71. Ibid., 229. See Colgrave's concluding paragraph where he revealingly distinguishes between the "external world" and the "human mind," not to mention the "rapid advance of knowledge" in Colgrave's time.
72. Jones, *Saints Lives and Chronicles in Early England*.

text also gives shape to his reading of Bede's *Historia*. Borrowing from and eventually correcting Colgrave, Jones reads the *Historia* as blend of history and hagiography.[73] Jones rightly says that these two genres are not necessarily in tension for Bede. Scholars often think they are, but that is because they operate in a "realist" mindset and methodology while others, in what he calls the Romanesque period, like Bede operate from a "romance" perspective.[74] Jones defines these via Lafcadio Hearn: "Realism is a truthful depiction of nature, especially human nature; romanticism is an elevation beyond the range of the familiar into aspiration. Aspiration, elevation, exaltation, edification are all words used to describe the purpose of Romance."[75] The common feature of both romance and realism is convention.

> If literature is to forsake the natural world it must provide a substitute, and that substitute is a man-created [sic] convention ... Though realistic writers, too, employ conventions, these serve them only as means to ends beyond. The romanticist enjoys the conventional for its own sake ... for it has the power of lifting men [sic] above or outside nature into their own created world ... The driving force of medieval romance is intellectual acceptance of abstraction as reality and the pleasure which the mind receives from the infinite adaptation of set pieces.[76]
>
> Romance attracts two types of mind—the credulous and the intelligently skeptical. These two approaches operate concurrently, even in the same reader or listener. No one can estimate how much of either approach any audience takes toward a romance ... It must be remembered that authors seldom write about the essentials of their art. A true convention in any age is accepted without comment.[77]

Since these conventions are presupposed, Jones seeks to find them within the hagiographical tradition in which Bede stood and wrote. In other words, Jones wants to find the common structures in Bede's genres and use them to help properly understand Bede, particularly his *Historia*. The difficulty is finding these conventions; how does one see them? Jones answers by looking at the texts "as strangers would."[78]

73. Ibid., 57, for his criticism of Colgrave.
74. Ibid., 51–52.
75. Ibid., 52.
76. Ibid.
77. Ibid., 53.
78. Ibid.

26 Allegorizing History

Regarding a hagiographer's intention, Jones's argument culminates, "It is immediately apparent that the lectors [and hagiographical authors] were not interested in giving history lessons when they read the lives of the saints."[79] And soon after, "I have said that the historian and annalist was *ipso facto* a hagiographer."[80] Jones makes this case by showing the different styles in which Bede wrote. He compares Bede's *History of the Abbots* and the *Life of St. Cuthbert*; the *History of the Abbots* is concise and contains a plentitude of detail to such a degree that no one disputes its historicity,[81] while the *Life of St. Cuthbert* is verbose and makes Cuthbert indistinguishable from St. Martin of Tours or other saintly persons who had their lives narrated in the hagiographical tradition.[82] Moreover, Eddius's *Life of St. Wilfrid* is copied nearly "word for word" from Bede's *Life of St. Cuthbert*.[83] Overall, Jones attempted to show the differences between the hagiographical traditions and more strict historical works and texts based on authorial intentions and audience expectations. More specifically, hagiography should edify its hearers and lift them to "ethical truth" and good deeds.[84] In light of this, Jones reads the *Historia* as both history and hagiography, and he uses Bede's own criterion, *uera lex historiae*, as the entry point into the combination.[85] However, he seems unaware of the inherent tension in this method that occurs by reading the texts "as strangers would," while also trying to understand it as the original audience would. He does not provide any details in how understanding the text via audience expectations fits with also reading it as a stranger would. Jones does not seem to think this a problem or tension as far as one can tell. Furthermore, through his distinction between realist and romantic, Jones continues to conceive of the authentic historical task as primarily conveying facts.

Bede's *uera lex historiae* is the conventional lynchpin for Jones because it connects Bede the historian and Bede the hagiographer. In the closing lines of the *Ecclesiastical History*'s preface, Bede says, "I also made it my business to add with care what I was able to learn myself from the trustworthy testimony of reliable witnesses. So I humbly beg the reader, if he

---

79. Ibid., 57. Here, "lectors" refers to those who audibly read the lives for the edification of the audience, which was the customary practice.

80. Ibid.

81. Ibid., 53–54.

82. Ibid., 54.

83. Ibid., 55.

84. Ibid., 74ff.

85. For more on Bede's *uera lex historiae*, see Ray, "Bede, the Exegete, as Historian," 125–40; idem, "Bede's *Uera Lex Historiae*," 1–21; Goffart, "Bede's *Uera lex historiae* Explained," 111–16.

finds anything other than the truth set down in what I have written, not to impute it to me. For, in accordance with the principles of true history [*uera lex historiae*], I have simply sought to commit to writing what I have collected from common report, for the instruction of posterity."[86] Previous scholars focus too much, according to Jones, on these particular sentences without placing them in the larger context of the preface that offers more clarity about what Bede thought the historian should be doing and what he thought himself to be doing. Bede addressed the preface to King Ceolwulf and told him,

> I gladly acknowledge the unfeigned enthusiasm with which, not content merely to lend an attentive ear to hear the words of Holy Scripture, you devote yourself to learn the sayings and doings of the men of old, and more especially the famous men of our own race. Should history tell of good men and their good estate, the thoughtful listener is spurred on to imitate the good; should it record the evil ends of wicked men, no less effectually the devout and earnest listener or reader is kindled to eschew what is harmful and perverse, and himself with greater care pursue those things which he has learned to be good and pleasing in the sight of God. This you perceive, clear-sighted as you are; and therefore, in your zeal for the spiritual well-being of us all, you wish to see my *History* more widely known, for the instruction of yourself and those over whom divine authority has [a]ppointed you to rule.[87]

Jones calls attention to Bede's pedagogical understanding of the *Historia* and places Bede's comments about the *uera lex historiae* within this broader purpose.

Bede first used the phrase *uera lex historiae* in his commentary on Luke. Commenting on Luke 2 Bede says, "It should not be forgotten that the evangelist was only expressing himself in common terms (*opinionem uulgi exprimens*), *quae uera lex historiae est*, when he called Joseph the father of Christ..."[88] Jones points out that Bede gets this from Jerome's *Perpetual Virginity of Blessed Mary* that uses nearly identical language.[89] In other words, when the gospel of Luke refers to Joseph as Jesus' father, it is not speaking literally but simply in ordinary terms in order to "express the common

86. Colgrave, *Ecclesiastical History of the English People*, preface.

87. Ibid.

88. Jones, *Saints Lives and Chronicles in Early England*, 83. Translation and Latin are from Jones.

89. Ibid. Jerome says, "opinionem vulgi exprimentes, quae uera historiae lex est," cited in ibid.

28   Allegorizing History

view" and communicate clearly without unnecessary distraction.[90] Jones therefore concludes that the *uera lex historiae* "is not a plea for literal truth, but for a truth which denies the literal statement or uses the literal statement to achieve an image in which the literal statement is itself incongruous."[91] And later, "The true law of history, then, in consonance with the gospels, is to express the common view—to use accepted symbols as tools for attaining the ideal end, though the words may not be factually true."[92] Thus, Jones understands that Bede conceives of the historical task as more than the conveying of facts.

The upshot of this analysis requires that scholars show more skepticism regarding Bede's narration of facts but also that they stop their quick dismissals of Bede's miracle stories, which misunderstand Bede's own intention.[93] For the first time since Plummer, a scholar recognizes Bede's theology and history together: "We might add that he [Bede] wrote history for no other than theological reasons."[94] More specifically, what distinguishes Bede's theological history from others (e.g., Eusebius) is its emphasis on ethical imitation and learning.[95] Jones ultimately concludes that Bede's history was written, "not, as we would view it, for its photographic shadowing out, but as a temporal representation of the state of souls in God's eternity—pulling that eternity down within the reach of the earnest, but none-too-imaginative, listener."[96] Hence, in the end, Bede's genius was that he combined hagiography and history in a way never before imagined or practiced. However, these two forms of writing are "incongruous" in Jones's view, and Bede never really integrated them well.[97] Nonetheless, if we fail to see the Romanesque or romantic features of Bede's *Historia*, we fail to understand what Bede believed and wanted to accomplish.

Jones offers a compelling description of Bede's own self understanding with much merit, especially in his examination of the *uera lex historiae* and its historical and biblical roots. However, the precarious tension in Jones's method creates a problem—a problem that continues to plague the practice of history. To find the conventions in Bede's *Historia*, Jones places himself outside Bede's audience as a "stranger," while still seeking to understand what

90. Ibid., 88.
91. Ibid., 83.
92. Ibid., 88.
93. Ibid., 90.
94. Ibid.
95. Ibid.
96. Ibid., 92.
97. Ibid., 92–93.

the original audience would have heard and understood. How is one both a stranger and an original listener? Can Jones be in Bede's original audience? Questions about temporality that history cannot answer must be presumed no matter what answers are given to these questions. It is more certain that Jones, as a historian, conceives of his task to know *about* the original audience, their expectations, and life while also remaining a stranger *because of* his temporal and historical location in the twentieth century. Thus, historians recover knowledge about the past, but this in no way connects them (or us) to it beyond the level of abstract knowledge.

This presumed separation allows for the very performance of Jones's work. However, the nature of the separation is a philosophical question, not a mere historical one. Furthermore, Jones's location as a twentieth century academic historian requires him to write in the realist mode and, therefore, describe Bede in this way. Is that a problem? Does his own (necessarily?) realist depiction of Bede distort Bede's "romantic" and "Romanesque" approach in the *Historia*? To put the question more pointedly and even in realist or modern historical terms: Is a realist reading of Bede's *Historia* anachronistic? Is it a projection back onto Bede that he would not recognize? This raises the very question about the nature of history itself, as well as the constitution of the practice and task of the historian. Later on, scholars eventually come to recognize that the nature of history itself is in question. Suffice it for now to have noted how the need for historians to avoid anachronism, which by definition requires some kind of significant and substantial separation between past and present, creates a helpful and yet unstable predicament. Helpful because it allows Jones to offer the best reading of Bede up to his time in the twentieth century without unnecessary condescension that marked previous scholarship; yet unstable because Jones finds himself needing to use terms like "romantic" to make sense of and truthfully describe Bede—words that Bede would have never known.

Scholarship on Bede and History in Second Half of the Twentieth Century

If the first half of the twentieth century could generally be described as "critical" in its reading of Bede, the second half mostly comes to Bede's defense, albeit in various and nuanced ways.[98] Several essays in the 1976 text *Famulus Christi* continue to address the question of Bede's understanding

---

98. The one glaring exception to this appraisal is by Carroll, *The Venerable Bede*. However, this text often reads more like a selective doctrinal summary (and defense) of Bede's texts than a summary of his spiritual teachings.

and practice of history.⁹⁹ More specifically, essays compare Bede to Eusebius, evaluate him as a scholar, address the impact his exegesis has on his historical work, and revisit the question of miracles. Paul Meyvaert makes the case that Bede is a scholar in the truest sense of the word; "real scholarship implies the application of sound critical judgement [sic] to a given body of material, and sound judgement [sic] of this kind is seldom applied without new insights being developed."¹⁰⁰ He argues that Bede fits this definition through his work on *computus*, Scripture, textual criticism, and even the *Historia*. Meyvaert believes he must address Bede's use of miracles since most scholars today would find affirming the miraculous in history as non-scholarly.

Meyvaert perceptively begins his short defense of Bede by noting how Bede's historical work previously has been framed by critics like Colgrave and Jones. He says:

> The modern scholar is above believing in miracles; in fact from his point of view "scholarship and "belief in miracles" are mutually exclusive terms. He will therefore seek to deal with the miraculous element in Bede's works ... in a sophisticated way, one that does the least damage to the portrait he wishes to draw of Bede as a scholar. He will point out the absence of miracles in Bede's Lives of the Abbots [e.g., Jones] conclude that this probably indicates a certain sceptical attitude on Bede's part towards the miraculous, and then go on to suggest that the presence of miraculous stories in the *Ecclesiastical History* and in Bede's hagiographical works must be explained on the basis that these works had a wider didactic or moralizing purpose. Bede wanted to edify. These stories therefore had a value somewhat parallel to his allegorical interpretations of Scripture. They did not belong to the world of history, or of scholarship, but occupied a world apart, on which Bede occasionally drew for a special purpose.¹⁰¹

Interestingly, Meyvaert finds these readings of Bede problematic on anachronistic grounds.¹⁰² He says that they are "trying to fit Bede into our own standards of scholarship"¹⁰³ and that hagiography and history were not

---

99. Bonner, *Famulus Christi*.

100. Meyvaert, "Bede the Scholar," 41.

101. Ibid., 51.

102. I say "interestingly" because anachronism is a later development in the practice of history after Bede, and I will discuss this in chapter 4.

103. Meyvaert, "Bede as Scholar," 51.

separate categories for Bede.[104] Instead, Bede must be understood in light of his own views and beliefs regarding miracles. Meyvaert then discusses how Bede believed in miracles and that he affirmed all the miracles in Scripture as fact. While Bede would not question Scripture, he would use critical thought to evaluate miracles in his own day, and "any careful study" of Bede's history of the *Life of Cuthbert* would bear this out.[105] Meyvaert handles the lack of miracle stories in Bede's history of the abbots by noting that Bede was writing from firsthand experience in this historical work, and since Bede did not experience any miracles, he simply did not include any.[106] Ultimately, the difference between Bede and modern scholars is how they see their entire world, according to Meyvaert. Bede expected marvelous things and inhabited a world where God was active, while we do not see the world that way; our world is "disenchanted." Thus, when Bede says that he has seen snake bites cured by drinking water that includes Irish parchment scraps, this does not necessarily mean that Bede thought it happened instantaneously, which would constitute a divine miracle, as he never said so. Instead, using the judgment he had in his own time, Bede believed this to be part of his everyday world. We see it as "miraculous" if in fact we believe it to be true. Therefore, when we read certain stories in the *Historia* we see them as "miraculous" and Bede would not have. In this way, Meyvaert avers, Bede must be understood on his own terms.[107]

Benedicta Ward continues defending Bede in her concise argument by placing Bede's miracle stories in historical relationship to other scholars and historians.[108] She notes how widespread the use of miracle stories was in the Middle Ages, which included the likes of Abelard, Anselm of Canterbury, Hugh of Cluny, John Salisbury, and also Herbert Bosham.[109] She contends that due to modern notions of causality modern obsession over the "how" of miracles will distort Bede because his primary concern was not how but why. The mechanics of the miracle did not matter but its significance.[110] She makes her case by rightly observing that Bede's favorite word for miracle is not "*miracula*" but "*signa*" thereby placing Bede in his broader Augustinian theological context where what was signified was more important than the

---

104. Ibid., 53.
105. Ibid., 54.
106. Ibid.
107. Ibid., 55.
108. Ward, "Miracles and History," 70–76.
109. Ibid., 70.
110. Ibid., 71.

sign itself.[111] However, she notes that Bede did take the time to attend to verifying material by citing how he sent his biography of Cuthbert to the monks at Lindisfarne who were unable to find fault in his account.[112] Hence, Bede was not naively credulous but sought verification. On Ward's reading, Bede was mostly concerned with the "inner meaning" and moral truths within the miracle stories.[113] Ward also notes the subtlety with which Bede used the miracle stories to make points that were beyond the sheer wondrous or miraculous status of the events. In fact, Bede was not interested in the miracle stories for the simple facts of them.[114] Ward says Bede freely altered facts to suit his purposes; this can be seen if one compares the anonymous *Life of Cuthbert* with Bede's *Life of Cuthbert*.[115] In light of this freedom, Ward ends her essay with a rhetorically pointed question and response:

> Do we then err if we look for factual information in the miracles recorded by Bede?" I think there is historical information there . . . but it is subject to more layers of interpretation than the other material. [. . .] Bede is using his miracle material from the inside, and he shapes it according to his purposes. If we try to see the miracles as a simple record of facts we show ourselves more credulous and naïve than Bede himself; perhaps it is not only in Bede's miracle material but in all his material that we should exercise some degree of this gift of discernment.[116]

In other words, modern historians must learn to think beyond their own conception of what constitutes history if they are to properly understand Bede.

The importance of Ward's posing of this question cannot be overstated. The very asking of it presumes that theology has something to say to history and that they are not merely separate disciplines with completely autonomous methods and spheres. While others before her begin to address the issue, they do not express it in the sharp terms that manifest some of the philosophical and theological presumptions that many historians unknowingly brought and continued to bring to Bede's work, even while trying to understand Bede in his own context via the methodological avoidance of anachronism.

---

111. Ibid., 71–72.

112. Ibid., 72. See the preface to Bede's *Life of St. Cuthbert*. Ward also mentions his citing of authors and authorities by name who were witnesses of miracles, which he does not do when relaying political or military history.

113. Ibid., 73.

114. Ibid., 75.

115. Ibid., 75–76. See also Blair, "Historical Writings of Bede," 197–221, esp. 202.

116. Ward, "Miracles and History," 76.

Building on the work of Robert Hanning,[117] Roger Ray offers a more substantive discussion of the relationship between Bede's exegesis and his practice and understanding of history.[118] He takes Plummer's warning cited as an epigram at the beginning of this chapter seriously that Bede must be seen first of all as a Christian thinker. Due to Bede's appended autobiography at the end of the *Historia*, Ray says "we can start to determine how his underrated work as an exegete affected his famous efforts as a historian."[119]

Ray begins by noting that English history was of secondary importance to Bede because Scriptural history took precedence. He cites Bede's attempts to understand orderings of events in the bible, as well as Bede's concern for finding the most faithful textual editions of Scripture.[120] Bede's *De schematibus et tropis* is also rightly brought into the conversation to make the point that Bede thought other histories, texts, and even grammars should be used in order to better understand Scripture; the study of *saecularis* literature is not an end in itself for Bede.[121] In short, scholars who want to read Bede's *Historia* as his most important work fail to take Bede's other writings, including his own self descriptions, seriously enough.

After the more formal discussion of how Bede conceived of the relationship between "secular" and Christian materials, Ray delves more deeply into how Bede's commentaries shaped his conception and practice of history. For example, Bede follows Augustine's lead and noted the importance that the intentions and purpose of the authors of the gospels play in proper interpretation.[122] The significance of knowing a book's purpose has less to do with finding out what really happened and more to do with moral edification, according to Ray.[123] Hence, when Augustine says that all truthful narrators subordinate concern for literal truth to the significance of the events, Bede follows his lead.[124] In this way, Bede's *uera lex historiae*, which was "greatly important"

---

117. Hanning, *Vision of History in Early Britain*.

118. Ray, "Bede, the Exegete, as Historian," 125–40. J. Campbell mentions the connection between Bede's exegesis and history but does so only briefly. See Campbell, "Bede," 159–90. His aforementioned brief statement comes on p. 165.

119. Ray, "Bede, The Exegete, as Historian," 125.

120. Ibid., 125–26.

121. Ibid., 127. For more on how Christians approached secular/classical culture and literature, see Shoedel and Wilkin, *Early Christian Literature and the Classical Intellectual Tradition*; Marrou, *History of Education in Antiquity*; Weltin, *Athens and Jerusalem*; Armstrong and Markus, *Christian Faith and Greek Philosophy*; Chadwick, *Early Christian Thought and the Classical Tradition*; Daniélou, *Gospel Message and Hellenistic Culture*.

122. Ray, "Bede, The Exegete, as Historian," 128, 130.

123. Ibid., 130–31.

124. Ibid., 131. See Augustine, *De consensu evangelistarum* 2.46.97.

to Bede,[125] does bear resemblance to ancient rhetorical methods, but Bede finds its significance in that the gospel authors utilized the principle.[126] Here, Ray reads Bede in his Augustinian heritage, especially Augustine's semiotics in *On Christian Teaching*. Bede's *Historia*, therefore, is Bede's attempt to follow the lead of Scripture's inspired authors but for his own purposes: to urge his contemporary Northumbrians unto holiness and salvation.

In sum, Ray follows Jones in understanding Bede's *uera lex historiae* as the orienting principle of history in a more technical sense that is borrowed from Jerome and indirectly from Augustine. However, Ray differs in how he relates the *uera lex historiae* to the *Historia* because of his attempt to understand it in light of Bede's exegesis.[127] A few years later, however, Ray changes his mind regarding Bede's *uera lex historiae*.[128] Ray argues that Jerome understood the *uera lex historiae* to be only *a* true law of history and "not the main principle in all historiography."[129] Jerome could never think that the gospels were simply an expression of the often mistaken vulgar opinion, which was the classical definition of the *uera lex historiae* found in the works of Cicero. Instead, Jerome recognizes this sometimes occurs in the writing of history for rhetorical purposes, but it is certainly not the primary principle. In fact, Jerome's preface to *Chronicon*, which Bede would have known, shows that Jerome believed that the practice of history required telling the actual truth.[130] Ray summarizes his reading of Jerome as such:

> Jerome took for granted that the evangelists had remained alert to the climate of opinion at the various stages of the unfolding drama. In the early period none but a few were aware that Mary had conceived of the Holy Spirit. The rest went on thinking the usual thing—that a woman who gives birth has lain with a man. [. . .] If the gospel writers, for their part, had not written the common view [that Joseph was the father of Jesus], they would have made their readers wonder about the reputation of Mary. Since her public image was in fact good, it would have been incongruous not to record the *opinio vulgi* about Joseph. [. . .] This *uera historiae lex* represents an exception to the main rule of

---

125. Ray, "Bede, The Exegete, as Historian," 129.

126. Ibid., 127.

127. This is Ray's own appraisal. See Ray, "Bede's *Uera lex historiae*," 1.

128. Ray, "Bede's *Uera lex historiae*," 1–21. Ray's latter account here goes against Blair, "Historical Writings of Bede," 197–221, insofar as Blair follows Jones in taking the *uera lex historiae* as a means for Bede to forego historical accuracy.

129. Ray, "Bede's *Uera lex historiae*," 2–6; quote from 2.

130. Ibid., 4.

history. It authorizes a brief strategic departure from the normal goal of factual truth.[131]

And later, Ray explains that Jerome was saying that "the evangelists accommodated their story to *opinio vulgi* because, as any schoolboy knows, all good narrators do."[132] In this way, Jerome and the gospel writers are simply noting and practicing the necessary connection between rhetoric and history.[133]

Bede understood Jerome's point and use of the *uera lex historiae* because of his exegetical works (specifically on Luke and Acts), and, therefore, the classical and mainly rhetorical use of the *uera lex historiae* "could not have become the major premise of the [*Historia*]."[134] On Ray's account, Bede's use of the *uera lex historiae* in the preface to the *Ecclesiastical History* "respected the factual basis of edifying narrative."[135] Hence, Ray revises Colgrave's translation from the preface: "I humbly implore the reader that he not impute it to me if in what I have written he finds anything other than the truth. For, in accordance with a true law of history, I have tried to set down in a simple style what I have collected from common report, for the instruction of posterity."[136] The *uera lex historiae* then is subordinate to *veritas*, and this disclaimer regarding potential errors shows this, and Bede's intention to write history that edifies is irrelevant insofar as factual events should be used for edification, as Bede's comments on history in book 1 of *De tabernaculo* manifest.[137] Moreover, the reception of Bede's *Historia* indicates that Bede was understood by subsequent thinkers as a man after the truth of the history.[138] Thus, to read the *uera lex historiae* in the preface of *Historia* as Bede's primary method and approach to doing history is greatly mistaken based both on Bede's own texts and in the decades and centuries of his reception.

The change in Ray's understanding of Bede over two of his essays illustrates how more recent scholarship has changed since the times of Levison and Jones. Criticism itself has been used to expose problematic readings of

---

131. Ibid., 5.
132. Ibid., 6.
133. Ibid.
134. Ibid., 10.
135. Ibid.
136. Ibid., 13.
137. Ibid.

138. Ibid., 20–21. For more on Bede's reception, especially in medieval England's monastic culture, see Gransden, "Bede's Reputation as an Historian in Medieval England," 397–425.

36   Allegorizing History

the *Historia* and Bede, though scholars have not yet named it as a theoretical problem. They continue to argue, presuming theoretical concerns, about historical matters. More specifically, from the work of Ward and the latter Ray, scholarship is beginning to take theological concerns more seriously and substantively as constitutive components of Bede's use and practice of history, while also showing how anachronism still creeps into some putative critical readings of Bede. This trend continues as the century unfolds.

If Ray attempted to secure an exegetical understanding of Bede's *uera lex historiae* solely from Bede's own texts and his sources, then Calvin Kendall and Jan Davidse sought to read Bede's history in even more explicitly theological terms. They attempted to place Bede's *Historia* inside Bede's larger theological framework that extends even beyond his commentaries, while still paying attention to Bede's texts and sources. In short, they seek to broaden the context in which the *Historia* should be understood.

Kendall argues that Bede utilizes a medieval form of rhetoric originating in classical Roman literature but was transformed by Christian theology at the hands of Augustine and Isidore of Seville.[139] Bede inflects this rhetorical tradition in a distinctly theological key with the help of preceding theologians. "I wish to suggest that Bede's conception of rhetoric in terms of 'figures' was a prime element in the making of a style which mirrored his vision of experience. It is a style grounded on the premise of a real correspondence between language and physical reality."[140] More specifically, the juxtaposition of miracle stories and more straightforward history in the *Historia* should not be understood as in tension for Bede; instead, it should be seen "as an accurate reflection of the discontinuity of the sixth age, conditioned by preexisting narrative conventions . . ."[141]

Kendall uses Bede's *De schematibus et tropis* as the central text to help understand Bede's rhetorical posture and writing in the *Historia*. In this meticulously detailed account, Kendall argues that Bede, like Gregory the Great, moves away from the more biblical uses of rhetoric, specifically *hyperbaton*.[142] The implication of this is that in the *Historia*, Bede uses complex forms of *hyperbaton* to "secure a pious tone or assert matters of faith" while in Scripture they are often used for simple historical narrative.[143] Bede's treatment of tropes in *De schematibus* and in the *Historia* is then

139. Kendall, "Bede's *Historia Ecclesiastica*," 145–72.
140. Ibid., 147.
141. Ibid.
142. Ibid., 157. *Hyperbaton* occurs when the usual or natural order of a word or phrase is reversed or reordered. In classical usage, the purpose was to offer more amenable speech patterns and rhythms and to place emphasis on particular words or phrases.
143. Ibid.

addressed by Kendall. Placing Bede in the Augustinian tradition where all of creation is a sign, Kendall continues to argue that the use of figures and tropes is necessary because Bede believed the fallen created realm to be fraught with contradictions. The use of rhetoric helps ease these tensions and points people to the unity and coherence which creation lost due to the fall.[144] Kendall even goes so far as to describe passages from the *Historia* as depicting a dualist view where the body is evil and the spiritual soul is good.[145] Kendall summarizes Bede's Christian semiotics and metaphysics through a reading of the healing of Imma in book 4 (chapter 22 in recent editions) of the *Historia*:

> If we consider the images of binding and loosing, it becomes apparent that the most "real" of them is the one that is hypothetical in terms of the story. That is, if Imma were dead, his soul "really" would be subject to binding, because that is the general proposition that is universally true in the Christian metaphysics within which Bede worked. The chains in the physical world are a sign of that reality; their failure to hold is a sign that the purgatorial bonds are loosed by the intercession of prayers for the dead.[146]

Putting aside this problematic and dualistic reading of Imma and Bede's metaphysics for the moment, Kendall believes this indicates that Bede used rhetoric in a specifically theological fashion to highlight the tensions in the sixth age that humans inhabit between the incarnation and the *eschaton*.[147] Kendall even discusses the importance of numerical symbolism in the *Historia* and links it to Bede's commentaries.[148] For my purposes here, the most important feature in Kendall's work is the fact that he attempts to make sense of Bede's *Historia* by understanding the larger theological and metaphysical framework that Bede articulated and inhabited. No one prior to Kendall attempted such a reading in any substantial or lengthy fashion.

In two essays, Jan Davidse continues this more explicitly theological rendering of Bede's *Historia*. In his earliest account, a condensed form of his dissertation written in Dutch, Davidse attempts to summarize Bede's "sense" of history.[149] After a historiographical summary of preceding re-

---

144. Ibid., 162–66.
145. Ibid., 165–66.
146. Ibid., 166–67.
147. Ibid., 162.
148. Ibid., 167–69.
149. Davidse, "Sense of History in the Works of the Venerable Bede," 647–95. In the same year, 1982, as Davidse's essay is published, Roger Ray published another essay building on his *Famulus Christi* piece. Ray goes so far as to say that exegesis is the "driving

search on Bede and history and the recent turn to understand it in light of his exegesis, Davidse begins his theological framing of Bede's history with a discussion of time and eternity.[150] Davidse argues that contrary to scholarly opinion that requires a distinction between history and redemptive history foreign to Bede,[151] Bede did not consider his historical writings to take place from a metahistorical perspective; metahistorical in that they lacked a sense of consciousness about time that led them to anachronistic views of time and history (i.e. that there is no distinction between past and present).[152] Instead, according to Davidse, Bede's conception of time did have a distinction between past and present, but this difference and distinction did not separate the past from the present.[153]

How does this presence of the past in the present occur for Bede? The historian is responsible for making it happen, according to Davidse.

> The task of the historian was to establish what happened in a reliable manner and in the proper sequence. [. . .] But the description of history had no significance in itself. It was important because the facts had a meaning in the eyes of the believer who was alive at the moment and at a later time and who read what had been written down. This held true for the description of the history of Jesus Christ just as much as it did for the history of the English church and people. To the believer, knowledge of the past could open the door to salvation in time and eternity by imitating the past.[154]

The ability for the historian to perform her task is based partly on mental processes the historian must necessarily go through, but it also rooted in the reality of change itself—which is to say time itself. Davidse attributes this view to Bede citing several commentaries.[155] Once Davidse describes Bede's view of time, he is ready to relate how time as transitory change relates to historical events and history. Bede's periodization of history into world ages provides the key to this relationship. Focusing on the sixth

---

force of all Bede's learning." See Ray, "What Do We Know about Bede's Commentaries?," 8.

150. Davidse, "Sense of History in the Works of the Venerable Bede," 652. Davidse and I share much in common in our reading of the twentieth-century Bedan scholarship.

151. See, for example, Brandt, *Shape of Medieval History*.

152. Davidse, "Sense of History in the Works of the Venerable Bede," 652–54.

153. Ibid., 655–56. Much of what follows in the section on time and eternity continues to argue this as well.

154. Ibid., 656–57.

155. Ibid., 657.

age in which Bede understood himself to live, the age between Christ's incarnation and his second coming, Davidse argues using *In genesim* that for Bede Christ's sacrifice on the cross consecrates the sixth age and gives it a unity. All persons "are his [Christ's] contemporaries because they share in the grace which descended into time with the incarnation of Christ."[156] Beyond the sixth age, the incarnation is the "central point of history" for Bede because it reveals the meaning of history prior to Christ's birth as well as the history that follows.

Davidse's characterization of the relationship between Bede's exegesis of Scripture and the *Historia* also requires summary but is more difficult to discern because Davidse rarely addresses the relationship explicitly. Davidse usually invokes Bede's commentaries in footnotes to make a larger theological or philosophical point. In one rare instance, Davidse says that Bede used allegory to "establish a link between the Old Testament and his own times" by often citing 1 Corinthians 10 which states several times that things happened to the ancients "as an example" (NRSV).[157] Thus, Bede connects the past and present by "the disclosure of the exemplary value of what has happened and, consequently, of the purpose of following the example."[158] While this is the one rare and explicit reflection on exegesis and history, it does summarize Davidse's approach to the question about how Bede relates exegesis and history, and it is also consistent with Davidse's view on the role of the historian relating past, present, and future. For Davidse, times are linked through a knowing subject (the historian or the exegete, whichever the case may be) studying texts about past events.

Recall Davidse's claim that "facts had a meaning in the eyes of the believer who was alive at the moment and at a later time and who read what had been written down. This held true for the description of the history of Jesus Christ just as much as it did for the history of the English church and people."[159] Historical events themselves do not necessarily contain any ontological similarity or linkage; a knowing subject provides that linkage through giving them "meaning." Thus, an exegete would give meaning to an Old Testament text or event in light of Christ. To be sure, Davidse does note that the very transitory nature of time itself allows for the historian or exegete to make such connections thereby connecting the process with a non-subjective reality. However, one is left wondering if events themselves have any real or non-subjective relations to the center of history: the incar-

---

156. Ibid., 660.
157. Ibid., 661.
158. Ibid.
159. Ibid., 656.

nation of Jesus Christ. Would Bede agree with such a claim, or is Davidse appropriating Bede in an anachronistic contemporary hermeneutical and idealist sense? More pointedly, is this Bede's sense of history or an idealist one? Davidse recognizes the problem with this account over a decade later.

In his latter essay, Davidse tries to demonstrate that Bede's *Historia* is "an original example of Christian historiography"[160] while simultaneously addressing the problems of using "modern historical awareness" to understand Bede.[161] Davidse outlines three distinctive approaches to the historical task in modern history in relationship to Bede, though all three "come down to the same problem of the 'facts' and their 'meaning.'"[162] 1). The objectivist or historicist approach which understands its task to be an objective rendering of the past; whatever does not cohere with this is dismissed as religion, theology, etc. Levison is an example of this. 2). The subjective or idealist account understands history to be formed in the "subjective consciousness" of the historian which is in turn imposed onto facts and data thereby making the historian the one who constantly breaks with the past with each new (and imposed) description. In this view, Bede becomes such an anomaly and perhaps even not an historian because Bede views history as mostly continuous. Past and present, while distinct, are not separate. Thus, Bede's theological view of how history hangs together is understood as an external imposition on "superficial, arbitrary, and naturally preceding events."[163] An example of this approach is Davidse's dissertation and earlier essay. 3). The narrative variant emphasizes form and function. Objectivity in the scientific sense is not the concern for the historian until the 19th century; thus, Bede is less concerned about an objective account and more concerned with a good story to keep tradition alive, and the criteria for a good story are products of Bede's culture and time.[164] The issue of relating facts and meanings appears to recede here, but Davidse says this is only apparent. "[T]he very possibility of this approach derives from the modern notion that fact and meaning must be brought together by the creative subject, via the language of his culture and tradition."[165]

Bede does not fit into any of these approaches, according to Davidse. Bede was influenced by his time, culture, and Roman historiography but he

---

160. Davidse, "On Bede as Christian Historian," 1–15; quote from 1.
161. Ibid., 2.
162. Ibid., 4.
163. Ibid., 5.
164. Ibid., 6–7.
165. Ibid., 7.

also Christianizes or biblicizes them in the tradition of Augustine.[166] More specifically, *historia* for those in the Augustinian tradition, like Bede, "relates what people in the past have done and it shows that that past had an order. For that reason *historia* cannot be reckoned with human institutions, for the latter are instituted by people. *Historia*, on the contrary, depends on research into what is effectuated by time or is instituted by God."[167] Therefore, the ordering of time and history are God's work (providence) and *historia* is decisively not a human institution.[168] Hence, Bede's *Ecclesiastical History* is neither an objective report of what happened, nor is it a subjective imposition of meaning on bare and arbitrary facts. Instead, the *Historia* narrates the coming of faith to Britannia (making it unique or original) and intensifies the very dynamics of history itself, the incarnation, which orients Bede's chronology via "in the year of our Lord."[169] Thus, history itself, *historia ipsa*, is the relation of events to the incarnation and God's providence, and the *Historia* is simply a narration of that relationship making it *historia ipsa*.

Davidse is the first to clearly articulate, in theoretical fashion, a potential conundrum for historians who seek to understand Bede.[170] Can contemporary uses and understandings of history understand and accurately represent Bede? This is not the question of skepticism in general regarding historical knowledge: can we know anything about the past? The question is based on substantive philosophical and theological differences between the position of the interrogator and the one being interrogated. Davidse does not name the issue in the same way I will, but he starts the conversation and sees what is at stake. Prior to Davidse, most Bede scholars presumed their historical method and its philosophical assumptions. There were some who raised questions about modern presumptions being read back into Bede, but these readings all required the use of anachronism, the modern staple of historical theory and practice because anachronism is precisely what all historians seek to avoid. If one historian can demonstrate that another historian is being anachronistic, then the accused historian ceases to be a true historian. I will address anachronism in chapter 4, but it must suffice for

166. Ibid., 8–9.
167. Ibid., 9.
168. Ibid.
169. Ibid., 12–13.

170. The wonderful and illuminating essays in DeGregorio, *Innovation and Tradition in the Writings of the Venerable Bede* demonstrate the more recent commitment to reading Bede in a more integrative disciplinary fashion, but they still fail to address more substantive theoretical issues that Davidse and I raise. That said, I still count myself as part of the more nuanced and integrative revival of scholarship on Bede, and, as my subsequent work will show, I am deeply indebted to contemporary scholarship as a result.

now to say that I think it is both useful and unavoidable, as my own practice has and will continue to show. However, it is not neutral or even "given" insofar as it was a development in the practice of history itself subsequent to Bede that occurred in the Renaissance.

Conclusion

From the very beginning with Plummer's introduction to his critical edition of the *Historia* in 1896, scholars recognized that Bede's faith, theology, and exegesis impacted his work as an historian. Throughout the century, however, many struggled in relating contemporary and modern understandings of history and its practice to what Bede was doing. Most of the conversation centered on miracles, but much more is at stake in the conversation than whether or not these particular occurrences are "historical" or "true." What is at issue is the very discipline of history itself.

Some scholars thought it best to relate Bede's theology, exegesis, and history in sheerly extrinsic terms such that any mention of the miraculous, or religious significance (or precedence) in events meant that Bede was forsaking the sphere of history for theology or hagiography (Browne, Levison, and Colgrave), leaving Bede to appear a conflicted monk moving back and forth between competing disciplines. This group of scholars also saw flashes of brilliance in Bede insofar as he was in advance of his own time when it came to the practice of history. By this, they supposed that Bede was one small step toward the development of the modern discipline of history, which they were all blessed and privy to practice.

Jones attempted to reorient the conversation by turning to a more detailed analysis of Bede's own texts and use of *historia* and the *uera lex historiae* and how they differed from modern conceptions. In this sense, Jones's treatment moves in the right direction because he seeks to get beyond modern condescension to Bede. However, Jones's analogues are mired in modern presumptions (realist v. romantic), but his attempt to read Bede in the hagiographical tradition cannot be neglected. Meyvaert and Ward provide critical fodder between Jones and Roger Ray who eventually comes to repudiate Jones's understanding of the *uera lex historia* in favor of a compelling case for an alternative and, to use Jones's own language against him, more realist *and* theological Bede. Specifically, Ray attempts to understand how Bede's exegesis and use of the *uera lex historia* actually impinges on Bede's *Historia* leading him to conclude that Bede believed himself to be telling accurate stories, at least as far as Bede was able to confirm; this is why Bede offers a caveat about his sources in the preface of the *Historia* regarding the subsequent material's veracity.

Calvin Kendall and Jan Davidse offer more theoretical and theological approaches to Bede's *Historia*. They attempt to makes sense of how Bede conceived of history as a whole in order to make sense of the *Ecclesiastical History*, and Davidse even brings contemporary philosophy and historical theory into his argument. The difference between time and history are also brought to the fore by Davidse and Kendall; they show that how an historian (implicitly or explicitly) conceives of time impacts how one narrates and understands history. Until this point few, if any, thought these more theoretical discussions were relevant to Bede and his *Historia*.

My work here raises several questions that I will be addressing throughout the rest of the book. First, how can we moderns read Bede given our divergent understandings of history? In other words, is it possible to avoid anachronism, like contemporary history requires of us, *and* understand Bede's conception of history that has no problem with anachronism? The second question must be answered before the first. How did this change in historical conception come about? I will address these two questions in chapters 4 and 5; the latter in chapter 4 in relationship to contemporary historical scholarship on the Renaissance, and the former in chapter 5 where I will suggest, using the work of Frank Ankersmit, that past and present are not ontologically separate. Third, what is the relationship between Bede's exegesis and his historical work? More specifically, I will inquire into how Bede relates them *theologically*. Chapters 2 and 3 address this relationship.

Overall, this chapter has sought to raise questions and provide a historiographical framework or context for the rest of my argument—to show how and why the argument I am making came about and can even make sense. My debt to the preceding scholarship on Bede is enormous, and my argument in what follows, despite its disagreements with preceding work on Bede and history, rests squarely on the shoulders of those who have gone before.

2

Can History Be Figural?
A Study of Bede's Historia Ecclesiastica *and* De Templo

Introduction

According to recent secondary literature, Bede is most famous for his *Ecclesiastical History of the English People*. Regardless of how subsequent generations have remembered him, Bede actually thought his primary task was to comment on the sacred page. In his conclusion to the *Historia*, Bede offers the clearest picture of what his life was actually like and how he understood his vocation.

> I, Bede, servant of Christ and priest of the monastery of St. Peter and St. Paul which is at Wearmouth and Jarrow, have, with the help of God and to the best of my ability, put together this account of the history of the Church of Britain and the English people in particular, gleaned either from ancient documents or from tradition or from my own knowledge. I was born in the territory of the monastery. When I was seven years of age I was, by care of my kinsmen, put into the charge of the reverend Abbot Benedict and then of Ceolfrith, to be educated. From then on I have spent all my life in this monastery, applying myself entirely to the study of the Scriptures.[1]

---

1. Bede, *EH*, 5.24 (293). "Domino adiuuante digessi Baeda famulus Christi et presbyter monasterii beatorum apostolorum Petri et Pauli, quod est ad Viuraemuda et in Gyruum. Qui natus in territorio eiusdem monasterii, cum essem annorum VII, cura propinquorum datus sum educandus reuerentissimo abbati Benedicto, ac deinde Ceolfrido, cunctumque ex eo tempus uitae in eiusdem monasterii habitatione peragens, omnem meditandis scripturis operam dedi . . ." (*HE*, 5.24.2).

Bede thought of himself not primarily as an historian but as an exegete of Scripture. If Bede is to be taken at his word, only in light of his exegetical activity, which was largely figural, can his history be understood, even if Bede recognizes differences between theological and historical work and writing.

Arthur Holder has argued that Bede intentionally separated his historical work from his exegesis in order to give preeminence to Scripture.[2] For example, Bede did not hesitate to allegorize every detail of the Temple and Tabernacle in his commentaries, but he did not feel free to allegorize the ecclesial structures of his own day or even the ones in his ecclesiastical history.[3] To be sure, church buildings were important to Bede, but the interesting point is that he rarely interpreted non-biblical architecture or history figurally, unlike other early Christian exegetes.[4] In Bede's own words, "These items of information on the structure of the temple, in our opinion, should indeed be passed on to the keen reader. But among them let us seek out figures of whatever mysteries sacred scripture has thought fit to relate and the rest let us use purely for historical knowledge."[5] Holder observes that this statement occurs late in Bede's exegetical career giving the impression that the separation between history and figural exegesis was part of the mature thought of Bede. So, on the rare occasion that Bede does allegorize a historical building or event, as he does in *De tabernaculo*, Holder claims that Bede acquired "sensitivity" to the difference between history and exegesis and their own distinctive methods as his thinking and writing matured.[6] In order to find out if Holder's analysis is correct a more detailed study of the *Historia* and its relationship to Bede's exegesis is required.

2. Holder, "Allegory and History in Bede's Interpretation of Sacred Architecture," 115–31.

3. Ibid., 121.

4. For example, Eusebius of Ceasurea, *Ecclesiastical History*, 10.4; Maximus the Confessor, *Mystagogia*, 1–5. In fact, in twelfth-century Paris at St. Denis portions of the internal structure (columns to be exact) were constructed based on figural readings and biblical symbolism; see Abbot Suger, *De consecratione*; In English, *Abbot Suger on the Abbey Church of St. Denis and its Art Treasures*; see also Augustine's *De civitate Dei* which could be read as an entire figural account of the history of the Roman empire. According to Holder, the only place where Bede allegorizes a historical event or building is in *De tabernaculo* 3.737–42. See also Frei's summary comments on the Christian tradition in "The 'Literal Reading' of Biblical Narrative in the Christian Tradition," 40.

5. Bede, *On the Temple*, 68. "Haec quidem de structura temple studioso lectori credidimus intimanda. Verum in eis quaecumque scriptura sacra referre commodum duxit figuras mysteriorum quaeramus ceteris pro historiae cognitione simpliciter utamur" (*De templo*, II, 73–76). Meyvaert concurs with Holder on this point in "Bede, Cassiodorus, and the Codex Amaitinus," 859–60.

6. Holder, "Allegory and History," 130–31.

While I will continue to refine my reading of Bede's exegesis, I need to introduce, albeit briefly, his figural approach in exegesis as a starting point. Recent literature provides a good overview of Bede's exegetical approach, even if it frequently falls short of seeing its relationship to his historical writings. Most Bede scholars rightly note that Bede follows Augustine and the more Alexandrian path in exegesis,[7] although the distinction between the Alexandrians and Antiochenes frequently misleads.[8] Bede spoke of three and four senses of Scripture as de Lubac rightly notes, and Bede fits quite well into his historical analysis of how the two senses (literal and allegorical, or historical and spiritual) became four senses.[9] Bede was also indebted to Tyconius's *The Book of Rules*.[10] For example, Bede speaks of allegories in factual events (*allegoria factis*) when describing Paul's exegesis of Galatians 4 and contrasts it to merely verbal allegories, a point I will revisit soon.[11] Thus, Bede functions with a polyvalent sense of allegory, and readers should never neglect these complexities.

Furthermore, Calvin Kendall shows how Bede uses the language of *mysterium*, *allegoria*, *arcanum*, and *sacramentum* in related, but not synonymous, ways regarding the spiritual sense of Scripture to go beyond the literal or historical sense.[12] He also makes the interesting observation that Bede wrestled with the distinction between sign and symbol—that is he struggled in expressing the difference, which he clearly believed to obtain, between commentators and Holy Writ itself because the language of symbol had not made a significant entrance into the Latin west by Bede's day.[13] Signs are the things themselves, like the cross of Christ; symbols remind us of signs, like the letter T reminds us of the cross in its empirical shape. The

---

7. Nearly all subsequent scholars follow Plummer in his translation of Bede's, *Opera Historica*, lvi; see most recently, Brown, *Companion to Bede*, 35–36.

8. See, for example, Young, *Biblical Exegesis and the Formation of Christian Culture*, and more recently, Ayres, *Nicea and Its Legacy*.

9. De Lubac, *Medieval Exegesis*, 2:33–39; cf. also, de Lubac, *Medieval Exegesis*, 1:90–105, 127, esp. 92–93, 127. Bede names three and four senses in the same paragraph. See *On the Tabernacle*, 25. Bede's reluctance to synthesize the three- and four-fold senses reveals he does not take them in a methodological or hierarchical order.

10. For a brief summary on the relationship between Bede and Tyconius see Brown, *Companion to Bede*, 39–40. On Tyconius, see *Book of Rules*, and Bright, *Book of Rules of Tyconius*.

11. See Bede's *De schematibus et tropis*, 251: "Notandum sane quod allegoria aliquando factis, aliquando verbis tantum modo fit." Latin text from Bede, *De schematibus et tropis*, which includes an English translation by Calvin Kendall.

12. Kendall, "Responsibility of *Auctoritas*: Method and Meaning in Bede's Commentary on Genesis," 106–11.

13. Ibid., 111–12.

example of the letter T and the cross comes from Bede himself where he uses *figura* for the letter T and *signum* for the cross.[14] However, Bede does not use these words technically with any consistency throughout his work thereby demonstrating Kendall's point about Bede's searching for the best ways to articulate such distinctions.[15]

In sum, Bede reads Scripture allegorically, in the tradition of the Church, while also trying to maintain the integrity of the letter, and he says as much, for example, in his commentary on Genesis: "But it must be carefully observed, as each one devotes his attention to the allegorical senses, how far he may have forsaken the manifest truth of history by allegorical interpretation."[16] How Bede works out this difference and relationship between the figural or allegorical and the literal or historical is the focus of the next two chapters. I will discuss the relationship between the *Historia* and *De templo* here because Bede was writing them simultaneously, though, quite interestingly, this fact is not immediately perceivable during a first reading.

Bede's *Historia* and *De templo*

Bede scholars generally agree that Bede was working on *De templo* and the *Historia ecclesiastica gentis Anglorum* simultaneously, since he most likely finished both of them in 731.[17] In fact, the relationship between these two texts was described by Henry Mayr-Harting as "a kind of diptych."[18] Hence, one must understand them in relationship to each other, especially if Bede's understanding of the relationship between theology, history, and exegesis is to come into sharper relief.[19]

14. This is Bede's example without the language of symbol. See *In genesim*, 97: "Nec frustra trecenti anni seorsum excipiuntur, quibus specialiter ambulasse cum Deo Enoch perhibetur. Hic etenim numerus apud Grecos per litteram solet notary. uero littera crucis figuram tenet; et si apicem solum qui deest in medio suscepisset, non iam figura crucis sed ipsum crucis esset signum manifesta specie depictum."

15. See Kendall, "The Responsibility of *Auctoritas*," 113–19; See Jones, "Some Introductory Remarks on Bede's Commentary on Genesis," 151–60.

16. Bede, *On Genesis*, 69. "Sed diligenter intuendum ut ita quisque sensibus allegoricis stadium impendat, quatenus apertam historiae fidem allegorizando derelinquat" (*In genesim*, 3).

17. On the dating of *De templo* see Jennifer O'Reilly, "Introduction," xvii; Mayr-Harting's, "The Venerable Bede, The Rule of St. Benedict, and Social Class," 12–13, 19; and Meyvaert's, *Bede and Gregory the Great*, 1, 9–10.

18. Mayr-Harting, "The Venerable Bede, The Rule of St. Benedict, and Social Class," 13.

19. The circumstances surrounding the occasion for Bede's writing of the *Historia* are debated and far from clear. The best and most meticulous work has been done by Goffart, *The Narrators of Barbarian History (A.D. 550–800)*, 235–328. My reading of

Bede stands in a long tradition of historians (both pagan and Christian) who thought of history's purpose as primarily pedagogical and moral.[20] "This you perceive, clear-sighted as you are; and therefore, in your zeal for the spiritual well-being of us all, you wish to see my *History* more widely known, for the instruction of yourself and those over whom divine authority has [a]ppointed you to rule."[21] More specifically, this instruction was morally and spiritually directed:

> Should history tell of good men and their good estate, the thoughtful listener is spurred on to imitate the good; should it record the evil ends of wicked men, no less effectually the devout and earnest listener or reader is kindled to eschew what is harmful and perverse, and himself with greater care pursue those things which he has learned to be good and pleasing in the sight of God.[22]

Furthermore, Bede specifically encouraged his readers to imitate the faith and virtue of preceding biblical figures while commenting on 2 Chronicles 4:8 in *De templo*, "When we take these [the examples of Joseph, Enoch and others] and countless things of the kind as models of virtue, what is it that holds them up before us but the five golden tables or vessels of the Lord or the loaves of proposition still on the left side of the temple?"[23] In this way, Bede's writing of history and his exegesis share a common purpose that keep them hinged together in their diptych: the moral and spiritual instruction of humanity. While interested in accurately describing the past, Bede never does so for its own sake. He always sought to teach his readers the truth for the sake of growing deeper into the mysteries of Christ and his

---

Bede presupposes Goffart's work with a much more theological edge by reading *De templo* and the *Historia* as a theological pair.

20. See, for example, Davidse, "On Bede as Christian Historian," 7–9; Ray, "Bede, the Exegete, as Historian," 125–40; Breisach, *Historiography*, 5–45.

21. *EH*, preface. "Quod ipsum tu quoque uigilantissime deprehendens, historiam memoratam in notitiam tibi simul et eis, quibus te regendis diuina praefecit auctoritas, ob generalis curam salutis latius propalari desideras" (*HE*, preface).

22. *EH*, preface. "Siue enim historia de bonis bona referat, ad imitandum bonum auditor sollicitus instigator; seu mala commemoret de prauis, nihilominus religious ac pius auditor siue lector deuitando quod noxium est ac peruersum, ipse sollertius ad exsequenda ea quae bona ac Deo digna esse cognouerit, accenditur" (*HE*, preface).

23. Bede, *On the Temple*, 112. "Haec et huiusmodi innumera nobis in exemplum uirtutis assumimus, quid nisi mensae quinque aureae siue uasa domini seu panes propositionis adhuc in sinistris temple nobis offerunt quia diuinae litterae iuxta historicum sensum ianuam nobis et recte uiuendi et aeterna praemia a domino speranda aperiunt?"(*De templo*, 229)

Church.²⁴ Thus, the discipline or practice of history as the mere accumulation of knowledge about the past is not an end in itself for Bede (in fact, it might not even be conceivable for him) because it should be used for moral, theological, and spiritual ends.²⁵ Goffart and DeGregorio are right to see that Bede's writing of the *Historia* itself was a form of moral advocacy and reform for the Northumbrian church that stretched throughout this later works.²⁶ Bede's Letter to Egbert, for example, details Bede's perceived decline of the Church in northern Britain.²⁷

However, it would be wrong to think that Bede considers history and exegesis as simply two different ways of saying or doing the same things. Immediately after he talks of Scripture's historical sense opening the door for salvation in *De templo*, he quickly adds and qualifies:

> But when on a deeper understanding of these things [Joseph's example and the tables and vessels], we catch echoes of either the plan of the Lord's incarnation or some other mysteries of the holy Church, we find, as it were, the five other tables for carrying the vessels of election and the food of the life of the spirit on the right side of the temple, because we recognize that these very same words of sacred history, which are to us an entirely new lightning-flash of heavenly wisdom, open the door to new understandings of the old. In which figure also, of course, are included in the five lampstands made in the temple.²⁸

Thus, it appears that Bede considers the study of history in need of transformation at the hands of figural or spiritual exegesis of Scripture. In other words, history can teach humans and even prepare them for the gospel and

---

24. See Bede's admonition against only reading Scripture according to the literal sense at the end of his commentary on Genesis. See Bede, *On Genesis*, 321–22; *In genesim*, 241–42.

25. Here I am in large agreement with Davidse, "The Sense of History in the Works of the Venerable Bede," 647–95.

26. See Goffart, *The Narrators of Barbarian History*, 296–328. See DeGregorio, "*Nostrorum socordiam temporum*: The Reforming Impulse of Bede's Later Exegesis," 107–22. Gunn extends Goffart and DeGregorio's work in interesting ways as well. See Gunn, *Bede's Historiae*

27. See *Bede's Letter to Bishop Egbert* in *The Ecclesiastical History of the English People*, 343–57.

28. Bede, *On the Temple*, 112. "At cum eadum altius intellegentes uel dispensationem dominicae incarnationis uel alia quaelibet sanctae ecclesiae sacramenta sonare uiderimus quasi alias quinque mensas ad portanda uasa electionis et alimoniam uitae spiritalis in dextris temple inuenimus quia eadem ipsa uerba sacrae historia nouum omnio fulgor nobis sapientiae caelestis nouos aperire sensus de ueteribus agnoscimus. In qua profecto figura et candelabra quina sunt facta in templo" (*De templo*, 229).

for Christ, but that same history will be understood in a "*novum omnio*" way in light of the incarnation.[29] While both history and exegesis have the same purposes, history itself does not have the internal resources to understand itself in the most comprehensible fashion—that is to say, to understand itself as under the command of the Triune God and God's providence.

Bede's History and Exegesis

Bede certainly wrote the *Historia* fully believing in divine providence, particularly in God's plan to bring the English into the Church, and he even explicitly recounts and narrates miracles and other acts of providence in the *Historia*.[30] However, this is not to say much at all; of course Bede wrote theological history that included divine actions. No one would ever dispute that. What I want to understand are the theological and philosophical presumptions or underpinnings that make that type of history writing intelligible and persuasive. In other words, what is the relationship between Bede's figural exegesis of the temple and his *Historia* and what theological claims are at issue in this relationship? I will have to uncover such presumptions by investigating the boundaries and differences between Bede's exegesis and historical works.

Before delving deeply into these borders, a brief summary of Bede's theology of history is necessary. I will revisit Davidse's scholarship on the theological sense of history in Bede that I previously addressed. Bede cited dates in relationship to Christ's incarnation. For example, in the opening pages of the *Historia* Bede mentions the reign of Julius Ceasar "in the year 60 before our Lord."[31] And then later recounting how the Emperor Claudis brought the Roman Empire to the British Isles, Bede refers to the end of a war: "in the year of our Lord 46."[32] Davidse rightly sees that for Bede all historical events get their significance from this moment in time, the incarnation of Christ, thereby making the incarnation essential for understanding history itself (*historia ipsa*).[33] In this way, the coming of the Church to England intensifies "the dynamics of history" because such conversion

---

29. While not nearly as philosophically adept, Bede is not far from Origen. See Dawson, *Christian Figural Reading and the Fashioning of Identity*, especially chapters 2–3, 5–6, and 9.

30. Jones actually takes one of the doctrinal loci of the *Historia* to be election. See his "Some Introductory Remarks on Bede's Commentary on Genesis," 125–31.

31. Bede, *EH*, 1.2. "ante uero incarnationis Dominicae tempus anno sexagesimo" (*HE*, 1.2.1).

32. Bede, *EH*, 1.3. "qui est annus ab incarnation Domini quadragesimus sextus," (*HE*, 1.3.1).

33. Davidse, "On Bede as Christian Historian," 9–12.

means the gospel is reaching the ends of the earth (Acts 1), and Bede intends his *Historia* to be read in just this way.[34] In other words, Bede's *Historia* is both focused on the concrete events in England but also the universal reign of Christ, since the Church's arrival in Britain instantiates that reign in Bede's own time and place. As Davidse puts it, "Bede's world is as wide as the *historia ipsa*, which encompasses all times and places; it is as wide as Christ's reign, which includes not only the past and the present, but also the future."[35] Therefore, history for Bede is concerned with the particular and the universal simultaneously. Bede's account of the world ages as taking place within the week of creation also fits within this larger theological framework, but this summary will suffice for now until I address the world ages in the next chapter.

In many instances and despite the theology of history sketched above, Bede surprisingly does not make figural connections between Scripture and his historical writings.[36] I will now treat several of those occurrences below focusing on what should be clear connections between *De templo* and the *Historia*. The first example has to do with snakes or *serpentes*. Given his close geographic location to Ireland, Bede has an interest in serpents. He mentions them several times in the first chapter of book one of the *Historia*.[37] Citing the authority of St. Basil and observing the beauty and plentiful resources of the British island, Bede says that glossy black jet (a hardened and dense type of coal often used in jewelry) repels snakes.[38] Then in describing Ireland, Bede notes that no reptile lives there and that serpents cannot even breathe its air without perishing; also, manuscripts from Ireland can be shredded, dissolved, and drunk in order to cure those suffering from poisonous snake bites.[39] Bede presumes the Christian tradition's association of sin with serpents, but he does not make any specific figural connections with serpents in Scripture. For example, it seems reasonable that Bede would connect the curing of snake bitten people by items from Ireland with the bronze serpent staff raised up in the camp of Israel when they were struck by poisonous snakes in Numbers 21. Moreover, in *De templo* Bede mentions that when cedar is burned its brightness drives snakes away. Nevertheless, no connec-

---

34. Ibid., 13.
35. Ibid., 15.
36. In what follows I use some of Mayr-Harting's appendix as well as my own findings that show connections between *De templo* and the *Historia*. However, Mayr-Harting does not note the lack of figural connection between similarities. See Mayr-Harting, *The Venerable Bede, the Rule of St. Benedict, and Social Class*, appendix.
37. Bede, *EH*, 1.1; *HE*, 1.1.2–5.
38. Bede, *EH*, 1.1; *HE*, 1.1.2.
39. Bede, *EH*, 1.1; *HE*, 1.1.4.

tions are made between the *Historia* and any other non-biblical event. This is especially puzzling given both passages' mentioning of fire: the burning of the cedar wood in *De templo* and the jet that is put to fire and kindled in the *Historia*.[40] I think this similarity would not be lost on Bede, but he never makes the explicit connection.

Second, there are at least two places in *De templo* that contain relevant material to Bede's recounting of the Synod of Whitby in the *Historia*. Bede was very concerned about the proper dating of Easter and the unity of the church in Britain because Celtic Christians celebrated Easter at a different time than Roman Christians. This difference included Christian practices that were seen to conflict creating possible temptation and went beyond mere factual argument as Bede's analysis shows.

> Hence it is said that in these days it sometimes happened that Easter was celebrated twice in the same year, so that the king had finished the fast and was keeping Easter Sunday, while the queen and her people were still in Lent and observing Palm Sunday... The dispute naturally troubled the minds and hearts of many people who feared that, though they had received the name of Christian, they were running or had run in vain.[41]

The Synod of Whitby which assembled in 664 sought to remedy this division and correct any false teachings regarding Easter and its proper date. In the end, the Celts ended up siding with the Romans and the differing practices ended.

Bede describes the arguments brought forth from each side, Celtic and Roman, to King Oswiu in chapter twenty five of book III of the *Historia*. The major theological rationale both sides used to make their case is apostolic authority. The Celts claimed to follow the apostle John and the Romans claimed to follow Peter, Paul, and John.[42] In *De templo*, Bede says that the two doors made of olive wood that serve as the entrance to the temple are figures of baptism into the one church which is to be identified with the apostles who were given the keys of the kingdom to "admit worthy ones inside the gates of the kingdom, and debar by excommunication or anathema the stubborn, the unclean, and the arrogant from entering eternal

---

40. Bede, *De templo*, 168: "Cedrus namque arbor est imputribilis omnino naturae odoris iocundi aspectus nitidi serpentes accensa nitore fugans ac perimens." Then, in *Historia*, 1.1: "... est autem nigrogemmeus, et ardens igni ammotus, incensus serpentes fugat adtritu calefactus applicita detinet aeque ut sucinum."

41. Bede, *EH*, 3.25; *HE*, 3.25.2.

42. Bede, *EH*, 3.25; *HE*, 3.25.3–6.

life."⁴³ Furthermore, when commenting on the three floors of the temple as described in 1 Kings 6, Bede uses King Ahaziah of Samaria's falling through the lattice in his Samarian palace (2 Kings 1:2) as a figural and biblical example of his separation from the house of David. Bede then goes on to directly link Ahaziah with heresy and schism.⁴⁴

> Ahaziah king of Samaria who had separated himself from the house of David did indeed go up to the upper-room, but he fell through the railings because, although heretics and schismatics seem to scale some peak of good work, nevertheless, because they lack the structure of the Church's unity, the protecting side walls are, as it were gaping wide open and weak, and consequently, they [the heretics and schismatics] are continually falling back into the depths of their vices until, deprived of God's help, they perish through their arrogance and obstinacy.⁴⁵

As Bede recorded in the *Historia*, at one point during debate at Whitby, Wilford, who represented the Roman Church, affirmed the good intentions, piety, and even good works of the Celts and their leaders but said that the Celts would be committing sin if they turned their backs on the truth now that they have heard it plainly.⁴⁶ In the words of *De templo*, they would be stubborn, obstinate, and arrogant. Bede describes the dispute at Whitby as finally being resolved on the grounds of apostolicity and the primacy of Peter when King Oswiu gets both sides to acknowledge that Christ gave the keys to Peter.⁴⁷ The figures, allusions, and similarities between the *Historia* and *De templo* vis-à-vis church dividing celebrations of Easter and apostolic authority and succession are obvious, but Bede does not mention them in the *Historia*. Again, a thinker with the intellectual acuity and theological imagination of Bede would seemingly discern these similarities and explicitly make the connections.

Third, the helpfulness of the Gentile King Hiram in helping Solomon build the temple is seen by Bede as a figure of God's inclusion of all nations and peoples. More specifically, Bede even makes a more general assertion about the helpfulness of secular leaders for the church.

> And since Hiram was a king and used his royal power to help Solomon in the building of the house of the Lord, there

---

43. Bede, *On the Temple*, 56; *De templo*, 186.
44. Bede, *On the Temple*, 26–27; *De templo*, 163–64.
45. Bede, *On the Temple*, 27; *De templo*, 164.
46. Bede, *EH*, 3.25; *HE*, 3.25.10.
47. Bede, *EH*, 159. *HE*, 3.25.10.

is nothing to prevent him from typifying [*typice*] masters of (worldly) affairs, themselves converted to the faith, by whose help, as is well-known, the Church has quite often been assisted and nobly increased, and has been supported by their imperial decrees against heretics and schismatics and pagans.[48]

A parallel with the immediately preceding example in the *Historia* aside, throughout the *Historia* Bede demonstrates great concern to show the faithfulness and apostasy of kings and how it impacts the spiritual life of the Anglo-Saxon people. Book II of the *Historia* spends a great deal of time discussing the reign of King Edwin, including his conversion to Christianity through the preaching of Paulinus and a vision. Bede recounts Edwin's acceptance of the faith and its effects:

> So King Edwin, with all the nobles of his race and a vast number of the common people, received the faith and regeneration by holy baptism in the eleventh year of his reign, that is in the year of our Lord 627 and about 180 years after the coming of the English to Britain. He was baptized at York Easter Day, 12 April, in the church of St. Peter the Apostle, which he had hastily built of wood while he was a catechumen and under instruction before he received baptism. He established an episcopal see for Paulinus, his instructor and bishop, in the same city.[49]

After Edwin's death, his successors, Eanfrith and Aelfric, led the people astray because they "abjured and betrayed the mysteries of the heavenly kingdom to which they had been admitted and reverted to the filth of their former idolatry, thereby to be polluted and destroyed."[50] At these places and throughout the *Historia*, Bede showed great concern for how kings

---

48. Bede, *On the Temple*, 7. "Neque aliquid prohibit quin Hiram quia rex erat regalique potential Salmonem in aedificio domus domini iuuabat conuersos ad fidem ipsos rerum dominos typice denuntiet quorum ope constat ecclesiam saepius adiutam nobiliter augmentatam et contra hereticos scismaticos et paganos principalibus erectam esse decretis" (*De templo*, 149).

49. Bede, *EH*, 2.14. "Igitur accepit rex Eduini cum cuntis gentis suae nobilibus ac plebe perplurima fidem et lauacrum sanctae regenerationis anno regni sui undecimo, qui est annus dominicae incarnationis DCXXVII, ab aduentu uero Anglorum in Brittaniam annus circiter CLXXX. Baptizatus est autem Eburaci die sancto paschae pridie iduum Aprilium, in ecclesia sancti Petri apostolic, quam ibidem ipse de lingo, cum cathecizaretur atque ad percipiendum baptisma imbueretur, citato opere construxit. In qua etiam ciuitate ipsi doctori atque antistiti suo Paulino sedem episcopatus donauit" (*HE*, 2.14.1).

50. Bede, *EH*, 3.1. "Qui uterque rex, ut terreni regni infalus sortitus est, sacramenta regni caelestis, quibus initiates erat, anathematizando prodidit, ac se priscis idolatriae sordibus polluendum perdendumque restituit" (*HE*, 3.1.1).

impacted the spiritual life of their people and nation. Bede strangely never actually makes an explicit figural connection between King Hiram in the Old Testament and the kings and leaders in the *Historia*.

There are still other places in the *Historia* where Bede could have made direct connections between historical events and biblical ones but chose not to do so. In narrating the rise of the apostate King Eadbald, son of faithful King Aethelberht, who committed multiple acts of fornication, including having his father's wife, Bede says that Eadbald "did not escape the scourge of divine punishment in chastisement and correction; for he was afflicted by frequent fits of madness and possessed by an unclean spirit."[51] While Bede does mention Paul's condemnation of "such acts not even known among the gentiles" in 1 Corinthians 5, the even more obvious connection with a king, fits of madness, and an evil spirit goes unmade. Bede, who spent time commenting on the opening chapters 1 Samuel, does not explicitly link King Eadbald and King Saul.[52]

Bede's Use of Scripture and History and Potential Objections

Before discussing why Bede might not have made the figural connections he could have, I need to address some potential objections to my argument thus far. But before I can even attend to objections, Bede's use of biblical figures and their relationship to other historical events must be considered.

Bede uses the presence of figures in Scripture in multiple ways. First, they can be mere examples or common illustrations. Second, they can represent or signify permanent ontological significance in the course of history, and third, figures that have ontological status act across time causally.[53] To some degree, I have already discussed the first two, so I will keep my treatment of them brief, and I will focus on the third, which has not been ad-

---

51. Bede, *EH*, 2.5; *HE*, 2.5.3.

52 For King Saul's possession by an unclean spirit and fits of madness see 1 Samuel 16–19. Bede's commentary on Samuel remains untranslated; for Bede's comments on this passage that mention nothing specifically in his *Historia*; see Hurst, *In primam partem Samuhelis*, 141–81.

53. Bede never discusses the ontological status on any figure in such language, so I fully recognize the imposition of categories that I am employing. My purpose here is to get at the various ways that figures function in Bede and to understand that issues of ontology necessarily arise. Furthermore, I do not think Bede (or any other church father for that matter) would object to a thoroughgoing theological and philosophical analysis of how figural exegesis works and functions. Also, my use of three categories here is not intended to be exhaustive. There could very well be more ways that Bede uses biblical figures.

dressed. While these differing uses are displayed throughout Bede's corpus, I will primarily focus on *De templo* in order to keep the conversation as germane as possible to the topic at hand in this chapter.

The first use of Scripture and history has already been mentioned above. King Eadbald serves as a good example. Bede clearly alludes to 1 Corinthians 5 when he says that Eadbald partook of actions that ". . . as the apostle [Paul] declares to have been not so much as named among the Gentiles, in that he took his father's wife."[54] Thus, Scripture functions as a prophetic denunciation of Eadbald's actions but not in a figural or symbolic sense. Bede simply applies Paul's text to the historical situation without any mediating categories of figure or symbolism.

Second, figures or events can have ontological significance beyond their own historical place and time. The temple is understood to be a figure of Christ and the Church. Again, "If, therefore, he [Christ] became the temple of God by assuming human nature and we become the temple of God through his Spirit dwelling in us, it is quite clear that the material temple was a figure of us all, that is, both of the Lord himself and his members which we are."[55] Because of this presence and figural significance, Bede says we should consider the material structure and building of the temple in order to better understand Christ and the Church. "This will be clearer if we consider the actual building of the temple systematically. That is to say, in this way the figure will apply to the Lord himself in some respects, in others to all the elect..."[56] Bede is implying that Christ and the Church are present in the material structure of the temple because for one to be able to understand Christ and the Church through the temple, they must in some way be present in or with the actual structure of the temple. In short, this is Auerbach's sense of *figura*, especially since Christ is the fulfillment of the temple's function.[57]

Lastly, in many places, Bede ascribes causative power to biblical figures. In book 2 of *De templo* Bede says that Solomon chose both Jews and

---

54. Bede, *EH*, 2.5. "Siquidem non solum fidem Christi recipere noluerat, sed et fornicatione pollutus est tali, qualem nec inter gentes auditam apostolus testatur, 'ita ut uxorem partris haberet'" (*HE*, 2.5.3).

55. Bede, *On the Temple*, 5. "Si ergo ille templum Dei per assumptam humanitatem factus est et nos templum Dei per inhabitantem spiritum eius in nobis efficimur, constat utique quia figuram omnium nostrum et ipsius domini uidelicet et membrorum eius quae nos sumus templum illud materiale tenuit..." (*De templo*, 147).

56. Bede, *On the Temple*, 6. "Quod melius considerate ex ordine ipso temple aedificio patebit ut in quibus dam uidelicet figura ad ipsum dominum in quibusdam uero ad omnes electos pertineat, in quibusdam intemeratam in caelis angelorum felicitatem in quibusdam inuictam in terris hominum patientiam describat..." (*De templo*, 147).

57 Auerbach's analysis of *figura* concurs with my analysis and conclusion of Bede on this point; see his *Scenes from the Drama of European Literature*.

gentiles to work on the temple because of what God was going to do with the gentiles in the New Testament.

> The point in Solomon's seeking help from Hiram in the work of the temple was that when the Lord came in the flesh and arranged to build a favourite home for himself, namely, the Church, he chose helpers for the work not from the Jews alone but also from the gentiles. For he picked ministers of the word from both peoples. Hiram sent Solomon cedar and pine-wood hewn in Lebanon to put in the house of the Lord *because* the converted gentiles sent to the humbled from the mountain of their pride by the axe of the Lord's reproof, to be trained according to the norm of evangelical truth to this merits or age. He also sent craftsmen *because* the gentiles offered to the Lord philosophers converted to true wisdom, people who because of their learning might deservedly be put in charge of people to govern them. Such, for instance, in the time of the apostles was Dionysius the Areopagite, such too was the most gentile and brave martyr Cyprian and countless others. He also sent gold which can be taken in the same sense, namely, that it symbolizes men renowned for wisdom and ability. For all these offerings the gentiles expect the gifts of heavenly grace from the Lord, namely, the wheat of the word of God and the oil of charity and of the unction and enlightenment of the Holy Spirit.[58]

In this fascinating passage, Bede says that Solomon sent for gentile help to build the temple *because (quia)* converted gentiles came to hear and be trained in the evangelical truth. Furthermore, the gentile aid to Solomon occurred *because (quia)* gentiles offered the Lord great thinkers and philosophers, and Bede actually gives an example of one, Dionysius the Areopagite.

58. Bede, *On the Temple*, 7–8, emphasis added. "Petit ergo Salomon in opere templi auxilium ab Hiram quia cum ueniens in carne dominus dilectam sibi domum uidelicet Ecclesiam aedificare disponeret non de Judaeis tantummodo, uerum etiam de gentibus adiutores operis elegit. Nam de utroque populo ministros sermonis assumpsit. *Misit Hiram Salomoni praecisa de Libano ligna cedrina et abiegna quae in domum domini ponerentur* quia conuersa gentilitas misit ad dominum uiros quondam ad saeculum claros sed securi dominicae increpationis de monte suae superbiae iam deiectos et humiliatos qui ad normam euangelicae ueritatis instituti in aedificio ecclesiae pro suo quoque merito, uel tempore collocarentur. *Misit etiam artifices* quia conuersos ad ueram sapientiam philosophos qui gratia eruditionis populis quoque regendis iure praeponerentur domino gentilitas obtulit qualis ipsis apostolorum temporibus Dionysius Areopagita qualis deinceps doctor suauissimus et fortissimus martyr Cyprianus aliique quam plurimi. *Misit et aurum* quod in eadem significatione accipitur quia nimirum uiros sapientia et ingenio praeclaros ostendit. Pro quibus cunctis oblationibus gentilitas a domino dona expectat gratiae caelestis triticum uidelicet uerbi Dei et oleum caritatis atque unctionis et illuminationis spiritus sancti" (*De templo*, 149).

Bede affirms that events that transpired after the construction of the temple were the reason for how and why it was constructed, namely with the help of pagan peoples. How can events and persons be affected by events and persons that come after them?

Bede says that the distance in space and time that separate believers is bridged by faith and the Holy Spirit. In commenting on the dimensions of the portico of the temple, Bede likens the length of the portico to the endurance of the faithful ancient saints who waited for God to fulfill his promises in the incarnation. "By their length, they equaled the breadth of the temple because through the forbearance of their devoted spirit they longed for the coming of the expansion of the Church in the love of God in Christ Jesus Our Lord for, although still separated in time from the mysteries of the Lord's incarnation, nevertheless by their faith and preaching they were very near."[59] Here, Bede says that the Old Testament saints become close to Christ (*fuere proximi*) by their faith and proclamation. Thus, the practice and "possession" of faith is not bound by temporal limitations and restrictions. This can occur because of the harmonious unity of the divine activity of providence (*diuinae operationis concordia*) at work in both the Old and New Covenants bringing the Old to fulfillment in the New.[60] Recalling the discussion above, faith is part of God's giving (*inditum*) separate temporal events figural significance they may otherwise lack. The work of the eternal Holy Spirit who was, is, and will always be at work weaves these events together as a whole.

> For these chains are woven together with wonderful craftsmanship because it is thanks to the absolutely marvelous grace of the Holy Spirit that the lifestyles of believers, quite removed from each other though they may be in space, time, rank, status, sex and age, are nevertheless linked together by one and the same faith and love. That this common fraternal bond of the righteous, separated in space and time, is effected by the union of the gift of the Spirit, is also shown by the following words, when, with reference to the making of the capitals, it is further remarked: Seven rows of nets were on one capital, and seven nets on the other capital. [. . .] The reason why there were seven rows of nets in both capitals is that it was through the grace of

---

59. Bede, *On the Temple*, 24. "Aequabant ergo longanimitatem deuotae mentis desiderabant uenire dilatationem ecclesiae in caritate Dei quae est in Christo Iesu domino nostro quia quamuis tempore adhuc fuerint a sacramentis dominicae incanationis separate fide tamen ac praedicatione fuere proximi" (*De templo*, 162).

60. See Bede, *On the Temple*, 77; *De templo*, 201.

one and the same septiform Spirit that the Fathers of both testaments received the privilege of election.[61]

The unifying work and providence of the Holy Spirit binds times and persons together across temporal boundaries. Since the same God who spoke to Moses and the Old Testament patriarchs and prophets is the God of Jesus Christ, limitations of time can be transcended or at least be understood as inconsequential or incidental to the life of faith. Ultimately this is why Bede can say that Moses taught the trinity, and many moderns can only be puzzled by this idea thinking that whoever wrote the Pentateuch did not teach the trinity because that was a later development in Christianity.[62] In other words, Bede commits the historical fallacy of anachronism here (and in many other places), while we simply "know better."

Now I am ready to handle potential objections. One might dissent that I have been too selective in appropriating putatively missed opportunities by Bede to make figural connections between history and biblical figures because Bede does allude to and use Scripture in the *Historia*. Of course Bede mentions Scripture and makes connections between the *Historia* and Scripture, but the *kinds* of connections and how he makes them is important to understand. I will show below how these connections do not attenuate my argument.

A good example of Bede connecting Scripture and an event in his *Historia* is King Raedwald. Bede mentions how King Raedwald was like (*in morem*) the "ancient Samaritans ... serving both Christ and the [idolatrous] gods whom he previously served."[63] At first glance, Bede does seem to be making a figural connection. However, Bede's connecting the events with "*in morem*" is linguistically quite weak if he were intending to make a figural or substantive

---

61. Bede, *On the Temple*, 78. "Hae etenim catenae miro sibi inuicem sunt opera contextae quia mirabilis prorsus gratia sancti spiritus actum est ut uita fidelium et locis et temporibus et gradu et conditione et sexu et aetate multum secreta ab alterutrum nihilominus una eademque fide ac dilectione sit ad inuicem coniuncta. Nam quia haec coniunctio fraternal iustorum locis et temporibus disiunctorum adunatione fiat doni spiritalis sequentibus quoque uerbis ostenditur cum de facture capitellorum adiungitur: Septena uersuum retiacula in capitello uno et septena retiacula in capitello altero ... Septena ergo uersuum retiacula errant in capitello utroque quia patres utriusque testamenti per gratiam unius eiusdemque spiritus septiformis ut essent electi acceperunt" (*De templo*, 202).

62. See Bede, *On Genesis*, 73; *In genisim*, 7.

63. *EH*, 2.15. 98. "Et quidem pater eius Reduald iamdudum in Cantia sacramentis Christianae fidei imbutus est, sed frustra; nam rediens domum ab uxore sua et quibusdam peruersis doctoribus seductus est, atque a sinceritate fidei deprauatus habuit posteriora peiora prioribus, ita ut in morem antiquorum Samaritanorum et Christo seruire uidere et diis, quibus antea seruiebat, atque in eodem fano et altare haberet ad sacrificium Christi et arulam ad uictimas daemoniorum" (*HE*, 2.15.1).

theological point. In *De templo*, Bede uses different vocabulary to show figural connections between the temple, Christ, and the Church. For example, forms of *figura, sacramentum, assimilare, designare,* and *signare,* dominate Bede's exegetical works when making figural connections.

In other places in *De templo*, Bede uses the adverb *ita* to connect events in mostly non-figural ways. He says of the workers building the temple,

> Notandum autem quod idem operarii ita errant distribute ut pars in monte lapides caederent pars item onera portarent. Diuersa sunt namque dona spiritus, et quidam maiorem dicendi ac proteruos arguendi constantiam habent, quidam mitiores ad consolandos pusillanimes et infirmos subleuandos existunt, quidam utriusque uirtutis munere praediti ad opus domus domini conueniunt, quales fieri uoluit eos quibus loquitur apostolus dicens, corripite inquietos consolamini pusillanimes suscipite infirmos patientes estote ad omnes.[64]

While Bede says this in the context of his spiritual exegesis of 1 Kings 5, his particular use of *ita* here does not function as language to figurally connect any events in Scripture to each other or even to history. He is merely stating that different workers had different tasks, which is simply what the Scripture under his consideration says. Bede then says how these different tasks represent the gifts of the Spirit, but in no way does his exegesis give *ita* any special figural or theological significance. Bede uses *ita* again in the same way in *De templo* in describing how beams were placed outside the temple:

> Legimus autem in libro paralipomenon quod trabes templi sicut et cetera eius interiora feurint auro uestitae. Quod ita factum esse non dubium est ut illae trabium partes quae intus in templo auri essent lamminis textae quae uero foris parebant hae minime deauratae ipsam cedri speciem formamque cunctis ostenderent in qua tamen imposita sibimet tabulata gestabant.[65]

64. Bede, *De templo*, 152–53. "But it is to be noted that the same workers were distribute in such a way that some cut stones on the mountain, others carried burdens. For in speaking and refuting the arrogant, other are gentler for the task with the gift of both virtues and are fitted for the work of the house of the Lord. Such did the Apostle wish those to become to whom he spoke the words: Admonish the disorderly, encourage the faint-hearted, support the weak, be patient towards all" (*On the Temple*, 12).

65. Bede, *De templo*, 164. "On the other hand, we read in the Book of Paralipomenon that the beams of the temple like the rest of its interior were adorned with gold. There is no doubt that this was done in such a way that those portions of the beams which were inside the temple were covered with gold leaf, but that those which showed outside were not gilded in order to show the actual graining and beauty of the cedarwood while supporting the floors which were laid on them" (*On the Temple*, 27). Another example of *ita* used in this way even in the context of figural exegesis:

The closest Bede comes to using *ita* to make spiritual or figural connections in *De templo*, comes in book 1, chapter 9. "*Auri autem lamminae quae marmori ac tabulis sunt abiegnis superpositae ipsa est latitudo caritatis de corde puro et conscientia bona et fide non ficta. Quae sicut aurum aliis pretiosius est metallis ita ceteris eximior uirtutibus in templo Dei singulari luce refulget.*"⁶⁶ In this case, *ita* functions to connect the superior value of gold in the overlay of the marble leaves and fir planks with the superiority of charity in comparison to other virtues. Thus, a connection is made between the objects of the temple (gold) with a figural referent (charity and virtue). However, in this example, a prior verb, *demonstrare*, governs the usage. The immediately preceding sentence reads as follows: "*Abies uero propter altitudinem sui et robur durabile mentem electorum infima quaeque desideria spernentem et caelestium contemplationi semper intentam virtute quoque patientiae singulariter excellentem non incongrue demonstrat.*"⁶⁷ Hence, the comparison between virtue and gold connected by *ita* (and *sicut*) depends on Bede's previous exegesis of the height and durability of the fir beams which demonstrate similarities (*non incongrue demonstrat*) to the minds of the elect.⁶⁸ Thus, *ita* can only function as the prime theological glue between gold and virtue because the fir beams, in a certain way, demonstrate the mind the of the elect.

All of the preceding analysis is also supported by the basic and varied uses that *ita* can have in differing contexts. In fact, the weaker sense of likeness, comparison, or commensurability is usually found when *ita* and *sicut*

"Sicut autem altitude parietis in altum exsurgens atque usque ad laquearia perueniens profectus uirtutum quibus electi ad regnum caeleste perueniunt uel certe ipsos electos choros sibimet per tempora uariantia succedentes significant, ita eaqualitas pauimenti concordem eorundem humilitatem aua in temporali adhuc uita positi socialite inuicem caritate dictante conuersantur non immerito demonstrat" (*De templo*, 170).

66. Bede, *De templo*, 170–71. "On the other hand, the gold leaf with which the marble and the fir planks are overlaid is the expansiveness of charity of pure heart and good conscience and faith not feigned. Just as gold is more precious than other metals so this is more outstanding than the other virtues and shines forth with alight all its own in the temple of God" (*On the Temple*, 36).

67. Bede, *De templo*, 170. "But on account of its height and lasting strength the fir tree is a quite appropriate analogy of the mind of the elect which spurns every lowest craving and is ever intent upon the contemplation of heavenly things and moreover, especially excels in the virtue of patience" (*On the Temple*, 36).

68. Bede, *On the Temple*, 36. Quite understandably, Connolly thought it best to get rid of the double negative present in the Latin and so translates it " . . . the fir tree is a quite appropriate analogy of the mind of the elect . . ." However, this elision makes one miss the dependence that subsequent sentences have on this sentence's verb and theological content.

are used together.[69] In short, if Bede wanted to make a serious theological or figural point or connection between a biblical event and something in the *Historia*, he had the strong theological vocabulary to do it, but he refrained from doing so.

In sum, Bede uses *ita* in mainly descriptive ways as a simile. That is, *ita* for Bede carries little or no special theological weight the way that *figura, signum, mysterium,* or one of the verbs he often uses (e.g., *designare, signare,* etc.) to ascribe figural significance to an event, object, or person does. Therefore, Bede does not intend any significant theological or figural point by comparing Raedwald to the ancient Samaritans, and the comparison should be understood to be an ornamental, extrinsic, or illustrative point to the overall historical description that Bede offers.

Another objection could be that while Bede may not make figural connections between the *Historia* and Scripture, he does write about miracles and other theologically significant events; in fact, the entire *Historia* should be understood as a piece of theological history. True enough. However, my point is not that the *Historia* is not theology; it certainly is, and I have nowhere suggested otherwise. Again, I am trying to get at what *kind* of theology it is because Bede clearly considered his task to be both theological and moral, not to mention that he clearly believed the *Historia* to be a piece of theological history, not unlike Augustine's *City of God*, albeit with the subtle yet significant theological and philosophical differences that will be further elucidated in the next chapter.

A final and potential point of opposition to my characterization thus far, which is in line with the immediately preceding objection regarding Bede's narration of miracles and obviously theological agenda in the *Historia*, would be that Bede is simply performing what Scripture already does in the gospels and the historical books of the Old Testament.[70] In other words, Bede's *Historia* imitates Scripture itself and the form it takes in various places. If this is the case, however, the puzzle as to why Bede does not treat certain events as being figurally linked to each other and to Scripture does not dissolve; it only becomes heightened because Scripture itself makes these kinds of connections and encourages its readers to do the same. Scripture was not timid in figurally interpreting preceding historical events or using allegory and figures. For example, in Galatians 4 Paul treats Sarah and Hagar as allegories of the old and new covenants, and likewise in 1 Corinthians 10 Paul read's Israel's history as a figure (type) for the Church. In Acts 8, Phillip explains Isaiah

---

69. See *Oxford Latin Dictionary*, first edition, sv "ita."

70. Some scholars have suggested this in different ways. See Kendall, "Bede's *Historia Ecclesiastica*: The Rhetoric of Faith," 145–72; Ward, *The Venerable Bede*, 114–29; Campbell, *Essays in Anglo Saxon History*, 2.

53 to the Ethiopian eunuch in terms of Christ, and there are other examples as well.[71] Overall, Bede makes many far less intuitive and indirect creative connections between objects in the temple, the Church, and Christian virtues, but he does not choose to make what seem to be obvious narrative and figural connections between figures and events in Scripture and those in his *Historia*. It should, therefore, not surprise us when Bede alludes to the fact that only Scripture should be read figurally as I have previously quoted. "These items of information on the structure of the temple, in our opinion, should indeed be passed on to the keen reader. But among them let us seek out figures of whatever mysteries sacred scripture has thought fit to relate and the rest let us use purely for historical knowledge."[72]

Conclusion

Chapter 1 addressed how modern interpreters of Bede have struggled to understand the relationship between Bede's *Historia* and exegesis. This chapter has shown that Bede himself, while not seeing a formal problem in relating history, theology, and exegesis, had a complex and perhaps even ambivalent approach in relating Scripture and history. Thus, I am suggesting that the struggle modern scholars have had in understanding Bede is not only a function of their own philosophical and theological presuppositions, though that is an important aspect of it. Instead, they are wrestling with Bede's own complexity and ambiguity in how he addressed the historical and exegetical tasks. Further inquiry into Bede's view of exegesis and history is necessary for an explanation to be found.

If an answer to the question posed in the title of this chapter on behalf of Bede must be given, we must conclude with a qualified no; qualified because he does affirm that historical events are figures or allegories of other historical events or theological truths, *allegoria factis*. Yet, no, because Bede does not, despite many opportunities, make the move to directly treat history as an allegory or figure even through the lens of Scripture. A more detailed reflection on why Bede might have taken this approach, as distinct from someone like Augustine, will be the subject of the next chapter.

71. See Wilken, "In Defense of Allegory," 35–50. Some other examples in the New Testament are the new Adam in Rom 5 and 1 Cor 15 and Heb 9 that says that Christ's sacrifice fulfills the high priest's sacrifice in the Old Testament. For more on this, see Auerbach's "Figura," 49–56.

72. Bede, *On the Temple*, 68; "Haec quidem de structura temple studioso lectori credidimus intimanda. Verum in eis quaecumque scriptura sacra referre commodum duxit figuras mysteriorum quaeramus ceteris pro historiae cognition simpliciter utamur" (*De templo*, 193).

3

Interpreting Genesis
Creation and the Relationship between the Literal and Figural Senses

Introduction

THE PRECEDING CHAPTER SHOWED that Bede did not figurally exegete events in the English Church's history, despite frequent opportunities to do so. I will argue in this chapter that Bede's commentary on Genesis and how he reads the creation of time, history, and the world displays a theological and philosophical ambiguity that factors into how Bede conceives of God's action or providential caring for history and humanity. Using *In genesim* as my point of departure, I am following Charles Jones who describes Bede's commentary as "God's Word on Nature and Grace."[1] In order to highlight what I think are Bede's strengths and weaknesses, I will engage Bede through a conversation with Augustine and his thought on creation in Genesis. The resulting argument will show that Bede did not learn as much from Augustine as he needed to regarding the literal interpretation of Genesis. Moreover, Bede's inability to think as profoundly about *creatio ex nihilo* as Augustine led him to make some of the problematic claims he does regarding creation in his exegesis of Genesis 1, which, in turn, causes problems in how Bede relates theology, exegesis, and history. Hence, I concur with Charles Jones who said, "We can best examine Bede's attitude toward the relationship of literal and allegorical by looking at his treatment of the work of the Six Days," though I will treat this relationship in more explicitly theological terms.[2]

---

1. Jones, "Some Introductory Remarks on Bede's Commentary on Genesis," 115.
2. Ibid., 157.

Before beginning an analysis of Bede's own commentary on Genesis, at least a cursory discussion of the preceding exegetical tradition and those distinguished *patres* that preceded him and to whom he often submitted his own thought and biblical commentary is necessary. Bede himself lists the most important commentators of Genesis from whom he has learned the most: "*Basilius Caesariensis quem Eustathius interpres de Greco fecit esse Latinum, Ambrosius Mediolanensis, Augustinus Hipponensis episcopus . . .*"[3] Bede leaves out one other influence, Isidore of Seville, who also greatly impacted his thought.[4] These commentators make up what some have called "the Genesis tradition," and I will summarize the salient aspects of this tradition for my study before engaging Bede's own work.[5]

The Genesis Tradition

Little work has been done on the overall trajectory and content of the early commentators in the hexeamoral tradition. Thomas O'Loughlin's *Teachers and Code-Breakers: The Latin Genesis Tradition 430–800* is the only comprehensive study available in English, and I will rely heavily on his research to place Bede's exegesis of Genesis within a larger theological and historical tradition and context.[6] One of the common threads in the Genesis tradition is how commentaries were handed on (*traditio*). Using an active understanding of tradition O'Loughlin describes how many early Christians often followed in the footsteps of the giants, like Basil, Ambrose, and Augustine, by simply summarizing and copying their work.[7] O'Loughlin uses Eucherius and Cassiodorus as examples of this type of traditioning. This form of *traditio* most commonly manifested itself as manuals for the instruction of students and neophytes in the faith.[8] Thus, what has previously been understood as a fear of innovation and indicative of a cruder culture (e.g., the so-called "Dark Ages"), fails to take into account the intentions of these authors. What appear as redundant pieces of scholarship are actually

---

3. Bede, *In genesim*, 1.

4. In his marginal notation, Bede only ever mentions four names: Augustine, Ambrose, Gregory, and Jerome; see Brown, *A Companion to Bede*, 40 and n. 32. Kaczynski argues that Bede was the first to establish such a Fathers' quadrumvirate, "The Authority of the Fathers," 1–27.

5. The phrase was first coined by Evans in *Paradise Lost and the Genesis Tradition*.

6. O'Loughlin, *Teachers and Code-Breakers*.

7. Ibid., 40–49. What makes this "active," according to O'Loughlin, is his focus on how Christian material is passed on from generation to generation as opposed to the content of that tradition.

8. Ibid., 52–54.

pedagogical attempts at clarifying and making accessible the work of great thinkers. Therefore, these manuals should be evaluated not in relationship to the more constructive works of Basil and Augustine but as teaching tools.[9] The writing of manuals and summaries of great thinkers also displays the importance the virtue of humility had in the larger theological tradition.[10] Despite his often overlooked exegetical trailblazing, much of this applies not only to Bede's interpretation of Genesis but also his entire corpus, making Bede very consonant with O'Loughlin's argument.[11]

A second important feature of the Genesis tradition is a narrowing in the understanding of revelation. Augustine clearly believed that God's revelation was discernable in the beauty of creation, the soul of human beings, and, of course, in Scripture.[12] Revelation was not solely located or simply commensurate with the text of Holy Scripture in Augustine's work. However, after disputes surrounding the canon of Scripture, Scripture seems to become the central locus of divine revelation, according to O'Loughlin.[13] Eucherius's work in the early 5th century is almost completely directed at the text in a way that Augustine's or even Basil's in the east was not. As O'Loughlin notes, "the creation anterior to the text is completely ignored..." by Eucherius.[14] In short, Eucherius's "underlying assumption was that if the book is understood, then the whole divine message is understood."[15] In other words, Scripture was understood to be a self sufficient guide on all matters it addressed, whether directly or indirectly.

The text also came to be understood as its own authority on all matters because to deny Scripture's words is to imply that Scripture is incorrect—an unacceptable conclusion, since the words are divinely inspired. Hence, all the ink spilled by some Christians to show that Scripture, in fact, is not mistaken even regarding minute details.[16] O'Loughlin suggests that part of the narrowing of revelation in the later Genesis tradition came from and is

---

9. Ibid., 54.

10. Ibid., 66–71.

11. For example, Bede, as far as we know, was the first to write a commentary on Ezra and Nehemiah, not to mention Bede's contribution to science, the Christian calendar, and his commentaries on the Temple and Tabernacle.

12. See, for example, *Confessions*, 10.6.9—10.7.11; *On the Trinity*, books 1–4, and 9–15; the entire *On Christian Teaching*, but especially the preface and books 1 and 2.

13. See Howorth, "Influence of St. Jerome on the Canon of the Western Church." See O'Loughlin, *Teachers and Code Breakers*, 58–59.

14. O'Loughlin, *Teachers and Code Breakers*, 58 n. 142.

15. Ibid., 58.

16. Despite his more complex view of revelation, this can still be seen in Augustine's *De consensu evangelistrarum*.

manifested by Isidore's *Etymologiae* where Isidore makes the explicit link between logic and true statements about nature in Genesis thereby making Scriptural sentences understood primarily as kinds of propositions.[17] The reason for this narrowing likely had to do with the teaching orientation of most of these later commentators and summarists of the earlier theological giants. Thinking through *creatio ex nihilo* in dialogue with the text of Genesis 1, after all, is an arduous task both exegetically and philosophically. It was much easier to teach Genesis to neophytes and ordinary believers as straightforward literal descriptions and propositions than not.[18] The consequence of this type of ordering of the text is that an external system is imposed on the text that the text itself may not in fact support or require. Thus, what one thinks to be the "literal sense" or "plain sense" may not be. Such an approach, moreover, also creates ambiguity in one's theology of nature and grace. As revelation is defined more and more narrowly in terms of Scripture's pages, then God's work in creation now becomes ambiguous insofar as his activity there would not, or even could not, constitute something we would call *revelatory* activity.

While still being a staunch Augustinian, Bede inherits the pedagogical reductionism of Isidore and previous thinkers and can never really make these approaches to Genesis fit together.[19] To solve this tension, and despite his noble intentions and at times brilliant exegesis, Bede ends up separating literal and figural exegesis in a way that makes it difficult for him to find theologically coherent and meaningful interaction between them when he reads the creation narrative of Genesis 1.

Bede's *In genesim*

Introductory Remarks

Bede authored *In genesim* in two parts. The first part ended with his commentary on Genesis 1–3, what is now book one of the four books that compose the entire commentary. Later, he commented on the next 18 chapters of Genesis.[20] Due to the pronounced change in content from Bede's com-

---

17. See Isidore's *Etymologiae*, 22–24. See O'Loughlin, *Teachers and Code Breakers*, 60, n146. While O'Loughlin goes further than I would in making his claims on some of these points, especially his view that revelation begins to take on a propositional character at these early stages, his overall observation is accurate. Also, Isidore is important for my work here because he was a large influence on Bede, especially Bede's *In genesim*.

18. O'Loughlin, *Teachers and Code Breakers*, 60.

19. On Bede's connection and use of Isidore, see Blair, *World of Bede*, 265ff; Brown, "Quotations from Isidore in Bede's Commentary on Genesis 4:25–26," 163.

20. Since my concern is with Bede's work on the opening chapters of Genesis, and

ments on Genesis 1—2:3 (Ia), the traditional patristic hexaemeron, Charles Jones argued that Bede produced his interpretation of 2:4—3:21 (Ib), with significant portions directly quoted from Augustine, in a "panic of haste" at a separate and later time—a time that precedes, however, the later portion.[21] Hence, Jones speculates there were three distinct phases or "recensions" of composition.[22] Calvin Kendall argues that Jones fails to consider that the change in content stems not from time constraints or haste but from Bede's actual agreement with St. Augustine on the Fall that led Bede to write what he did on Genesis 2—3.[23] In Kendall's own words, "In all probability, however, Jones's 'first recension' (Ia) is nothing more than an unauthorized, truncated form of the 'second recension' (or shorter version), Ia + Ib."[24] Kendall concludes that even if Ia and Ib were composed at different times they were "written within a short time of each other" and not more than 15 years apart like Jones advocates.[25] In my opinion, it makes theological sense that Bede would follow Augustine's interpretation of Genesis 2 and 3 given Bede's own polemic against Pelagianism in his corpus. Hence, I find Kendall's view persuasive, albeit while noting its own speculative nature.

The exact date of *In genesim* is disputed. Charles Jones argues for dating Ia of *In genesim* between 703 and 709 and the final version somewhere around 730.[26] Charles Plummer, on the other hand, dated the final version of *In genesim* to 720.[27] Kendall follows Plummer and gives an extensive argument for why it is probable that Bede was finishing *In genesim* in 720.[28] Since we can be relatively confident in the sequential order of Bede's commentaries under investigation in my study (*In genesim* follows *In Ezram et Neeiam*, which is followed by *De templo* and *Historia ecclesiastica gentis Anglorum*), the exact date of *In genesim* and the other texts are, fortunately, only of secondary importance. As will become clear, the trajectory and progression of Bede's thought matters the most for my purposes.

When reading *In genesim* it is imperative to bear in mind Bede's purpose in writing, which he reveals in the preface, a letter to Bishop Acca.

Bede did not appear to subsequently change his original exegesis, we need not spend time rehearsing the details regarding the composition of later portions of *In genesim*.

21 Jones, "Introduction" to *In genesim*, vi-x; quote from viii. Also see Jones, "Some Introductory Remarks on Bede's Commentary on Genesis," 115-98.

22. Ibid., vi-x.

23. Bede, *On Genesis*, 40-45.

24. Ibid., 41.

25. Ibid., 44; see Jones's "Introduction" to *In genesim*, 8.

26. Jones, *In genesim*, viii.

27. See Plummer, *Venerabilis Baedae opera historica*, 1:cxlix.

28. See Kendall, *In Genesis*, 323-26.

Ever concerned about the evangelization and education of the Anglo-Saxon people, Bede wanted to offer something of a simplified summary of previous exegetes in addition to his own basic interpretation that would be useful for rudimentary readers and for a starting point for those wanting to ascend to higher readings.[29] Judith McClure summarizes, "For the weaker students, the content of Bede's Notes would provide a basic commentary on each phrase in the text of Genesis covered, with a certain degree of coherence and logical development provided by transitional sentences, references forward and back, and rhetorical questions."[30] To be sure, as McClure notes, there are elements in *In genesim* that would not be suitable for less sophisticated readers, but these were probably useful for instructors and teachers who might be training the unskilled priests and monks.[31] In other words, Bede's commentary functions as a kind of textbook; much of it can be useful for students studying on their own, but some portions would require additional explanation and exploration that only a *magister* could provide. Bede's overall pedagogical posture as a thinker and exegete is also supported by his own oeuvre. Bede wrote grammatical treatises that were influential through Charlemagne (*De arte metrica* and *De schematibus et tropis*) along with other instructional scientific works (*De temporum ratione*, *De natura rerum liber*, and *De orthographia*).[32]

Before I begin my analysis of Bede's own exegetical work on the hexaemeron with attention to its relationship to Augustine in the next section, some preliminary comments must be made about Bede and Augustine. The influence of Augustine on Bede can hardly be overstated. As Bernard Robinson said, "Augustine stands behind every sentence of Bede; to Augustine, with his stress on the unity of Scripture and on Christ as its centre, Bede owes the very programme and goal of his exegetical activity."[33] Bede explicitly mentions two

29. *In genesim*, 1: "Verum quia haec tam copiosa tam sunt alta ut uix nisi a locupletioribus tot uolumina adquiri, uix tam profunda nisi ab eruditioribus ualeant perscrutari, placuit uestrae sanctitati id nobis officii iniugere ut de omnibus his, uelut de amoenissimis late florentis paradisi campis quae infirmorum uiderentur necessitate sufficere decerperemus. Nec segnior in exequendo quae iubere es dignatus extiti, quin potius statim perspectis patrem uoluminibus college ex his ac duobus in libellis distinxi, quae rudem adhuc possent instituere lectorem, quibus eruditis ad altiorem discreet fortioremque maiorum ascendere lectionem."

30. McClure, "Bede's Notes on Genesis and the Training of the Anglo-Saxon Clergy," 25. For more on Bede's uneducated audience, see also Gunn, *Bede's Historiae: Genre, Rhetoric, and the Construction of Anglo-Saxon Church History*, 24–35.

31. McClure, "Bede's Notes on Genesis and the Training of the Anglo-Saxon Clergy," 24–29.

32. For more on Bede's educational works, see Brown, *Bede, the Venerable*, 24–41.

33. Robinson, "The Venerable Bede as Exegete," 205.

of Augustine's three commentaries on Genesis (*De genesi contra manichaeos* and *De genesi ad litteram*), as well as Augustine's reflections on creation in books XII and XIII of *Confessions* in the preface to *In genesim*.[34] Furthermore, ample textual evidence suggests that Bede had access to these three works from Augustine readily available to him at Wearmouth-Jarrow's library.[35] In accord with this Augustinian influence, my subsequent reading of Bede will take place as a conversation or *disputatio* of sorts between the two eminent doctors of the Church who share much in common but diverge on important points that have salient consequences for how history, Scripture, and theology are conceived. I will focus on Genesis 1 and Bede's adaptation of Augustine's world ages. Augustine's and Bede's theological and cosmological logic are what I am seeking to highlight in what follows.

Augustine and In principio

I think that it is necessary and fitting to observe the profound and speculative nature of commenting on such a topic as the beginning of the world at the outset. Painfully aware of this difficulty, Augustine repeatedly expressed how difficult and sublime a task it is to write on the creation of time, history, and the world.[36] My goal is to model this humility, without succumbing to post-Kantian bias against the possibility and intelligibility of such metaphysical, theological, and philosophical claims and speculations.

Augustine describes "in the beginning" as having several senses. One possible reading of "in the beginning" refers to the genesis of temporality—the creation of time itself.[37] Augustine notes the difficulty of this reading due to verse 14 of Genesis 1 that narrates the creation of the lights in the sky that are intended to mark time via days and years. If there were no markers of time created yet in verse 1, how could this be the beginning of time, at least in an intelligible sense? Augustine does try to conceive of a kind of time before time in which angels were created—a non-human form of temporality, yet

---

34. It appears that Bede did not know or have access to Augustine's unfinished commentary on Genesis.

35. Kendall makes note of the many and various quotations in footnotes throughout his translation, and Laistner in "The Library of the Venerable Bede," 237–66, provides a list of the books we can safely assume Bede had access to based on textual quotation.

36. For example, see Augustine's introductory comments to his unfinished literal commentary on Genesis.

37. Augustine, *On Genesis*, 116. I will use Hill's translation unless otherwise noted. Some clarifications must be made regarding citations of Augustine's commentary on Genesis. For the English translation, *On the Literal Meaning of Genesis*, numeration refers to book, section, paragraph; in the Latin text (see next note) there are only sections. I will use pagination notation for Latin quotations to Augustine's other works on Genesis.

still a type of time—but he names these kinds of inquiries "*res enim secretissima est et humanis coniecturis inpenetrabilis.*"[38] In his later work on Genesis (*Ad litteram*), Augustine settles on "in the beginning" as referring to in the Wisdom of God, the eternal Son, so that the creation of the world took place simultaneously and not in a temporal sequence of one day subsequent to another, though the days are important in understanding creation's order.[39]

The precise details of how creation takes place are of utmost importance for understanding the difference between Bede and Augustine. First, it must be recalled that this is Augustine's *literal* commentary on Genesis. In other words, Augustine thinks this is how creation actually took place; "*quae facta narrentur,*" he says.[40] Many biblical scholars today would find Augustine's treatment far from "literal" because, despite the fact that Augustine thinks his words have a referent, the referents are not necessarily physical or empirical. Though space does not permit a direct comparison between contemporary literal readings and Augustine's literal interpretation, the basic difference between Augustine and many biblical scholars today is a philosophical one, and this will become more evident in what follows.

For Augustine, Christian readers should conclude that God created the heavens and the earth simultaneously because for God to have spoken the world into existence through a physical sentence would imply both change within God and that time pre-existed creation when, in fact, time is also created.[41] As Augustine says in his *Confessions*,

> That word [The Son and creative word] is spoken eternally, and by it all things are uttered eternally. It is not the case that what was being said comes to an end, and something else is then said, so that everything is uttered in a succession with a conclusion, but everything is said in the simultaneity of eternity. Otherwise time and change would already exist, and there would not be a true eternity and true immortality.[42]

38. Augustine, *De genesi ad litteram inperfectus liber*, 463. See also Book XI of his *Confessions*.

39. Augustine, *Literal Meaning of Genesis*, 1.10.18–22, 4.33.51—5.11.27.

40. Augustine, *De genesi ad litteram*, 1. In the next sentence Augustine again reiterates and clarifies that the literal sense is what actually took place: "In narratione ergo rerum factarum quaeritur, utrum omnia secudum figurarum tantummodo intellectum accipiantur, an etiam secundum fidem rerum gestarum adserenda et defendenda sint." See *Ad litteram*, 1.

41. See, for example, Augustine, *Ad litteram*, 1.15–22; Augustine, *Confessionum*, 11.6–12. English translations of *Confessionum* are from *Confessions*.

42. Augustine, *Confessions*, 11.9. ". . . quod sempiterne dicitur et eo sempiterne dicuntur omnia. Neque enim finitur, quod dicebatur, et dicitur aliud, ut possint dici omnia, sed simul ac sempiterne omnia: alioquin iam tempus et mutation et non uera

Hence, and also drawing on Wisdom 11:20, Augustine suggests that God did not create through some kind of physical utterance but through the infinite and eternal Word, in whom all perfections are contained. So the orderly arrangement of all created things in weight, number, and measure are pre-contained in God, albeit not in the same way our thoughts are pre-contained in our mind.[43] Augustine is at pains to demonstrate the problems of conceiving of God's act of creating as similar to human acts of making or thinking which, to borrow later language from the scholastic tradition, are composite. He says that God's creation is not perceived, "outside himself, to be sure, as we perceive bodies with our eyes . . . Nor did he perceive them inside himself in the way that we perceive in our thoughts the appearances of bodies which are not there before our eyes, but which we form in our imaginations from what we see or have seen."[44] In short, Augustine here is wrestling with the utter simplicity of God and how that impinges upon a right literal reading of Genesis 1.[45]

Keeping in mind creation's simultaneous creation "in the beginning" and God's utter simplicity, I will now turn to Augustine's interpretation of "the heavens and the earth" in Genesis 1:1. Noticing the absence of God's speaking in the creation of the heavens and the earth, Augustine affirms that "heaven and earth" refer to a formless and imperfect spiritual reality. "That is why allusion is made to the Son, not because he is the Word but only because he is the beginning, when it says, in the beginning God made heaven and earth; here he [the Son] is being suggested as the source of creation still in its formless imperfection."[46] Augustine speculates that "water" is the name given to this created spiritual formlessness in verse 3 because of its fluid and shifting state.[47] What Augustine seems to be describing here is God's plentiful gifting/

---

immortalitas" (*Confessionum* 11.9).

43. Augustine, *Ad litteram*, 4.5–6.

44. Augustine, *Literal Meaning of Genesis*, 4.6.12. "Cum ergo haec ita disponerentur, ut haberent mensuras et numerous et pondera sua, ubi ea cernebat ipse disponens? Neque enim extra se ipsum, sicut cernimus oculis corpora, quae utique nondum errant, cum disponenerentur, ut fierent. Nec ita intra se ipsum ista cernebat, sicut cernimus animo phantasias corporum, quae non praesto sunt oculis, sed ea, quae uidimus, uel ex eis, quae uidimus imaginado cogitamus" (*Ad litteram*, 4.6).

45. Augustine's most detailed treatment of divine simplicity and human knowing and speaking can be found in books VI through VIII in *De trinitate*.

46. Augustine, *Literal Meaning of Genesis*, 1.4.9. " . . . propterea filii commemoratio non ita fit, quia uerbum, sed tantum, quia principium est, cum dicitur: in principio fecit deus caelum et terram; exordium quippe creaturae insinuatur adhuc in informaitate imperfectionis" (*Ad litteram*, 1.4). See also *Confessions*, 11.4, 11.9–14 where Augustine mentions Col 2:3 and other scriptures in a similar discussion.

47. Augustine, *Literal Meaning of Genesis*, 1.5.11.

othering of creation; creation as not-God, as not-simple, as composite, albeit spiritually composite, since Augustine does not think heavens, earth, and water have a physical referent at this point in the narrative.[48] Since this othering of a spiritually shapeless creation is not a temporal occurrence, God's othering of a formless creation is not temporally prior to its receiving of form. Instead, it is logically prior.[49] Hence, Augustine can later summarize the seven days of God's creative work by affirming that all creation is inchoately primed in the Word and in the initial simultaneous act of creating.

> In all these cases things already made received the characteristic activities of their own proper time, which came forth in manifest forms and natures from the secret formulae that are causally latent [*causaliter latent*] in creation; things like grass which sprang up over the earth, and the man made into a living soul, and other things of this sort whether shrubs or animals, which belong to that work of God at which he is working until now. But these things too carry within them a repetition [*iterum*], so to say, of their very selves, invisible in some hidden power of reproduction, the world that was created "when the day was made," before they ever burgeoned into the visible manifestations of their specific natures.
>
> Now, however, the truth is that those things which were due to be "unwrapped from their unwrappings" in the course of subsequent ages, and which God created simultaneously with all things when he made the world, were both completely finished then in a certain way and also started off in a certain way; completely finished indeed, because they have nothing in their natural manner of running their course in time which was not made causally in that primordial creation; started off, however, since they were seeds in a sense of future realities, destined to germinate in suitable places from hidden obscurity into the manifest light of day through the course of the ages.[50]

---

48. See Augustine, *Literal Meaning of Genesis*, 5.12.28–25.15.33.

49. See, for example, Augustine, *Literal Meaning of Genesis*, 1.15.29–30, 4.34.53–55, and 5.5.12–13.

50. Augustine, *Literal Meaning of Genesis*, 6.10.17, 6.11.18. "In quibus omnibus ea iam facta modos et actus sui temporis acceperunt, quae ex occultis atque inuisibilibus rationibus, quae in creatura causaliter latent, in manifestas formas naturasque prodierunt, sicut herba exorta super terram et homo factus in animam uiuam et cetera huius modi, siue frutecta siue animantia ad illam operationem dei pertinentia, qua usque nunc operatur. Sed etiam ista secum gerunt tamquam iterum se ipsa inuisibiliter in occulta quadam ui generandi, quam extraxerunt de illis primordiis causarum suarum, in quibus creato mundo, cum factus est dies, antequam in manifestam speciem sui generis exorerentur, inserta sunt . . .

These logically prior primordial causes within the spiritual shapelessness are then called back to the Word and given form: "... we should understand an incorporeal utterance of God in the substance of his co-eternal Word, calling back to himself the imperfection of creation, so that it should not be formless."[51] Likewise in his *Confessions*, "That word is spoken eternally, and by it all things are uttered eternally."[52] The form given to creation through the Father's uttering of the Word comes to abide in creation through the Spirit, according to Augustine.[53] Thus, in the end, creation itself images or repeats in a composite manner the activity that is Father, Son, and Holy Spirit and is imbued with form from the Triune God, a form that resembles this same God. Augustine continues on in his commentary to discuss more specifically how this form looks and how to discern it as the days of creation progress throughout Genesis 1.[54]

In sum, Augustine's literal commentary sought to understand how creation in its multitudinous and seemingly infinite manifestations of plants, animals, and ultimately all creatures and geographic terrain can find its source in the one and simple God who is Father, Son, and Holy Spirit. More pertinent to my concerns here is the fact that time and history inflect or compositely repeat their eternal source making them intrinsically good and imaging their triune creator. The difficult part is saying more than this: how are they good and what can be said about time and eternity? These questions led Augustine to make his famous statement about the nature of time: "*Quid est ergo tempus? Si nemo ex me quaerat, scio; si quaerenti explicare uelim, nescio . . .*"[55]

Nunc autem, quia et consummate quodam modo et quodam modo inchoate sunt ea ipsa, quae consequentibus euluenda temporibus primitus deus simul omnia creauit, cum faceret mundum—consummata quidem, quia nihil habent illa in naturis propriis, quibus suorum temporum cursus agunt, quod non in istis causaliter factum sit inchoate uero, quoniam quaedam errant quasi semina futurorurm per saeculi tractum ex oculto in manifestum locis congruis exerenda . . ." (*Ad litteram*, 6.10, 6.11)."

51. Ibid., 1.4.9. "... intellegamus dei dictum incorpeum in natura uerbi, eius coaeterni, reuocantis ad se inperfectionem creaturae, ut non sit informis..." (*Ad litteram*, 1.4).

52. Augustine, *Confessions*, 11.9. "Vocas itaque nos ad intellegendum uerbum, deum apud te deum, quod sempiterne dicitur et eo sempiterne dicuntur omnia . . ." (*Confessionum*, 11.9).

53. Augustine, *Literal Meaning of Genesis*, 1.6.12–11.8.14.

54. The *prima facie* resonance of Augustine's metaphysics here with evolutionary theory and science should not be dismissed or overlooked.

55. Augustine, *Confessionum*, 11.17.

Bede and In principio . . .

Bede was deeply influenced by Augustine's commentary on Genesis. More specifically, like Augustine, Bede recognized the difficulties in using composite human speech to describe such mysterious actions as the founding of the world.

> By introducing the creation of the world in the first sentence, Holy Scripture appropriately displays at once the eternity and omnipotence of God the creator. For by asserting that God created the world at the beginning of time, Scripture signifies that he indeed existed eternally before time . . . Hence, it is well said that *In the beginning God created heaven and earth*, in order that it may be clearly understood that he did both simultaneously, although it could not be said simultaneously in human language. Finally, the prophet says, *In the beginning you founded the earth, O Lord*. Here, however, the Lord is said *in the beginning* to have *created heaven and earth*; hence it is clearly inferred that the creation of each part was completed simultaneously, and this with such great swiftness of divine power that the first moment of the infant world had not yet passed.[56]

Thus, Bede agrees with Augustine that time is a created reality and that we must understand that God creates from eternity without change. However, a significant shift occurs between Augustine and Bede because Bede reads philosophical/theological interpretation as allegorical whereas Augustine saw it as literal.

> Moreover, that *in the beginning God made heaven and earth* can very probably be understood in the words of the only-begotten Son who, when the Jews asked why they should believe in him, replied, *(I am) the beginning, which I also speak unto you*. For, as the Apostle says, *in him were all things created in heaven and on earth*. But it must be carefully observed, as each one devotes his

---

56. Bede, *On Genesis*, 68, italics in original to indicate biblical quotation. Subsequently, I will maintain the italics in the original without notation, unless the quotation is not from Scripture. "Creationem mundi insinuans scriptura diuina apte primo statim uerbo eternitatem atque omnipotentiam Dei creatoris ostendit, quem enim in principio temporum mundum creasse perhibet, ipsum profecto ante tempora enternaliter extitisse designat . . . Vnde benedictum est quia *In principio creauit Deus caelum et terram*, uet aperte detur intellegi quia utrumque simul ab eo factum est quamuis utrumque simul ab homine dici non possit. Denique dicit propheta, *Initio terram tu fundasti, Domine*, hic autem *Dominus in principio caelum et terram creasse* narrator; unde liquido colligitur quia factura utriusque elementi partier expleta, et hoc tanta uelocitate diuinae uirtutis ut necdum primum mundi nascentis momentum esset transcensum" (*In genesim*, 3).

attention to the allegorical senses, how far he may have forsaken the manifest truth of history by allegorical interpretation.[57]

Here, Bede cautions readers against forsaking the manifest truth of history for allegorical interpretation thereby implying a tension between the historical and figural/allegorical senses in a way that Augustine did not. Bede's concern is to stay as close as possible to what Holy Scripture actually says. Thus, he attempts to circumvent any unnecessary speculation on what "heaven" refers to in Genesis 1:1 immediately following the above admonition. "And which and what sort of heaven it is which was made in the beginning with the earth is made known in the following words, when it said: And the earth was void and empty, and darkness was upon the face of the deep."[58] To be sure, Augustine was not looking for ways to side step the words of Scripture, so we must read further to find the specifics on how he and Bede differ.

Bede certainly does not read Genesis 1 in a completely empirical or "overly" literal fashion. For example, he discusses how the "heaven" of verse 1 is not visible to human eyes, yet it exists just the same. In fact, Bede reads "heaven" quite similarly to Augustine mentioning how "heaven" refers to the realm of angels.[59] Bede departs from Augustine, however, in his interpreting of "earth." Bede says that the earth refers to the earth as we know it now in its geographic, continental boarders and confines. In Bede's reading the earth existed as it does now but was completely covered by water. "For these were not, as some argue, mixed together formlessly, but the earth, confined in every direction by the same borders as it is now, was then in its entirety just as it still partly remains under the deepest depth of the sea."[60] Bede interprets "earth" in this way because of his discomfort with saying that God created something that was "unformed" (see Wis 11:18); Bede understood form and beauty to go together. Thus, Bede was seeking to avoid implicitly affirming that God made something that was not beautiful.[61] He says,

---

57. Ibid., 68–69. "Potest autem non inprobabiliter intellegi *in principio* fecisse *Deum caelum et terram* in unigenito filio suo qui, interrogantibus se Iudeis quid eum credere deberent, respondit, *Principium quod et loquor uobis.* Quia *in ipso,* ut ait apostolus, *condita sunt omnia in caelis et in terra.* Sed diligenter intuendum ut ita quisque sensibus allegoricis stadium impendat, quatenus apertam historiae fidem allegorizando derelinquat" (*In genesim,* 3).

58. Ibid., 69. "Quod autem uel quale sit caelum quod in principio cum terra factum est sequentibus uerbis insinuator cum dicitur: Terra autem erat inanis et uacua et tenebrae super faciem abyssi." (*In genesim,* 4).

59. Ibid., 69–71; *In genesim,* 4–5.

60. Ibid., 71. "[S]ed terra ipsis quibus et nunc est finibus undique uersum circumscripta, talis tunc erat tota qualis adhuc sub imo maris profundo ex parte remanet." (*In genesim,* 5–6).

61. Ibid., 71–72n20.

> To this extent only is that matter of which the world was made unformed, as Scripture declares, which says *in praise of God*, *'You who made the world of unformed matter'*. For all things which we are accustomed to see in the world made up of waters and earth either derived the origin of their nature from them or from nothing. But earth and waters themselves get the name of unformed matter because, before they came into the light from which they recieved their beauty, it did not exist.[62]

Bede, following Basil quite faithfully on this point, offers a scientific explanation for this reading insofar as he thought the earth to be composed of four elements: air, fire, water, and earth. Since water was covering the unlit earth, this did not allow its form to be what it is now. Bede understands "unformed" in this context simply to be the earth's status prior to the separation of the water and the earth and prior to the creation of light.[63] In other words, it was not a wrong mixture of elements (earth and water) that made the earth unformed because this would be God's doing; instead, "unformed" is simply a description of the water's fluidity covering the earth in the absence of light. At this point, it seems Bede is reading this passage as if he (or Moses) were actually watching creation take place or at least witnessing the immediate result of the simultaneous creation of the heavens, earth, and water.[64] More support for Bede's spectator reading can be seen in his commenting on Genesis 1:2 where Bede contrasts the incorporeal nature of "heavens" with the corporeal and visible creation or earth.[65]

Bede still believes that the heavens and the earth were created simultaneously, and there is certainly no logical problem in holding that a spiritual reality can be created simultaneously with a physical one. Bede has not forgotten this important doctrinal point by which he began his reading of Genesis. However, once Bede begins to read the passage in a way that requires "water" and "earth" to have a physical referent, he must conclude that verse 5 means that "there was evening and morning one day" was "without a doubt a day of twenty-four hours" as Kendall so aptly translates it.[66] As was

62. Ibid., 71."Ad haec tantum est informis illa materies, de qua mundum esse factum testatur scriptura, quae in Dei laudibus dicit, Qui fecisti mundum de material informi. Nam cunctua quae cum aquis et terra uidere solemus in mundo, uel de ipsis exordium naturae, uel sumere de nihilo; ipsa autem terra et ipsae acquae propterea nomen sortitae sunt materiae informis, quia priusquam in lucem uenirent, unde formositatem haberent, non erat" (*In genesim*, 6).

63. Ibid., 71–72; *In genesim*, 6.

64. Ibid.

65. Ibid., 72–73; *In genesim*, 7.

66. Ibid., 75. "Et huc usque dies expletus est unus, uiginti scilicet et quatuor horarum" (*In genesim*, 9).

previously mentioned, Bede was attempting to solve another theological issue in reading the text this way: he wanted to avoid saying that God created something ugly or formless. While it seems quite awkward to say, especially in our current philosophical and theological context, it is a true theological statement nonetheless: beauty as such does not necessitate a body or physicality for Christian thought because God, as infinite, eternal, and incorporeal, is beauty as such and is not a physical thing or creation; this theological claim is what actually allows for creaturely and physical beauty to reflect God's beauty in the first place.[67] It seems that Bede did not think through this more trenchant philosophical and theological point, and perhaps for good reason, since his primary goals in writing and commentating were to train neophytes in the faith. I am not accusing him of being ignorant of such a doctrinal claim; I am simply pointing out how what he says requires certain conclusions to which he later comes.

In fact, while interpreting Genesis 21 and closing his commentary on Genesis, Bede says that readers of Scripture should not take refuge in *umbras figurarum* because such literal readers remain ignorant of the spiritual and figural referent of such figures that is the New Covenant in Christ.[68] I do not think the ending of Bede's commentary is intrinsically contradictory to Bede's earlier admonitions regarding allegorical exegesis. In this way, therefore, one could argue that Bede is not necessarily putting forth a "right" reading of Genesis in his own view, but instead leading those young in the faith towards higher and higher realities as he comments on the first 21 chapters of Genesis. Therefore, it is possible that Bede is not just "mistaken" in his reading of Genesis 1, if we take his purposes in writing into consideration. Nonetheless, his reading of Genesis 1 remains theologically ambiguous.

Creation and the World Ages

Augustine on the World Ages

As previously mentioned, Augustine believed that Genesis taught that God created the entire world simultaneously. However, he also takes the words of Scripture very seriously and now has to do something with the "six days" in which Genesis describes the creation of the world. In short, his answer to how creation was both simultaneous and in six days is that both are true.

---

67. At least I would argue this and invoke Plato's *Symposium* and Hart's *Beauty of the Infinite*.

68. *In genesim*, 241. See Kendall's "Responsibility of *Auctoritas*: Method and Meaning in Bede's Commentary on Genesis," 101–19.

> The creator, after all, about whom scripture told this story of how he completed and finished his works in six days, is the same as the one about whom it is written elsewhere, and assuredly without there being any contradiction, that he created all things simultaneously (Sir. 18:1). And consequently, the one who made all things simultaneously together also make simultaneously these six or seven days, or rather this one day six or seven times repeated.[69]

Augustine then goes on to say that Scripture uses the language of days in order to help those who cannot understand the texts that teach God created all things simultaneously. Thus, Augustine privileges, for theological and philosophical reasons already stated above, descriptions of creation in Sirach and Wisdom and uses them to guide his reading of Genesis.

The days are not dismissed exegetically but must be understood to be in relationship with the primal formulae (*rationes*) embedded in heaven and earth's simultaneous creation. Heaven and earth are created "primed" and teeming with potentiality.[70] After a brief and insightful exploration of the kinds of ways creation could develop from these *rationes* (the usual sequence of birth through adulthood that we ordinarily see or emerge in maturity; e.g., Adam was a man who never was a child), Augustine settles on a more complex reading that can only be intelligible in light of creation *ex nihilo*: "It remains, therefore, that they were created with an aptitude for each mode, whether for this one by which temporal events most commonly transpire, or for that one by which rare and miraculous things are done, as it may please God to do whatever is appropriate at the time."[71] By this subtle metaphysical (and exegetical!) move, Augustine allows creation to have both a created form (a type of formal causality) along with constant and immediate divine providence that is not in competition with creation or the causal *rationes*.[72] The consequences of this view sound more like a contemporary reading of

---

69. Augustine, *Literal Meaning of Genesis*, 4.33.52. "de quo enim creatore scriptura ista narrauit, quod sex diebus consummauerit opera sua, de illo alibi non utique dissonanter scriptum est, quod creauerit omnia simul. Quid ergo opus erat sex dies tam distinct dispositeque narrari? Quia scilicet hi, qui non possunt uidere, quod dictum est: creauit omnia simul, nisi cum eis sermo tardius incedat, ad id, quo eos ducit, peruenire non possunt" (*Ad litteram*, 4.33).

70 "Quaeri autem merito potest, causales illae rationes, quas mundo indidit, cum primum simul omnia creatuit, quomodo sint institutae:..." (*Ad litteram*, 6.14).

71. Augustine, *Literal Meaning of Genesis*, 6.14.25. "Restat ergo, ut ad utrumque modum habiles creatae sint, siue ad illum, quo rara et mirabilia fiunt, sicut deo facere placuerit, quod tempori congruat" (*Ad litteram*, 6.14).

72. See also *Literal Meaning of Genesis*, 6.14.25—6.15.26, 6.18.29 where Augustine says God does not go against his own arrangement (*dispositionem*) of creation .

Genesis than that from the fourth century: "When he [Adam] is said to have been made among them, it was surely, the actual cause that God made, by which the man was to come to be in his own time, and in accordance with which he was to be made by the one who both finished what he had started on account of the perfect completeness of the causal formulae, and started what was to be finished on account of the ordered march of time."[73] As Augustine previously stated in book 5, God created by endowing his creation with "an order that is not set by intervals of time but by the linking of causes, so that the things made simultaneously might also be brought to perfection by the sixfold representation of that day."[74] Augustine concludes by emphasizing that any form/shape/necessity that creation possesses comes from the will of God.

This theological and philosophical exegesis impinges directly upon how Augustine then sees and understands history.[75] Since creation is given a form in the primal *rationes*, not only does creation have form and structure but so does the entire course of human history. In other words, if all of creation and human history are inchoately present in the six days of creation, then the actual happenings of history must be intrinsically related to them in some fashion. This line of reasoning gives way to Augustine's world ages theological history that is most discernable in his *De ciuitate Dei* books 15—22. While Augustine does not delimit the world ages specifically in *De ciuitate Dei*, he does specify them in his *On Genesis: A Refutation of the Manichees*[76] and: the first age is from Adam to Noah, the second from Noah to Abraham, the third from Abraham to David, the fourth from David to the Babylonian captivity, the fifth from the captivity to the Incarnation of Jesus, the sixth age, in which we currently live, from the incarnation to the second coming.[77]

Exactly how specific historical repetitions of the initial days of creation are discerned is less clear. Augustine makes some general observations likening humanity's history to the individual development of a human being

---

73. Augustine, *Literal Meaning of Genesis*, 6.15.26. "In quibus cum dicitur factus, ipsam causam utique fecerat deus, qua erat suo tempore homo futures et secundum quam fuerat ab illo faciendus, qui simul et consummauerat inchoate propter perfectionem causalium rationum et inchoauerat conummanda propter ordinem temporum" (*Ad litteram*, 6.15).

74. Ibid., 5.5.12. ". . . praestans eis etiam ordinem non interuallis temporum, sed conexione causarum, ut ea quae simul facta sunt, scenario quoque illius diei numero praesentato perficerentur" (*Ad litteram*, 5.5).

75. I am indebted to the following works on Augustine's view and writing of history: Markus, *Saeculum*; Vessey, Pollman, and Fitzgerald, *History, the Apocalypse, and the Secular Imagination*; Daly, Doody, and Paffenroth, *Augustine and History*.

76. Augustine, *On Genesis*, 1.35–43.

77. Augustine, *On the Catechizing of the Uninstructed*, chapter 22.

growing from infancy through adulthood.[78] For example, the first age from Adam to Noah resembles human infancy insofar as Adam and Eve experience the light of day for the first time with their creation and because, like the flood, "our infancy is sort of blotted out by a flood of oblivion" (lack of memory)[79] and reaches old age, or the status of the "old man" (or self), in the sixth age.[80] The key here is that "maturity" is reached when Christ arrives at the dawn of the sixth age because history and humanity do not, and cannot, mature or find their end/fulfillment in this created life.[81] Echoing the creation of a living soul on the sixth day in Genesis 1, God renews and redeems humanity through rebirth in baptism in the advent of Christ.[82]

The difficulty in understanding Augustine's connections between world ages and created history as we experience it stems from the simultaneity of creation and the inchoate *rationes*. In other words, Augustine does not "stretch" history or understand it simply to correspond or parallel the six days of creation as if history *must* follow the progress of the days of creation, which would be a tempting interpretation. However, as his analogy of history and the development of humans implies, Augustine still maintains a teleological view of history, and this is where the world ages become more intelligible as repetitions of the original act of creation. Nearly all the connections, parallels, and repetitions that Augustine notes between human history and the biblical narrative (e.g., Cain and Romulus's fratricidal actions) presuppose the theological and philosophical account he has already given of creation. Hence, when Augustine reads Cain as a figure of Romulus, Augustine is not giving an explanation in terms of efficient causes within the sphere humans call "history": that Romulus killed his brother because God foreknew it and the story of Cain and Abel predict it in some way, or even that Cain killed Abel because "that is what happened." Instead, Augustine, believing that Scripture is the truth *of* the world (not that it just tells truths *about* the world), draws attention to a theological truth at work in history. In the case of Cain and Romulus, the truth is about the divisions and animosity within the earthly city itself and between the city of God and the earthly city that come from malformed desires and the objects to which

---

78. Augustine, *On Genesis*, 1.35.

79. Ibid.

80. Ibid., 1.40.

81. Perhaps a clearer way of putting it would be that humanity is ripe for redemption (as opposed to mature) in the sixth age in the advent of Christ.

82. Augustine, *On Genesis*, 1.40–42.

our desire attaches itself.[83] In a similar fashion, Augustine calls the founding of Rome a kind of second Babylon.[84]

More specifically, humans always desire something and that we cannot choose not to desire is a result of being created as good bodily beings by God.[85] Sin enters when we desire the wrong things which we mistake to be good or desire good things inappropriately. Thus, while Cain and Romulus's conceit and fratricide obviously parallel one another, more fundamentally they are a commentary, albeit a counter intuitive one, on the goodness of the original creation as created in Genesis 1 because their sinful actions seek an explanation: Why would someone kill a sibling? Ultimately, this drives one back to the origins of the world and to creation by reasoning through evil's necessarily dependent relationship upon some logically prior good. In the end, Augustine's literal commentary on Genesis, which includes all of its metaphysical, theological, and philosophical moments, is both the most and the least speculative account of the world. The most speculative because of the difficulty of grasping the mystery of creation; the least speculative because the question of origins is implied in all human acts and history, even ones of privation. Put differently, what most contemporary commentators understand as history and as explaining events and happenings on a literal level, Augustine intrinsically sees as products of a greater, prior, and more mysterious cause that makes those occurrences even possible. Note here as well that while the contingency of the world is obviously part of Augustine's main point, it is not an empty "it could have been otherwise" understanding of contingency because of the *rationes* embedded in creation. Consequently, for Augustine history as such is that which points beyond itself educating humanity about their origin and forward toward their end, and any narration of history that does not take this into account is problematic and not properly called "history."[86] In other words, the question, "Why is there something rather than nothing?" is a question latent in all aspects of existence and to neglect this question is to misunderstand existence and history as such for Augustine. The City of God is the wayfarer on earth who keeps this knowledge of our origin and end before itself at all times, and the

---

83. Augustine, *City of God Against the Pagans*, 15.5.

84. Ibid., 18.22.

85. See Augustine's *De libero arbitrio* and Augustine's reflections on sin and desire in book II of *Confessionum*.

86. To be sure, Augustine does get himself in some muddles, despite his own insight. For example, later in book 15, he takes great pains to make the biblical chronology and age of humans make 'historical' sense, though he does so in a very interesting way that most contemporary "conservatives" would be uncomfortable with.

world ages structure that knowledge in order to keep our origin and end constantly before us.

Bede on the World Ages

Bede's theology of the world ages must be considered in light of both *De genesim* and *De temporum ratione*. *De temporum ratione* was composed in 725, according to Charles Jones, which is very close to when Bede wrote *In genesim*.[87] However, many perplexing differences arise in these two works. For example, in *De temporum* Bede says that the first three days of creation could not be counted by hours, since the sun had not been created yet.[88] However, while commenting on Genesis 1:5, which states that there was evening and morning the first day, Bede says that this first day was "certainly" or "naturally" (*scilicet*) twenty-four hours long.[89] Even more confusingly, *In genesim* says of 1:14, "For that whole period of three days had earlier passed in the undivided progress of its course, having internally no measurement of hours . . ."[90] seemingly switching to his position in *De temporum*. The best theological sense I can make of these statements so close together is that Bede did think the first day of creation was twenty-four hours, but the measurement is external to creation, i.e., that time has an objective status apart from measurement. However, Bede clearly denies the possibility of time without measurement in chapter 2 of *De temporum*.[91] I think Bede runs into an unnecessary conundrum here, which I will highlight in what follows. For my purposes now, I will engage *De temporum* in relationship to *De genesim*, while focusing on *De genesim*, since Bede considered his primary task in life to comment on Holy Scripture.[92]

While Bede basically followed Augustine in demarcating the times of the world ages, Bede theologically appropriated the world ages in

87. See Jones's introduction to *De temporum ratione liber*, 241. Bede's very early *De natura rerum libra* and *De temporibus* also discuss the world ages, but I want to focus on Bede's latter and mature thought on these matters. For the new translation see Bede, *On the Nature of Things* and *On Times*.

88. Bede, *The Reckoning of Time*, 24.

89. Bede, *In genesim*, 9.

90. Bede, *On Genesis*, 81. "Nam totum illud triduum superius indiscreto cursus sui processu transierat, nullam penitus dimensionem habens horarum . . ." (*In genesim*, 16). Unfortunately, the apparent rescensions which Bede wrote *In genesim* do not help solve these apparent contradictory statements since both comments come in chapter 1 of Genesis.

91. These statements are just one instance of the tension inherent in Bede's commentary on Genesis that I attempt to highlight below.

92. See Bede, *EH*, 5.24 (293).

significantly different ways. Bede transitions into his discussion of the world ages by leaving his literal exegesis of Genesis behind: "*Huc usque de primordia mundi nascentis iuxta sensum litterae dixisse sufficiat.*"[93] Thus, where Augustine maintains some connection between the literal and figural regarding of the world ages via the embedded primal *rationes*, Bede does not offer any mediation between the days of creation and the world ages allowing Bede only to offer more "straightforward" connections between the days of creation and world ages. In *De temporum*, Bede calculates the world ages with as much precision as can be gleaned from the biblical text by counting days and years from each occurrence. "On the sixth day God made the earthly creatures and man, Adam . . . from Adam's side God brought forth Eve. This day is the 10 kalends of April [March 23]."[94] Bede then goes on to count the years from Adam and Eve's children using these for dates: "A.M. 130, Adam annorum centum et triginta, genuit Seth . . . A.M. 235 Seth annorum CV genuit Enos . . ."[95] In Bede's commentary on Genesis, and since he presumes the literal twenty-four-hour days of creation, the dawn and evening of each day of creation are more important than for Augustine.

> Now the first day, on which God said, *Let light be made, and light was made*, corresponds to the first age, in the beginning of which this same world was made and man was placed in the delights of the paradise of pleasure, where, free and ignorant of all evils, he might enjoy the immediate grace of his creator. But this day now began a decline toward evening when the first created humans lost the happiness of their heavenly country by sinning, and were sent for into the *vale of tears* . . . But the full evening of this day [day one] arrived when the whole *earth was corrupted* by the increasingly frequent sins of the human race *before God, and was filled with iniquity* to such an extent that all flesh, except those creatures which he had shut in the ark, deserved to be destroyed in the flood.[96]

93. Bede, *In genesim*, 35.
94. Bede, *The Reckoning of Time*, 159.
95. Bede, *De temporum ratione liber*, 273. The actual textual layout of his work here shows the structure Bede thought Genesis was describing as well.
96. Bede, *On Genesis*, 100–101. "Primus namque dies in quo dixit Deus, Fiat lux et facta est lux, prima aetati congruity in cuius initio mundus idem factus et homo in deliciis paradise uoluptatis positus est, ubi praesente gratia sui conditoris malorum omnium liber ac nescius frueretur. Sed hic dies ad uesperam iam coepit declinare cum protoplasti peccando filicitatem patriae caelestis perdiderunt atque in hanc conuallem lacrimarum dimissi sunt . . . Plena autem uespera diei huius aduenit cum crebrescentibus uitiis humani generis corrupta est omnis terra coram Deo et iniquitate replete, adeo ut deleri diluuio omnis caro praeter quos arca mereretur" (*In genesim*, 36).

Though Augustine draws a similar parallel,[97] the connection is not as wooden or identical since he understands the "days" of creation to be pedagogical for those who cannot understand simultaneous creation, which more *literally* describes how the heavens and earth were made. In other words, dawn and evening are pedagogical literary tools to drive the reader back to contemplate the original creation and its mysterious constitution. Thus, Augustine has no theological stake in whether a cycle of sin and redemption mark the ages, though he is happy to use them for such purposes. Ultimately, Augustine's explanation of the ages hinges on the incarnation more than getting the exact times of world history to match up with the days of creation.[98] In fairness to Bede, he (along with many other patristic and medieval exegetes) was not primarily concerned with working out and maintaining a completely consistent exegetical method.[99]

Even with the methodological caveat, it is clear that Bede tended to "stretch out" the creation narrative in Genesis to fit with historical events. In *De temporum ratione*, Bede engages in an argument surrounding the exact day the earth was created. Again displaying that his literal exegesis presumes a bystander's perspective of the act of creation, Bede argues that the world was created on the 15th calends of April (or March 18), which is exactly three days before the equinox when God created the sun and the stars to mark the seasons.[100] Bede's purposes in this section of the *De temporum* are clearly theological, more specifically in determining the proper date and time of Easter.[101] Hence, Bede is not separating theology and science or history here at a *prima facie* level, but the conclusions he draws could make for an easy split between faith and science and faith and history. For example, since we now know quite decisively the age of the earth is much greater than

---

97. "This age [first age] stretches from Adam up to Noah in ten generations. A kind of evening of this day is made by the flood, because our infancy too is sort of blotted out by a flood of oblivion" (*On Genesis*, 1.35–37). Augustine does relate the sin in the world prior to the flood and to the evening of the first age. Instead, the metaphor of the development of a human life dominates his use here. However, since Augustine did not read the days of creation as twenty-four-hour days, his description of "evening" has a different sense, which Hill seeks to highlight by calling it "a kind of evening." Moreover, when Bede and Augustine's overall approach to figural and literal exegesis is taken into consideration, the difference between their uses of "evening" becomes more dramatic.

98. Of course, Christ was the center of Bede's exegesis as well and the key to understanding all of Scripture, but my point here is one of emphasis and how Bede's particular theological/exegetical logic ended up where it did.

99. For Bede, see Holder, "Bede and the Tradition of Patristic Exegesis," 399–411; See also Young, *Biblical Exegesis and the Formation of Christian Culture*, 119–213, esp. 186–213.

100. Bede, *De temporum ratione liber*, 153–57.

101. Ibid., 154–55.

86   Allegorizing History

six or seven thousand years, this makes Bede's reading of Genesis 1 (not to mention much of the rest of his *computus* in Genesis), directly contradictory to later understandings of time, history, and science, thereby giving the impression that Scripture and theology are intrinsically at odds with "natural" knowledge. It is this inherent tension, which Bede instantiates far more than Augustine, that I am interested in understanding.

Recalling the separation of figural and literal exegesis that Bede appears to follow in his commentary on Genesis, Bede disallows himself the opportunity to read non-biblical history itself in specific figural terms. As previously discussed, Arthur Holder has argued that Bede intentionally separated his historical works from his exegesis in order to give preeminence to Scripture.[102] Bede did not hesitate to allegorize every detail of the Temple and Tabernacle in his commentaries, while he did not allegorize the ecclesial structures of his own day or in his ecclesiastical history.[103] Although other Christians did so, Bede withheld from figurally interpreting non-biblical architecture and history.[104] Recall that Bede says, "These items of information on the structure of the temple, in our opinion, should indeed be passed on to the keen reader. But among them let us seek out figures of whatever mysteries sacred scripture has thought fit to relate and the rest let us use purely for historical knowledge."[105]

Holder fails to mention what import, if any, Bede's naming of the *Greater Chronicle* of "The Sixth Age" or any remnants of Bede's theology of history in *De temporum* has in his historical work. My contention, however, *pace* Holder, is not that Bede became increasingly more discerning in understanding the difference between exegesis and history (interestingly, quite like a modern historian) but that he did not develop the philosophical and theological skills necessary to read Genesis 1 in an appropriately literal way. Thus, in my view, we should not credit Bede with making a sharp distinction between exegesis and history (like we moderns are fond of doing), but we should learn from Bede that such theological and philosophical caesurae between disciplines actually impair both historical practice and proper exegesis. In other words, Bede attempted to integrate theology and history,

---

102. Holder, "Allegory and History in Bede's Interpretation of Sacred Architecture," 115–31.

103. Ibid., 121.

104. See 34 n. 4 above.

105. Bede, *On the Temple*, 68. "Haec quidem de structura temple studioso lectori credidimus intimanda. Verum in eis quaecumque scriptura sacra referre commodum duxit figuras mysteriorum quaeramus ceteris pro historiae cognitione simpliciter utamur" (*De templo*, 193). Meyvaert concurs with Holder on this point in "Bede, Cassiodorus, and the Codex Amiatinus," 859–60.

but was unable to do so in a coherent way that made theological sense of Genesis 1, and this manifests itself in various ways throughout his oeuvre. It may seem like the literal reading of Genesis 1 and the writing of history is completely separate (or should be), but they are not. I will continue this argument in the final chapters via contemporary historical theory.

Conclusion

So, why was Bede different? Why did Bede restrict figural interpretation to Scripture alone and not extend it to historical events in his *Historia*? I think Bede knowingly does not make such connections. One plausible explanation for why he does not make explicit connections between Scripture and the *Historia* is to allow his readers to learn to do so. In other words, Bede wants readers to use what he has already taught them and see the figures in history as just that, figures of deeper divine truths. The problem with this reading is that given the low level of education in England in Bede's day, it seems unlikely that people and even priests were ready for such a task or test.[106] However, it is certainly not outside the realm of possibility.

Another possibility, and the one I am inclined towards, is that Bede intentionally would not figurally exegete history because of his narrower understanding of revelation and his literal exegesis of Genesis 1. Recalling O'Loughlin's work, after Augustine Scripture increasingly began to be understood as the primary of locus of revelation in opposition to revelation in history and creation. The reason for this was not inherently theological and was likely the result of an uneducated laity and clergy who needed simpler answers and a basic catechetical education. As a result, Scripture was used in a quasi-propositional manner to instruct Christians ignorant in their own faith.[107] Whatever the reasons may be for this shift between Augustine and Bede, as mentioned previously, Bede apparently received this understanding of revelation and Scripture most directly from Isidore.[108]

Bede's view of Scripture as the primary locus of revelation discouraged him from looking into extra-biblical areas or signs as having intrinsically revelatory significance. This is not to say that Bede thought that God did not act in the world outside the pages of Scripture. He did, as the *Historia*

---

106. On the low level of education in Anglo-Saxon England, even among the clergy, see Eckenrode, "Venerable Bede and the Pastoral Affirmation of the Christian Message in Anglo-Saxon England," 258–78; Thacker, "Bede's Ideal of Reform," 149; DeGregorio, "Bede's *In Ezram et Neemiam* and the Reform for the Northrumbrian Church," 1–25; Gunn, *Bede's Historiae*, 24–35.

107. O'Loughlin, *Teachers and Code Breakers*, 42–64.

108. Ibid., 92–94, 185–99.

plainly demonstrates. However, there is a subtle and important distinction between events and persons having intrinsic revelatory significance and events and persons that God can use for revelation but that do not intrinsically possess such significance apart from divine action. I am claiming that in consonance with the later Genesis tradition Bede viewed extra-biblical history in this latter fashion as a consequence of his exegesis of Genesis and his elevation of Scripture as the primary locus of divine revelation. Since Bede thought that only divinely inspired signs (biblical signs that are intrinsically revelatory) should be figurally exegeted, he did not think it appropriate to figurally exegete the signs of history which God can and certainly did use, since they lacked any theological significance apart from God's taking them up into his providential care. While this may only seem like a fine theological or philosophical distinction it has important consequences for the practice of history and how one conceives it. On this score, Bede and Augustine are quite different, as I attempted to show, since Augustine does figurally exegete history.[109]

I find this a plausible reading because it fits, and is perhaps the consequence of, Bede's reading of creation in Genesis. First, as I noted in the previous chapter, Bede sharply distinguishes figural and literal exegesis and, as articulated here, he tended to read Scripture's literal sense as if he were standing alongside events watching them transpire, including the creation of time and history. Hence, Bede cautions against philosophical and theological speculation as proper exegetical practice and can collapse the literal and the empirical into the same category, especially when it comes to interpreting what "earth" refers to in Genesis 1:1.[110] Moreover, and because of his empirically literal interpretation of the "earth," Bede says that each day of creation was a twenty-four hour day in Genesis 1.[111]

Bede's reading of Genesis is relevant to his understanding of history in a very interesting way. Since God is actively making each particular thing on a particular day, these events can have figural significance because of God's immediate and direct action in or on them, especially because creation is from nothing. Thus, the days of creation can be figures of the world ages for

---

109. By "figurally exegete," I am going beyond Auerbach's type and anti-type definition of *figura*. I will specifically argue for this understanding of *figura* in chapter 5. Suffice it for now to say that my understanding does not contradict Auerbach's but seeks to find what constitutes it.

110. Bede, *In genesim*, 3–4. I recognize that I mentioned that Bede thought heaven was not a physical referent. My point here is simply to highlight Bede's tendency in his exegesis.

111. Ibid., 9.

Bede.¹¹² However, the key at this point is that the development subsequent to the first six days where God was directly involved now becomes theologically and providentially precarious. Does God actively create and sustain subsequent creation in the direct way that Bede's literal exegesis of the first six days of creation implies? In other words, does God directly act on creation in the ways that Bede conceived of Genesis 1 as having transpired? I do not think that this question actually ever occurred to Bede, but it seems he would answer it in the negative, since he refuses to recognize figural significance as being intrinsic to many following events and persons, unless God deems otherwise (e.g., God calls Abraham; God speaks to Moses; God provides instructions for the construction of the temple, etc.).

My point here can be made more perspicuous by another comparison with Augustine. Where Bede's exegesis of Genesis seems to imply differences in God's providential care (direct and indirect, for lack of a better way of putting it), Augustine can simply affirm God's immediate and non-competitive presence to all of creation, regardless of temporal location via the eternal *rationes* in God, since he reads the six days as being simultaneous and not temporal. Thus, for Augustine, every historical event, person, and object is intrinsically charged (appropriate to its nature) with revelatory significance, and therefore capable of figural exegesis given God's immediate presence to it as its creator from nothing.¹¹³ Bede, on the other hand, must have God act and take up historical events in order to give them revelatory significance capable and worthy of figural exegesis. Therefore, extra-biblical historical events, persons, and objects can be figurally exegeted for Augustine but not for Bede. I am suggesting this is why the connection between the founding of the earthly city in fratricide is connected to the fratricide at the founding of Rome by Augustine, while Bede lets other obvious figural connections between his own history and Scripture go by the wayside.¹¹⁴

Other examples of Augustine figurally exegeting both biblical and non-biblical history also occur in books 15—18 of the *City of God*.¹¹⁵ For example, Augustine finds the human city at work in Noah's line in the con-

---

112. See Bede's, *On Genesis*, 100–105; *Reckoning of Time*, 39–41; and esp. *Greater Chronicle*, 157–249.

113. See, e.g., Augustine's discussion of causation in relationship to Cicero's understanding of divine foreknowledge and freedom in *De ciuitate Dei*, 5.9. Here Augustine argues for the non-competitive nature of God's causal power with his free creation and his discussion continues through 5.10.

114. Augustine, *De ciuitate Dei*, 15.5.

115. For a helpful summary of some of these, see O'Daly's *Augustine's City of God*, 160–95, esp. 171–91.

fusion of languages at Babylon.[116] Furthermore, Augustine ends up "synchronizing" biblical history with non-biblical history in book 18 all for the purpose of performing his theological reading of the entire scope of history in light of his exegesis of the origins of the two cities.[117] Augustine also says that discrepancies between the Hebrew text of Scripture and the Septuagint are intended to spur readers to higher spiritual readings.[118] In sum, for Augustine, each created thing and/or event by virtue of having being is intrinsically revelatory of its creator in some fashion.[119] Hence, Augustine can figurally explain the decline of the Roman Empire in light of various ages of the world and the origin of the two cities that spans through the world ages without temporal and revelatory limitation in the *City of God*.[120]

Bede might abstain from figurally exegeting history for two reasons; one more perspectival, the other more ontological. The more perspectival reason would be that for Bede one does not have access to the knowledge of when God will take up an event, person, or figure and give them revelatory significance, but one is able to know that God does act in such a way because of the revelation of Scripture. In other words, all historical objects are ontologically present to God in the way that Augustine clearly describes, but humans fail to see them as such until they are shown otherwise. The more ontological reading would be that Bede thinks historical events themselves lack revelatory significance unless God acts upon them and gives them such significance. While the perspectival reading might be a more generous and charitable reading (at least from my perspective), Bede's own writings do not lead in this direction. For example, if Bede thought the issue was perspectival, then figurally exegeting subsequent historical events in light of Christ and Scripture would not be a problem. Actually, that should encourage Bede to figurally exegete history to show its revelatory significance in light of Christ and Scripture. Bede, however, fails to perform such exegesis.

---

116. Augustine, *De ciuitate Dei*, 16.4.

117. See Augustine, *De ciuitate Dei*, 18.1. Another salient point worthy of note is that Augustine's defense of God's universal providence in *De ciuitate Dei* 5.11 fits nicely with his account of the divine *rationes* in his commentaries on Genesis. Bede's *World Chronicle* also integrates biblical and non-biblical history, but his recounting and synchronization does not lead to any different conclusions than the ones I have already drawn. See Bede, *Reckoning of Time*, 157–249.

118. Augustine, *De ciuitate Dei*, 18.44.

119. While it is true that in *De ciuitate Dei*, 17.3, not to mention other places, Augustine says that not all historical (and even biblical) events have symbolic significance, he also says that he would not condemn anyone who finds spiritual or allegorical significance in all the events, which he should be committed to saying given his views of creation.

120. The most extended treatment of this is book 18 of *De ciuitate Dei*. See also O'Daly's *Augustine's City of God*, 160–95.

From what I can discern, Bede likely thought of historical events as lacking any intrinsic revelatory value apart from God's activity of taking them up into his providential care.

Of course, Bede never explicitly says anything like what I just summarized regarding the relationship between creation, history, and providence. I am simply trying to make connections that Bede did not make between his own works. I want to be clear that I do not think Bede intended for the relationship between history, creation, and providence to take on this quasi-extrinsic character. In fact, my immediately preceding analysis is in tension with how he articulates the nature and purpose of the discipline of history in other places. Recall from the introductory remarks that Bede never thought history should be practiced for its own sake; history has moral and even theological purposes. While Bede did seek to order his history to theological ends, as his naming of the major chronicle "The Sixth Age" demonstrates, not to mention the spiritual instruction in the *Historia*, his exegesis of Genesis, creation, and understanding of God's relationship to history continues to cause tension and issues for his historical and exegetical writings and *this* could be why he limits figural exegesis to only Scriptural events, persons, and words.[121]

My argument here is more exploratory than demonstrative insofar as it must be noted that Bede never explicitly examined the relationship between creation, history, exegesis, and divine providence theologically in the ways I have been doing, though his work certainly encourages it. Regardless of my reading of Bede being accurate, my fundamental point is one of theological instruction and observation, attending to the importance of properly conceiving revelation, interpreting the creation of the world in Genesis 1, and how that impacts understandings and practices of history. In short, philosophy and theology matter in the writing of history and in the reading of the literal sense of Scripture. I will get more specific in how they matter in the next two chapters.

---

121. See Bede, *Greater Chronicle*, 307–40.

4

Anachronism and the Status of the Past in Bede's *Historia* and Figural Exegesis

Argument Recapitulation

BEFORE TRANSITIONING TO THE subject for this chapter, a brief recounting of my argument to this point seems appropriate. Along with summarizing contemporary scholarship on Bede's *Historia* and exegesis, Chapter 1 alluded to the fact that reading Bede in light of modern historical methods and presumptions results in distortion. Part of that discussion revolved around the status of the past and its relationship to the present. The work of Charles Jones made such issues come to the fore in my historiography, specifically Jones's application of the categories of realist and romantic to Bede, and Jan Davidse applied such concerns to the work of Bede in criticism of some modern Bedan scholarship. I concluded with lingering questions needing an answer: 1). How can we moderns read Bede given our divergent understandings of history? In other words, is it possible to avoid anachronism, like contemporary history requires of us, *and* understand Bede's conception of history that has no problem with anachronism? 2). How did such a change in historical understanding take place—that is, how did anachronism become an historical fallacy? 3). What is the theological relationship between Bede's exegetical writings and his history?

Chapters 2 and 3 sought to answer the third question by clarifying the theological relationship between Bede's exegesis and the *Historia*. I attempted to show how Bede's exegesis of Genesis 1 and understanding of *creatio ex nihilo* relates to his figural exegesis and historical writings. I have argued that while Bede clearly thinks that history is a theological practice and should be ordered according to its moral and theological ends, he was not able to maintain such integration insofar as he was theologically disallowed (whether intentionally or unintentionally is unclear) from figurally exegeting extra-biblical historical events and persons. My purpose for making this argument is largely intended to highlight and explore theologically and philosophically the relationships between figural exegesis, history, and *creatio ex nihilo* as Bede saw and practiced them in order to demonstrate how seemingly unhistorical speculations on theoretical and exegetical issues impact how history, creation, exegesis, and divine providence are conceived and practiced. Put differently, philosophy and theology matter in the practice of history.

The first two questions remain largely unanswered. In short, how philosophy and theology matter for history occupies the subject of this chapter and the following chapter. While I outlined how Bede related them and the consequences of that relationship, I will now discuss that with an intentional eye to the present and more constructive theological moments. Now, I will discuss the rise of anachronism and its concomitant sense of the past. Furthermore, I will make explicit and discuss in more theoretical fashion some of the differences between Bede and modern historians by bringing contemporary historical theory and Bede together through an analysis of the nature and role anachronism plays in the practice and theory of history.

Introduction

According to Frank Manuel, to commit anachronism in the writing of history is to commit the "historical sin of sins," and thirty years later the historian and theorist Constantin Fasolt concurs.[1] There is little scholarship specifically devoted to the development of anachronism as a concept in historical practice and theory. Therefore, what follows will be a summary of the work available on anachronism in historical writing and theory as well as the philosophy and history of art. I want to emphasize that my interest in anachronism itself is less important than the sense of the past and the past's relationship to the present that anachronism presumes. In other words, forms of anachronism reveal a way of thinking about the past and its relationship to the present, and *that* is my primary concern.

What exactly am I looking for when looking for anachronism? The most common usage occurs as an accusation or formal attack on an historian or scholar who has supposedly and illicitly read the present back into the past. I used this form of anachronism several times in chapter one. For example, I chastised Plummer's defense of Bede's figural exegesis as non-arbitrary because it gives the impression that Bede had similar epistemological fears as

---

1. Manuel, "Use and Abuse of Psychology in History," 218; Fasolt, *Limits of History*, 6–7.

a nineteenth-century scholar regarding subjectivity and objectivity. David Fischer defines this kind of anachronism as such; "It generally consists in the description, analysis, or judgment of an event as if it occurred at some point in time other than when it actually happened."[2] This broad definition, according to Fischer, encompasses an entire host of anachronistic fallacies: the presentism fallacy, the antiquarian fallacy, the tunnel history fallacy, the false periodization fallacy, the interminable fallacy, the fallacy of archtypes, the chronic fallacy, the static fallacy, the fallacy of presumptive continuity, the genetic fallacy, and the didactic fallacy.[3]

Most of Fischer's extensive list of anachronistic fallacies are just more specific versions of the more general definition he provides. What is noteworthy for my purposes is that the anachronism fallacy, according to Fischer, consists in the historian's description, analysis, and judgment. In this way, anachronism is not understood to be rooted in a philosophical or ontological claim, at least not explicitly. Thus, anachronism is simply a methodological control for acknowledging when something has gone awry in the writing and narrating of history. Descriptions of events and times are out of place; the present is read back into the past or norms from one time are imposed on another.

Harry Ritter, on the other hand, defines anachronism in a more theoretical and philosophical fashion. In the *Dictionary of Concepts in History*, Ritter says anachronism is an "[a]wareness that the past differs in fundamental respects from the present."[4] Thus, there are two ways to understand anachronism; the one more ontological, the other more methodological. While I have no objection to the more formal view on anachronism, such distinctions are often murky in practice since there are no strictly formal claims or judgments, as contemporary philosophy of language has demonstrated. (The next chapter will address the point about formal and analytic judgments specifically). Next, I will answer the question about when and how this shift regarding anachronism took place.

The Rise of Anachronism and Its Sense of the Past

Peter Burke addresses three differences between modern and pre-modern understandings of history that began to take shape during the early Renaissance period.[5] He calls this developing conception the "sense of

2. Fischer, *Historians' Fallacies*.
3. Ibid., 131–63.
4. Ritter, "Anachronism," 9–13.
5. Burke, *Renaissance Sense of the Past*. Haddock also makes similar claims in *An*

history,"⁶ and its three components are "the sense of anachronism," "the awareness of evidence," and "the interest in causation."⁷ Medieval historical thought and practice often lacked these or at least construed them in radically different ways.⁸

The "sense of anachronism" deals with a sense of historical perspective. In short, medieval people generally lacked a "sense of change" or a sense of the pastness or significant differences of the past.⁹ To be sure, they knew the present was not identical to the past. "They knew, for example, that the ancients had not been Christians. But they did not take the difference very seriously."¹⁰ In other words, they did, of course, have notions of the past, present, and future. They, like everyone, wrote in and understood tensed language. However, they did not think that serious or fundamental differences existed between themselves and preceding peoples and generations. Burke details several examples of this lack of historical curiosity from attitudes toward ruins, the bible, and law.¹¹ As for Scripture:

> Since it [Scripture] was the work of God, who was eternal, there was no point in asking when the different parts of it were written down. It was treated not as a historical document but as an oracle; that is, what it had meant was subordinated to what it could mean. From the time of the Fathers of the Church, the Bible was interpreted in four senses; the literal or historical sense, and three spiritual senses, allegorical, moral, and anagogical.¹²
>
> The allegorical interpretation of the Bible is of a special kind. It is 'figural.' The German literary historian Erich Auerbach defined *figura*, in his famous essay on the subject, as 'something real and historical which announces something else that is also real and historical.' [. . .] It is not that Adam is simply like Christ [referring to Paul's discussion in 1 Corinthians 15], that he may be compared by us to Christ. In an objective sense he announces Christ. It is as if God is writing the history we live, and Adam is one of his metaphors. This kind of interpretation clearly worked against the sense of the past, for it depends on taking men and

---

Introduction to Historical Thought, 1–5, though his entire text supports this conclusion.

6. Haddock, *Introduction to Historical Thought*, 1.
7. Ibid.
8. See also Kemp, *Estrangement of the Past*, 3–65.
9. Burke, *Renaissance Sense of the Past*, 1.
10. Ibid.
11. Ibid., 2–6.
12. Ibid., 3.

events out of their historical context, and putting them into a spiritual one.[13]

While some of Burke's comments (quoted and unquoted here) misconstrue Christian figural exegesis, his insight still holds: The nature of figural exegesis requires a certain conception of the past that differs from the way most contemporary historians and scholars conceive of it.[14] Furthermore, Christians who lived in medieval times and read Scripture figurally did not think of themselves as distanced from the past; the past was not a foreign country difficult to understand from which they were fundamentally separated.

The history of the development of the sense of anachronism contains complex variations and developments, but Christian art can provide a helpful foray into the discussion. Many icons and paintings of saints from the first millennium depict characters from the first century in later liturgical garb. As late as the high Middle Ages and during the Renaissance, Carpaccio's *The Vision of St. Augustine* commits many anachronisms.[15] Many nativity scene paintings likewise read contemporary themes and garb into the first century. For example, Hugo van der Goes's (1475) painting of the nativity has shepherds and even Mary dressed in medieval clothing.

However, in 1564 Gilio da Fabriano published *The Errors of Painters* where he famously attacks the painting of Michelangelo and demonstrates a keen sense of anachronism.

> The prudent painter should know how to paint what is appropriate to the individual, the time and the place . . . so that he does not represent Aeneas as coming to Italy in the time of the emperor Justinian, or the battles of the Carthaginians in the presence of Pontius Pilate . . . They represent St. Francis as fat and red, well-dressed, with his beard and moustache carefully combed, perfumed, with a cap of fine cloth carefully folded, with a silken cord round his waist, looking more like a general or provincial of an order than the mirror of penitence that he was; they do not realize that he wore nothing but a rough gown.[16]

So when did this arrival of a new sense of the past take place? Many historians trace the arrival of a perceived distance between the ancient world and

---

13. Ibid., 4.

14. While I do not address Burke specifically, I will spend significant time in the next chapter discussing how figural exegesis should be understood, at least in Bede's usage.

15. See Nagel and Wood, "Toward a New Model of Renaissance Anachronism," 403–15, for an analysis of Carpaccio's *The Vision of St. Augustine*.

16. Da Fabriano, *The Errors of Painters*, quoted in Burke's *Renaissance Sense of the Past*, 28.

the Middle Ages to the 14th century in the work of the renaissance scholar and humanist Francesco Petrarca or Petrarch.[17] Petrarch, who many think was the first to understand the early Middle Ages as "dark ages," longed for the ancient Roman world.[18] He sought to restore classical learning and did not take historical artifacts, like the ancient ruins in Rome, for granted.[19] In fact, he was awe-struck by such artifacts to the point of silence.[20] Petrarch was also one of the first to state that laws have a history, but his ideas were not developed until the middle of the 15th century by Lorenzo Valla.[21] Furthermore, Petrarch's letters to classical persons like Livy and Cicero demonstrate his desire to bring back or inhabit a time like the classical period.[22] In sum, the sense of anachronism "was born of a sense of cultural loss."[23]

Furthermore, one can also see how the Reformation in the sixteenth century requires a sense of the past that Petrarch also presumed.[24] Many reform-minded scholars began to perceive differences between the church of the sixteenth century and apostolic church in Acts, and they wanted to reinstate or go back to these previous and putatively more pristine times. Thus, in order for Petrarch or Luther to want to renew or revive a specific epoch in history, or judge the contemporary scene as corrupt, he would have had to feel alienated from the past in some sense. This perceived and observed distance between the present one inhabited and the past brings forth a concern for anachronism and a conception that the present is

17. See, for example (along with their bibliographies), Burke, *Renaissance Sense of the Past*, 21–25; Trinkaus, *Poet as Philosopher*; Mommsen, "Petrarch's Conception of the Dark Ages," 226–42, as well as the many works by art historian Panofsky from the mid-twentieth century. In fact, Dempsey goes so far as to say that "[m]any historians (well before Panofsky) had agreed that a sense of historical distance from the classical past seems first to have appeared with Petrarch ..." "Response: *Historia* and Anachronism in Renaissance Art," 416–21. More recently, Dupré discusses the importance of Petrarch and the new understanding of the past. See Dupré, *Passage to Modernity*, 120–65.

18. See Mommsen, "Petrarch's Conception of the Dark Ages," who attempts to settle the argument for good whether or not Petrarch thought of the early middle ages as the "dark ages." He concludes on page 242 that Petrarch should be considered the first to characterize this time period as the "dark ages."

19. Burke, *The Renaissance Sense of the Past*, 21–23.

20. Mommsen, "Petrarch's Conception of the Dark Ages," 230.

21. Burke, *The Renaissance Sense of the Past*, 33. Following in the wake of Petrarch and Vallo, in the sixteenth century, Richard Hooker criticized the Puritans for applying OT laws to modern society. See Hooker's *Of the Laws of Ecclesiastical Polity*.

22. See, Petrarch, *Letters*.

23. Haddock, *Introduction to Historical Thought*, 2. For more on Petrarch's influence on subsequent philosophy and political thought, see Gillespie's *Theological Origins of Modernity*, 44–92.

24. See Kemp, *Estrangement of the Past*, 75–83.

fundamentally different from the past, as Ritter's definition above states. Consequently, even a mere methodological avoidance of anachronism that reigns in current historical practice was born out of the deeper sense that the past has been lost or is deeply different and alienated from the present.

Bede's Conception of the Past

Although I have been infrequently noting places where Bede commits anachronism, I now want to turn to a more detailed analysis of this conception of history and the past. In the very home of Bede at the Northrumbian double monastery, a miniature portrait of the prophet Ezra rewriting the sacred books graces one of the front pages of the Codex Amiatinus; Bede may have even composed the inscription above the portrait (see Image 1).[25] The couplet reads, "Codicibus sacris hostili clade perustis / Esdra Deo fervens hoc reparavit opus."[26] The details of this painting, however, are its most fascinating aspects. The dress of Ezra attempts to be faithful to Old Testament descriptions given the depicted priestly insignia on his head and chest as well as the tallith and breastplate with precious stones. He is seated copying something indiscernible into a book seemingly from memory. The conclusion that should be drawn here stems from the tradition that Ezra preserved the Hebrew Scriptures by copying them down from memory after they had been destroyed by the Babylonians. Thus, the painting depicts Ezra penning the sacred books.

---

25. See Nees, *Early Medieval Art*, 164–65. For more on the argument favoring Bede's authorship see Meyvaert, "Bede, Cassiodorus, and the Codex Amiatinus," 827–83, and idem, "Date of Bede's *In Ezram* and His Image of Ezra in the Codex Amiatinus," 1087–1133.

26. "After the sacred books were destroyed in hostility, Ezra, fervent for God, repaired the works" (my translation).

Image 1: Ezra/Cassiodorus miniature in front matter of the Codex Amiatinus

Or does it? Closer inspection may reveal a different conclusion. In the cupboard behind Ezra are nine volumes. With the help of infrared and ultraviolet light, scholars have been able to identify the titles on the spines of these volumes (depicted in formal arrangement as they appear in the cupboard):

OCT.LIB LEG   REG.PAR.L.VI
HIST.LIB.VIII   PSAL.LIB.I
SAL.LIB.V   PROP L.SVI
EVANG.L.IIII   EPIST.AP.XXI
ACT.AP.APOC.IS[27]

These abbreviations stand for (left to right, top to bottom) 1) the eight books of the Octateuch and the law, 2) six books of Kings and Paralipomenon, 3) eight historical books, 4) one book of Psalms, 5) five books of the Wisdom of Solomon, 6) sixteen prophetic books, 7) four gospels, 8) twenty one epistles, and 9) Acts and the Apocalypse.[28] Interestingly, in his *Institutions*, Cassiodorus consistently refers to one of the bibles he commissioned as nine volumes in length including commentary, and Benedictine scholar Dom. Bonifatius Fischer says the other two books (the one being written in and the one on the floor) represent the other two bibles that Cassiodorus's monks penned at his request.[29] In light of these similarities, Bruce-Mitford concludes that the figure represented in the front matter of the Codex Amiatinus is Cassiodorus in the guise of Ezra.[30] Bruce-Mitford argues the painting is intended to compliment Cassiodorus and his achievements at his monastery in Squillace by depicting him as Ezra because Cassiodorus also helped save sacred writings after he was unable to start a theological school due to upheaval in his day.[31]

My argument has little stake in which scholar is right about who the miniature portrays. After all, even if the miniature depicts Ezra, he is writing books of the New Testament (NT)! Sufficient for my purposes is that the artist in Wearmouth-Jarrow monastery who created this painting had no problem depicting Cassiodorus in the garb and image of Ezra who lived hundreds of years before Cassiodorus.[32] No gap was understood to have existed between the past and present to the extent that it disallowed or gave pause to a monk in Bede's context who created this beautiful work.

27. See Bruce-Mitford, *Art of the Codex Amiatinus*, 9.

28. Ibid.

29. Ibid., 14. These two bibles would be the *Codex Grandior* and *minutiore manu conscriptus*—both of which are now lost. See also Cassiodorus, *Institutions of Divine and Secular Learning*.

30. Bruce-Mitford, *Art of the Codex Amiatinus*, 14.

31. See Cassiodorus, *Institutions of Divine and Secular Learning*. See also Bruce-Mitford, *The Art of the Codex Amiatinus*, 14.

32. For a treatment of the originality of the painting to Wearmouth-Jarrow in its earliest years, which is now accepted by English scholars, see Bruce-Mitford, *Art of the Codex Amiatinus*. Even if the miniature is of Ezra, my point still stands, since the volumes include New Testament texts that Ezra himself would not have copied.

Moreover, and as Scott DeGregorio argues, the very activities the monks were engaged in, like copying the Codex Amiatinus, are perhaps the precise reason such figures like Cassiodorus and Ezra would be portrayed on the Codex's front matter.[33] Consequently, the very biblical text that Bede frequently used for this commentaries and scholarship opened with this putatively anachronistic image.[34] Bede likely believed the image to be of Ezra and not Cassiodorus. He did not have access to Cassiodorus's *Institutes*,[35] and if he penned the inscription above the image, he certainly believed the image to be of the Old Testament (OT) priest, Ezra.[36] Bede's ignorance of the "real" depiction of the image does not damage my argument insofar as my point is only to demonstrate the differences in conceptions of the past between contemporary scholars and those in Bede's day. More specifically, the Ezra-Cassiodorus depiction shows that anachronism was not a problem within Bede's monastic and ecclesial culture.

One could object at this point that paintings are not like the writing of history and thus my analysis thus far is misguided. I have two responses to this objection. First, the writing of history is more like painting than many might like to admit. However, why this is so must wait until the next chapter. Second, I would contend that the fact these images grace the pages of a text show how the monks and medievals did not draw such sharp distinctions between visual and verbal art and representation. Again, I will say more about this in chapter 5.

Though anachronism was unproblematic for Bede and his contemporaries, time and history were not stable or unchanging things, like Burke can at times imply.[37] Instead, as Davidse says, "It is only possible to experience the past in its similarity to the present on the basis of the fact that things do change. This aspect of transitoriness is evident to him [Bede] from the mere fact that a monastery can become a nunnery."[38] Moreover, Bede's nar-

---

33. See DeGregorio, Appendix 2, in Bede, *On Ezra and Nehemiah*, 231–33.

34. For more on Bede's relationship to the Codex Amiatinus see Meyvaert, "Bede, Cassiodorus, and the Codex Amiatinus," 827–83; Marsden, "*Manus Bedae*: Bede's Contribution to Ceolfrith's Bibles," 65–85.

35. See Meyvaert, "Bede, Cassiodorus, and the Codex Amiatinus," 827–31.

36. For the claim that Bede penned the inscription, see Nees, *Early Medieval Art*, 165.

37. See, for example, Bede, *In Lucam*, 130: "Apostoli qui electionis merito bonitatem generis humani multis excesserant modis supernae bonitatis intuit mali esse dicuntur quia nihil est per semet ipsum stabile nihil immutabile nihil bonum nisi deitas sola. Omnes uero creaturae ut beatitudinem aeternitatis uel immutabilitatis obtineant non hoc per suam naturum sed per creatoris sui participationem et gratiam consequuntur."

38. Davidse, "Sense of History in the Works of Venerable Bede," 657. On the monastery becoming a nunnery, see Bede, *The Life and Miracles of St. Cuthbert*, chapter 3.

ration of the victories and challenges the English church faced demonstrate that Bede understood history to be a movement that includes good times and bad, especially since much of his latter exegesis was aimed at church reform, as Scott DeGregorio has rightly maintained.[39] More specifically and most significantly, one's particular temporal locale gets its meaning from the center point of history: the incarnation, death, and resurrection of Jesus.[40]

Augustine's philosophy of history has had a great influence on Bede here.[41] In *On Christian Teaching*, Augustine distinguishes between two types of human learning or the types of things studied by humans. There are humanly instituted things and divinely instituted things—or things observed—which is to say uncreated by humans.[42] Among the useful non-superstitious variety are dress, currency, weights and measures, the alphabet, and coinage.[43] Surprisingly, the task of the historian is not one of these human institutions for Augustine:

> Historical narrative also describes human institutions of the past, but it should not for that reason itself be counted among human institutions. For what has already gone into the past and cannot be undone must be considered part of the history of time, whose creator and controller is God. There is a difference between describing what had been done and describing what must be done. History relates past events in a faithful and useful way, whereas the books of the haruspices and similar literature set out to teach things to be performed or observed, and offer impertinent advice, not reliable information.[44]

The following paragraphs that address Bede are deeply indebted to Davidse and his departure from scholars like Brandt who thought Bede's historical narrations were "static." See Brandt, *Shape of Medieval History*, 65–73; quote from 70.

39. See Davidse, "Sense of History in the Works of the Venerable Bede," 657; DeGregorio, "Bede's *In Ezram et Neemiam* and the Reform of the Northumbrian Church," 1–25; idem, "*Nostorum socordiam temporum*," 107–22. See also Bede's *Letter to Egbert* for the challenges the Northumbrian church was facing.

40. Davidse, "Sense of History in the Works of the Venerable Bede," 661.

41. For more specifics on the influence of Augustine's philosophy of history on Bede, see Rector, *Influence of St. Augustine's Philosophy of History on the Venerable Bede in the Ecclesiastical History of the English People*.

42. Augustine, *On Christian Teaching*, 2.66–152.

43. Ibid., 2.103.

44. Ibid., 2.109. "Narratione autem historica cum praeterita etiam hominum instituta narrantur, non inter humana instituta ipsa historia numeranda est, quia iam quae transierunt nec infecta fiery possunt, in ordine temporum habenda sunt, quorum est conditor et administrator dues. Aliud est enim facta narrare, aliud docere facienda. Historia facta narrat fideliter atque utiliter, libri autem haruspicum et quaeque similes litterae facienda vel observanda intendunt docere, monitoris audacia, non indicis fide"

History, then, as the study of the past, is a divine institution in some sense for Augustine. As Davidse points out, Bede likely draws on Augustine's understanding of *historia* as that which "depends on research into what is effectuated by time or is instituted by God . . . The order of time is God's work, and that is why *historia* is not a human institution, even though it concerns" human matters.[45] History relates the past in ways that anticipate the actualization of its truth or fulfillment in the incarnation or the consummation of all creation, depending on when one is writing.[46]

One conspicuous example from Augustine will be sufficient to demonstrate the point, but let me briefly recount Augustine's understanding of signs as a precursor. In *De doctrina Christiana*, Augustine defines signs in two ways. First, signs are "those things which are employed to signify something."[47] Hence, all signs are things but not all things are signs, and signs are understood in terms of their user. The three components here are the sign, the thing signified, and the user. Second, "For a sign is a thing which of itself makes some other thing come to mind, besides the impression that it presents to the senses."[48] This slight recasting includes the sign, the thing signified, and the receiver or perceiver of the sign.[49] In sum, there are four aspects in the use of signs: the user or speaker, the sign, the signified, and the receiver/perceiver of the sign. Augustine also distinguishes between two types of signs, natural (*signa naturalia*) and given signs (*signa data*).[50] Natural signs are "those which without a wish or any urge to signify cause something else besides themselves to be known from them . . ."[51] For example, smoke makes us think of fire and animal tracks make us think of the animal that left them.[52]

(*De doctrina Christiana*, 2.109). Latin text from *Corpus Scriptorum Ecclesiasticorum Latinorum*.

45. Davidse, "On Bede as Christian Historian," 9.

46. Ibid., 9.

47. Augustine, *On Christian Teaching*, 1.5. "Ex quo intellegitur quid appellem signa: res eas videlicet quae ad significandum aliquid adhibentur" (*De doctrina Christiana*, 1.5). All subsequent Latin quotations of *De doctrina Christiana* will be from *Corpus Christianorum Series Latina*.

48. Ibid., 2.1. "Signum est enim res, praeter speciem quam ingerit sensibus, aluid aliquid ex se faciens in cogitationem venire." *De doctrina Christiana*, 2.1.

49. Here I am following Markus, "Signs, Communication, and Communities in Augustine's *De doctrina Christiana*," 97–108; Jackson, "Theory of Signs in St. Augustine's *De doctrina Christiana*," 9–49.

50. Augustine, *On Christian Teaching*, 2.2–4.

51. Ibid., 2.2. "Naturalia sunt quae sine voluntate atque ullo appetitu significandi praeter se aliquid aliud ex se cognosci faciunt . . ." (*De doctrina Christiana*, 2.2).

52. These are the examples that Augustine gives.

Given signs or conventional signs are more complicated and broadly construed.[53] They must include some level of intention making them encapsulate not only human communication but also animals, though Augustine only focuses on human use.[54] Given signs include head nods, hand waves, eye winks, and any other physical display that communicates; Augustine calls these "*verba visibilia*."[55] Of course, the most common given signs humans use are linguistic words, *verba*. There are two kinds of words, spoken words and written words. Spoken words are fleeting in existence: they "cease to exist as soon as they come into contact with the air, and their existence is no more lasting than that of their sound."[56] Hence, humans write in order to have their communications, wishes, and desires expressed in a more permanent fashion; we use written words as signs of verbal words.[57]

Therefore, the written word has the status of sign in two ways. First, it signifies the spoken word or communication of the speaker, and second, words signify other things; words simultaneously signify back to their source and outward toward a referent or thing, either literal or metaphorical.[58] The sentence "There is a cat on the mat" signifies the wishes or mind of the communicator (as complex or as simple as that may be is irrelevant at this point), as well as signifying the cat on the mat, if it is a literal sign. Metaphorical signs or *translata signa* refer *both* to literal and to non-literal things. Augustine uses the example of an ox. The word ox literally refers to the animal we call by that name, but metaphorically it can also refer to a worker in the gospel.[59] Note that *translata signa* include the literal meaning according to Augustine, which is precisely why knowledge of the original languages of Scripture is so important for him.[60] Knowledge of the original language helps the reader better know how the *signum* refers back to its source. However, understanding metaphors requires more than knowledge of languages; an understanding of things is also necessary,[61] not to mention

---

53. For the use of "conventional" see Markus, "Signs, Communication and Communities," 99–100.

54. Augustine, *On Christian Teaching*, 2.2–7.

55. Augustine, *De doctrina Christiana*, 2.3.

56. Augustine, *On Christian Teaching*, 2.4. "Sed quia verberato aere statim transeunt nec diutius manent quam sonant . . ." (*De doctrina Christiana*, 2.4).

57. Augustine, *On Christian Teaching*, 2.9.

58. Ibid., 2.32. "Sunt autem signa vel propria vel translata" (*De doctrina Christiana*, 2.32).

59. Augustine, *On Christian Teaching*, 2.33.

60. Ibid., 2.34–58.

61. Ibid., 2.59–61.

numbers,[62] and music.[63] For example, general knowledge about snakes can help clarify Jesus' command, "Be as wise as serpents."[64] Thus, an exemplary reader and communicator must possess good linguistic skills and virtues in addition to a fecund and liberal knowledge of the created order and all its beautiful multiplicity.

Now the specific example to illustrate my point about Augustine's thought on historical events signifying other historical events. The OT Scriptures signified the incarnation, life, death, and resurrection of Jesus, especially the story of Abraham. "This, I say, is the universal way for the deliverance of believers, concerning which the faithful Abraham received the divine oracle, 'In thy seed, shall all nations be blessed'. . . Hence, when, so long afterwards, our Savior had taken flesh of the seed of Abraham, He said of Himself, 'I am the way, the truth, and the life.'"[65] Augustine is arguing that prior to Christ's advent, history, and especially the OT, was primarily concerned with pointing to the coming of the Messiah. Then, after the incarnation, history comes into clearer focus and now takes into account the incarnation and the promised consummation of all things.[66] "And we see so many of these promises fulfilled that we righteously and piously trust that the rest will also be fulfilled in time to come."[67]

Augustine does not specify which sense of sign is at work in the OT when it points to Christ, but the bidirectional account of the linguistic sign works well here. The text of the OT signifies "back" to the historical covenantal promise to Abraham, while also pointing forward to the advent of Christ. Hence, two historical events are signified by the same text and are internally related to one another through God's providential design.

As a result of Augustine's influence, when Bede cites a date as "*anno Dominicae incarnationis*," he was not merely using rhetorical flare. He was signifying and placing historical events into their proper relation—to that of Christ and his incarnation. For Bede, history can only be rightly understood in its entirety when seen in light of the Light of the world who inaugurated the sixth age.[68] The eight ages of the world that Bede is well known for affirming

62. Ibid., 2.62–147.
63. Ibid., 2.66–72.
64. Ibid., 2.59.
65. Augustine, *City of God Against the Pagans*, 10.32.
66. See Augustine, *City of God Against the Pagans*, 10.32: "Then came the mediator himself, in the flesh, and His blessed apostles. In revealing the grace of the New Testament, they showed more clearly those things which, in earlier times, had been signified only in a veiled way."
67. Ibid.
68 See Bede, *On Genesis*, 73–74.

reflect or follow "in all respects" the actual creation of the world according to Genesis.[69] In fact, the eight world ages take place within the week of creation.[70] *On Genesis* says, "But I want to make clear, briefly, that the order of those six or seven days in which it was created is also in harmony with the same number of its ages."[71] And *On the Reckoning of Time* clarifies when it affirms that the world ages follow "in all respects the pattern of the first week."[72] Even more specifically regarding each day's relationship to the world ages: the creation and division of light from darkness on the first of creation reflects the creation of humanity (light in paradise) and their fall (darkness), which is the first age up to the flood; God adorned the sky with lights on the fourth day of creation reflecting the glory of David and Solomon's rule and the glory of the temple in Jerusalem, but evening came when the Babylonians destroyed the temple and carried off God's people into exile.[73]

The age we inhabit now is the sixth age, the age of the Lord and his incarnation, which began with Christ's incarnation and lasts through the persecution of the anti-christ.[74] Chronicling the historical content of the sixth age, Bede narrates in detail generations and leaders of the West from Christ up to the 8th century English people.[75] This is significant because Bede does care about historical detail, as any cursory reading of his *Ecclesiastical History* reveals, while simultaneously and theologically placing the events in the larger arena of God's providence in history understood in relation to Christ. The fact that Bede orients the very first date he gives in the *Historia* in relation to the incarnation shows his intention to read history in light of Christ.[76] Specifically in the *Historia*, the coming of the Christian faith to the English, in its Roman form, was part of the spread of the gospel to come during the sixth age.[77] In *De templo* Bede says,

69 Bede, *On the Reckoning of Time*, 40.

70 Ibid., 39–41. See also Bede, *On Genesis*, 100–105.

71. Bede, *On Genesis*, 100. "Libet autem paucis intimare ut etiam ordo sex illorum siue septem dierum in quibus factus est totidem eius aetatibus conueniat" (*In genesim*, 35–36).

72. Bede, *On the Reckoning of Time*, 40. "Octaua species hebdomadis uniformis et sola sine circuitu reuolutionis extans ad figuram per omnia primae hebdomadis labentibus huius saeculi conficitur aetatibus" (*De temporum ratione liber*, 310).

73. Ibid., 40, 157–58.

74. Ibid., 40–41, 158.

75. Ibid., 195–237.

76. Bede, *EH*, 1.2: "Now Britain had never been visited by the Romans and was unknown to them until the time of Gaius Julius Caesar who, in the year of Rome 693, that is, in the year 60 before our Lord, was consul with Lucius Bibulus." Of course, Bede follows this way of citing dates throughout the *Historia*.

77. Davidse, "Sense of History in the Works of the Venerable Bede," 668.

> The wheels placed underneath to support the laver of the temple raised the base from the ground when the blessed Pope Gregory recently in our own day ruled the Roman Church on the strength of the words of the Gospel; the same wheels fitted beneath God's chariot transported people long distances when the most venerable Fathers, Augustine [of Canterbury], Paulinus and the rest of their companions backed by the oracular sayings of the Gospel came to Britain at his command and a short while ago entrusted the word of God to believers.[78]

The *Historia* is Bede's theological and historical account of the how Christ's work in the Church continues forward after Pentecost.[79] (When I mentioned in previous chapters that Bede's *Historia* was theological, despite Bede's distinguishing between exegesis and history, I was referring to this point).[80] Therefore, Bede undertakes history for theological reasons and even narrates events in accordance with such concerns. As I recounted in chapter one, Bede's theological approach draws the ire of many contemporary historians when investigating his historical endeavors and presuppositions.

Similarly, and as a result of my entire argument up to this point, Bede's *Ecclesiastical History* and all his historical writings must be read in accordance with his theology for it to be properly understood. Thus, Bede's *Historia* should be read not in terms of the present, like many 20th century scholars did and as usual forms of anachronism would have it, but in terms of a past event—an anachronism nonetheless, however. The present is read in terms of the incarnation and the sixth age.[81]

I must be careful in using the language of "reading" at this point because it gives the impression that Bede thought history was about the subjective imposition of categories onto the past where Jesus and the incarnation

---

78. Bede, *On the Temple*, 98. "Rotae basem subpositae ad portandum luterem temple a terra sustollebant cum nostris nuper temporibus beatus papa Gregorius euangelicis roboratus eloquiis Romanam rexit ecclesiam; rotae eaedem currus Dei subnexae longe gestabant cum reuerendissimi patres Augustinus Paulinus et ceteri socii eorum eisdem euangelicis confirmati oraculis iubente illo uenere Brittanniam et uerbam Dei incredulis dudum commisere gentibus" (*De templo*, 218).

79. See Davidse, "Sense of History in the Works of the Venerable Bede," 668. Also, *pace* Smalley who intimates that Bede's historical concerns were much more secular than other Christian historians; see Smalley, *Historians in the Middle Ages*, 55.

80. Moreover, this theological view of history that Bede gets from Augustine in no way mitigates my argument regarding the lack of figural exegesis of historical events in Bede's work, since my concern was more in the details of how this theology of history and Bede's exegetical practice were related. My analysis of Bede's refusal to figurally exegete historical events therefore obtains.

81. I am following and in agreement with Davidse, "On Bede as Christian Historian," 1–15.

are simply one among many such lenses, albeit the true ones for Bede, by which to read or understand the past.[82] Nothing could be further from the truth. More precisely, events are related to the order of time, as that which structures history, by their temporality in light of the incarnation. Broadly speaking, Bede believed he was simply describing history in its relationship to the revelation Jesus Christ.

The Function of Anachronism

As a transition to the final chapter, I want to explore how anachronisms, like the ones described above, functioned for Bede with regard to the presence of the past in the present. Alexander Nagel and Christopher Wood have argued that medieval anachronism was often used as a form of substitution: to perceive something (a word, artifact, etc.) under

> substitutional terms was to understand it as belonging to more than one historical moment simultaneously. The artifact was connected to its unknowable point of origin by an unreconstructible chain of replicas. That chain could not be perceived; its links did not diminish in stature as they receded into the depths of time. Rather, the chain created an instant and ideally effective link to an authoritative source and an instant identity for the artifact. If under the performative theory of origins a given sequence of works is seen perspectivally, each one with a different appearance, under the substitutional theory different objects stack up one on top of another without recession and without alteration. The dominant metaphor is that of the impress or the cast, allowing for repetition without difference, even across heterogeneous objects and materials.[83]

Furthermore,

> The literal circumstances and the historical moment of an artifact's material execution were not routinely taken as components of its meaning or function; such facts about an artifact were seen as accidental rather than as constitutive features. Instead, the artifact functioned by aligning itself with a diachronic

---

82. I have intentionally eschewed the language of interpretation because this carries the subjective conceptual framework even more so.

83. Nagel and Wood, "Toward a New Model," 407. For the full historical argument see idem, *Anachronic Renaissance*. I will be using both the summary essay and their full length text in what follows.

chain of replications. It substituted for the absent artifacts that preceded it within the chain.[84]

In other words, the image, event, or artifact is substantively constituted by its relationship to a diachronic chain of causation; the effect (the artifact or image) stands in for the original cause or another preceding cause because of its likeness and relationship to it. Much depends on what Nagel and Wood mean when they say that substitution allows "for repetition without difference, even across heterogeneous objects and materials."[85] They offer an example using the iconoclastic controversies and cite St. Theodore the Studite: Theodore "compared the relation of image to prototype to the impress of a seal on different materials at different times: 'The same applies,' he wrote, 'to the likeness of Christ irrespective of the material upon which it is represented.'"[86] The dominant metaphor here is one of an imprint or cast. An artifact made an "imprint" on subsequent objects and artifacts creating replicas across time where the diminutive effects of time have no impact or effect on the replicas ability to make present the original. Thus, a "replica" icon of Christ made in the twelfth century imitating a fourth-century icon has the same ontological status as the "original," despite its historical and cultural contexts as well as material conditions.

These ersatzes have a "double historicity" that allowed those who gazed upon them or read them to know both that the object had been recently fabricated but to value it as if it were as old and as if it was the original.[87] Furthermore, "the literal circumstances and the historical moment of an artifact's material execution were not routinely taken as components of its meaning or function. Instead, such facts . . . were seen as accidental rather than as constitutive features."[88] This view of historicity was not universal and did not apply to all works of art or artifacts. For example, relics could not be substituted; a horse bone could not be a substitute for a saint's bone because the particular circumstances and historicity of the saint's bone were constitutive of its power and essence.[89] In this way, art and some architecture were understood to organize time like ancient biblical exegetes. An artifact "stitched" apposite temporal realities together and collapsed the temporal gap between them; chronological time would be disrupted.[90] This also had a

84. Nagel and Wood, "Toward a New Model," 405.
85. Ibid., 407.
86. Ibid. For more examples see idem, *Anachronic Renaissance*, 7–28, 35–44.
87. Nagel and Wood, *Anachronic Renaissance*, 29.
88. Ibid.
89. Ibid., 31.
90. Ibid., 32.

pastoral function because these artifacts and physical structures were seen and understood by all in this way.[91] In other words, substitutionary understandings of objects and figural readings of Scripture were not the possession of elite intellectuals; everyday masses used them and relied upon such common understandings.[92] Visual artifacts, however, made the collapsing of times easier to understand, since its wholeness is more apparent than in discursive text, though the glosses on texts like the Sentences and other Scriptural commentaries demonstrate an effort and perspective to treat texts in a substitutionary manner as well.[93]

While I doubt that the Ezra-Cassiodorus miniature was believed to function as an ontological substitute, the point to be gleaned from Wood and Nagel is that through such a substitutionary imagination, the monks at Wearmouth-Jarrown were able to stitch two time periods together, second temple Judaism and their own Northumbrian context, in nearly a seamless fashion and without intellectual balking. Hence, the monks, and perhaps even Bede, considered themselves new types of Ezras working on the *Codex Amiatinus*, within the sixth age, in order to spread the gospel to all nations. Whether this self understanding was explicit or implicit is hard to discern, especially for Bede, since I have shown how he refused to read history in explicitly figural ways. However, the essential point that past and present were not thought to be, or even experienced as, fundamentally separated, albeit distinct, obtains.

Conclusion

This chapter has shown that Bede's conception of the past differs from modern understandings of anachronism that seek to keep the past and present separate or believe them to be fundamentally unique. Furthermore, this newer sense of the past arose between the times of Bede and contemporary developments in historical inquiry, specifically in the work of Petrarch in the early Renaissance. While maintaining that the past and present were different, Bede did not understand there to be a barrier that should be erected or maintained between them. I used the Ezra/Cassiodorus miniature, several

---

91. For more on substitution in architecture see ibid., 51–70.

92. Ibid., 32–33.

93. Ibid., and Carruthers, *Book of Memory*, 216–17. The similarity here between contemporary scholars who argue for a "narrative" view of Scripture, like Hans Frei and his followers, or "echoes" within Scripture that appeal to the whole of a prior text, like Richard Hays, should not go unnoticed and deserves further attention. See Frei, *Eclipse of Biblical Narrative*, and Hays, *Echoes of Scripture in Letters of Paul*; idem, *Conversion of the Imagination*.

passages from Bede, and the work of Wood and Nagel to demonstrate the historical and conceptual point that the past could be considered present for many thinkers in medieval times and for Bede himself.

Finally, I want to clarify that my argument regarding anachronism in this chapter does not attend to all versions of anachronism. I only address and object to those who would argue for and maintain a fundamental or ontological boundary between the past and present, or those who, prior to actual investigation of the past, think the past and present *must* be separate and unique. My preceding argument does not, for example, directly address the work of someone like Gadamer where the understanding of the past arises out of the "temporal distance" between the past and present leading to a different conception of how the past and present relate.[94] Gadamer's argument that prejudices are the "conditions for understanding" makes this point quite well[95] where Gadamer ultimately concludes that "The true locus of hermeneutics is this in-between," in-between the differences and similarities of subjects and objects each within different traditions.[96] The specifics of how Gadamer relates the present and past through his history of effects is not my immediate concern, so I need not rehearse his view here, but the account of representation I provide in the next chapter certainly could be compared to Gadamer's proposal. In fact, Ankersmit, whose work I will draw heavily from, presumes Gadamer a great deal, while also departing from his account of historical experience.[97]

94. See, for example, Gadamer, *Truth and Method*, 265–379; quote from p. 291. See also some of his later reflections as well in Gadamer, "The Universality of the Hermeneutical Problem," 3–17. I want to thank Frank Ankersmit for pointing this out to me.
95. See Gadamer, *Truth and Method*, 277–307, esp. 291–300.
96. Gadamer, *Truth and Method*, 295; originally in italics.
97. See, e.g., Ankersmit, *Sublime Historical Experience*, 78–80, 193–239.

5

Bede and Frank Ankersmit
The Inevitability of Figural History

Introduction

UP TO THIS POINT, I have tried to show how Bede's practice of history was deeply theological yet ran into some difficulties that someone like Augustine was able to avoid when he came to the literal sense of Genesis 1. One of these problems revolves around how language refers in its literal and historical usage. Recall that Bede read the days in Genesis 1 as literal 24-hour days, despite Augustine's unwillingness to affirm such a reading in his literal commentary on Genesis. For Bede the literal and the allegorical were in tension with each other; when one moves to allegory, one leaves the history behind.

> Moreover, that *in the beginning God made heaven and earth* can very probably be understood in the words of the only-begotten Son who, when the Jews asked why they should believe in him, replied, *(I am) the beginning, which I also speak unto you. For,* as the Apostle says, *in him were all things created in heaven and on earth.* But it must be carefully observed, as each one devotes his attention to the allegorical senses, how far he may have forsaken the manifest truth of history by allegorical interpretation.[1]

---

1. Bede, *On Genesis*, 68–69. "Potest autem non inprobabiliter intellegi *in principio fecisse Deum caelum et terram* in unigenito filio suo qui, interrogantibus se Iudeis quid eum credere deberent, respondit, *Principium quod et loquor uobis. Quia in ipso*, ut ait apostolus, *condita sunt omnia in caelis et in terra*. Sed diligenter intuendum ut ita quisque sensibus allegoricis stadium impendat, quatenus apertam historiae fidem allegorizando derelinquat" (*In genesim*, 3).

Moreover, Bede says in his transition to his discussion of the world ages in *In Genesim*, "Let it suffice to have spoken thus far of the beginnings of the infant world according to the literal sense."[2] Bede thought he was leaving the literal sense when he began reading the days of creation as the world ages, whereas Augustine's reading was more complex through his use of the *rationes* in the days of creation. In *On Ezra and Nehemiah*, Bede opts for the literal *instead* of the allegorical: "it behooves us not to scrutinize the allegorical meaning but to observe the literal meaning of the text itself . . ."[3] Again, the literal and the allegorical or figural appear to be exclusive of each other or at the very least have very firm boundaries. Much of Bede's reading is rooted in his view of how language refers to the world. He is at pains in his commentary on Genesis to show how the creation account is an accurate *description* to the point where he gives the dates of the first days of creation. As a result of this tendency, when a reading of Scripture ceases to be understood as a *description*, one has therefore left the literal sense in Bede's mind. What would it mean, after all, to say that the beginning describes the only-begotten Son?[4] Quite obviously, his *Historia* follows a similar rationale, since it is history, as Bede's qualifications regarding sources and their reliability attest.

There is no question that historical work should be descriptive. History should make claims about the world and the past. In this way, Bede is an unexceptional historian concerned with truth. However, history is more complicated than merely describing what happened. Bede actually knew this too, and this is why Bede always read events in the larger context of the world ages and the incarnation. As described in the last chapter, such placement ordered Bede's historical work giving it the theological intelligibility he thought necessary in the writing of history. Many historians, some of whom I summarized in chapter 1, scoff at such putatively unhistorical claims arguing that Bede left the historical realm for the theological too often. In what follows I will argue that Bede's theology of the world ages is an historical claim after all, despite the fact that Bede frequently separated the literal and allegorical senses. More specifically, using the work of Frank Ankersmit, I want to propose that a distinction between description

---

2. Bede, *On Genesis*, 100. "Huc usque de primordia mundi nascentis iuxta sensum litterae dixesse sufficiat" (*In genisim*, 35).

3. Bede, *On Ezra and Nehemiah*, 185. "In qua uidelicet lectione non nos allegoriae sensum inquirere sed ipsum litterae textum oportet diligentius operando . . ." (*In Ezram et Neemiam*, 360).

4. Bede did not read *every* passage in his literal commentaries as descriptions. When he does not do so, it is usually because the passage is ascribing something unfitting to God. For example, Bede rejects that God literally rested after creation and that God's rest is not like our rest from labor. See Bede, *On Genesis*, 98–99.

and representation intrinsically constitutes the practice of history. In other words, if one ceases to describe a person or event that does not require the leaving behind of historical writing.

Description, Representation, and Truth Claims

Frank Ankersmit has published copiously on historical theory and the practice of history writing, especially in relationship to the philosophy of language.[5] He has been influenced by many twentieth century philosophers and historical theorists,[6] especially analytic philosophy of language.[7] As a whole, these influences have culminated in an interest in aesthetics that lead Ankersmit to relate historical writing to works of art, specifically portraits.

My use of Ankersmit here will focus on one of his most recent texts: *Historical Representation*.[8] The overall argument in *Historical Representation* makes the case that historical writing should be robustly realist, granting us access and knowledge of the past. However, this does not always imply that propositional or referential notions of truth and falsity apply to every aspect of historical writing. This non-referential component Ankersmit calls "historical representation." He describes it as such:

> I intentionally use the term "historical representation" instead of alternative terms, such as "historical interpretation," "description," "explanation," or "historical narrative." For as will become clear in a moment, the relevant secrets of the nature of historical writing can only be discerned if we see the historical text as a representation of the past in much the same way that the work of art is a representation of what it depicts—or, for that matter, in a way that Parliament or Congress is a representation of the electorate.[9]

---

5. I want to specifically thank Ankersmit for his comments on this chapter—my use of his work helped improve the argument's overall quality.

6. Perhaps the most significant thinkers and their works: Collingwood, *Idea of History*; Ricoeur, *Memory, History, Forgetting*; White, *Metahistory*.

7. Wittgenstein, *Philosophical Investigations*; idem, *On Certainty*; Gadamer, *Truth and Method*; Danto, *Narration and Knowledge*; Quine, "Two Dogmas of Empiricism," 20–43; Rorty, *Philosophy and the Mirror of Nature*. See Ankersmit's recently published book for his own responses and treatments of some of these figures, *Meaning, Truth, and Reference in Historical Representation*.

8. Ankersmit, *Historical Representation*.

9. Ibid., 80.

Ankersmit arrives at his view of "historical representation" through engaging the so called linguistic turn in philosophy.[10] Quine's problematizing of the analytic/synthetic distinction functions as the lynchpin for what Ankersmit argues regarding historical representation.

Quine argues that analytic truths—truths which are true or can be deduced to be true by definition and inquiry into the words/concepts alone—are not as easily distinguishable from synthetic truths or truths of fact—that is, truths that need to be verified by experience. For example, the sentence "All bachelors are single" is analytically true because singleness is part of what it means to be a bachelor. "My office chair has four legs" is a synthetic truth because one has to actually look and see if, in fact, the chair has four legs; there are pedestal chairs and three legged chairs after all. Quine shows this distinction, at the time thought to be air tight, to be much murkier than formerly believed.[11]

I need not rehearse all the intricacies of Quine's argument here, but his main point is that terms like "synonymous" and "definition" need clarification, while the term "analyticity" rests upon them as unproblematic. In short, to call a statement or truth "analytic" is not clear in every sense because these terms often turn out to be synthetic judgments or uses by a lexicographer (or scientist, or philosopher, or whoever): "the definition which is the lexicographer's report of an observed synonymy cannot be taken as the ground of synonymy."[12] The result of this argument is that words like "bachelor" and "unmarried man" are not synonymously interchangeable making it a non-analytic truth. Hence, Quine's famous example: "Bachelor has less than ten letters."[13] The seemingly synonymous terms "unmarried man" cannot be exchanged for bachelor in that sentence without falsifying it.[14] Thus, distinguishing between analytic and synthetic truths is not as simple as one might like.

Ankersmit uses Quine's argument to distinguish between speaking and speaking about speaking. History, Ankersmit argues, is as much about speaking—that is simply making claims about the world—as it is about speaking about speaking, and often we cannot easily distinguish between them. He offers an example regarding the use of the term/description "revolution." Some historians may characterize the eighteenth-century American

---

10. The "linguistic turn" is the subject of Ankersmit's first chapter in *Historical Representation*, 29–74.

11. I am using Quine's original version published as, "Two Dogmas of Empiricism," 20–43.

12. Quine, "Two Dogmas of Empiricism," 24.

13. Ibid., 27.

14. Ibid.

war for independence as a revolution, while some may not. Marxist historians would not call the American Revolution a revolution at all because it lacks the essential aspect of class struggle. Thus, "the problem of the systematization of phenomena such as revolutions [or the Renaissance or the Reformation, or the . . .] is that they seem to depend as much on what one actually finds in the past as in how one decides to define the word 'revolution.'"[15] Therefore, characterizing a war as a revolution is as much about what actually happened as it is about conceptual definition.[16] Truths of speaking and truths of speaking about speaking shade into one other and depend on each other.

As a result, there is nothing wrong with characterizing the American war for independence as a revolution or not as a revolution; either way is fine. However, the ambiguity between synthetic and analytic truths need not result in skepticism regarding the historical enterprise: that we cannot know if America had a revolution. In other words, just because seemingly straightforward descriptions and apparent deductions from historical evidence are not as air tight as they appear to be, like the American battle for independence was a revolution, does not require the conclusion that history offers no reliable knowledge of the past. At this point, Ankersmit makes his clever and fascinating move. Since the American Revolution can and cannot be described as a revolution, criteria other than propositional (referential) truth and falsity will have to surface and help solve the problem. Thus, compulsion to seek propositional truth and falsity in the question regarding the status or name of the dispute between Britain and the colonies is unnecessary.

We can apply this reasoning to my preceding work on Bede in quite straightforward and productive ways. Take the picture of Ezra/Cassiodorus from the Codex Amiatinus as an example: The identity of the figure, whether Ezra or Cassiodorus, frames what can and cannot be said about other images in the painting. If we take it to be Ezra, then the books on the shelf cannot be Cassiodorus's; they would most likely be the books of the Law that Ezra was rewriting from memory. If we take it to be Cassiodorus, then the books cannot be Ezra's rewritten Law but Cassiodorus's own manuscripts of Holy Scripture. The belief regarding who is depicted in the painting then "creates" or structures what can be true about it subsequent to this determination. One can make a case either way for who the priest-like figure is, but once a person is selected, it therefore determines the rest of the painting, at least in some circumscribed manners.

15. Ankersmit, *Historical Representation*, 33.

16. For more on the impact of defining a revolution in historical inquiry see Kabede, "Religion and Revolution."

But is not the truth or falsity of the Ezra/Cassiodorus figure still in question here? That is, that the figure is truly or falsely Ezra or Cassiodorus? Yes, but this is not a problem. However, once a determination is made it becomes a claim of a different level in relation to the rest of the drawing because it begins to determine other truth claims; thus, it moves from a mostly synthetic claim to the realm of analyticity and its truth is no longer questioned, while interpreting the rest of the painting. Hence, what happens in historical writing is that analytic and synthetic claims slide back and forth. Put differently, they move from speaking to speaking about speaking and without warning. Who one takes the Ezra/Cassiodorus figure to be can be a claim of truth or falsity at the beginning. However, once one decides on its truth, it then slides into analyticity insofar as it determines how the rest of the painting is understood; it begins to function on the level of speaking about speaking, not just speaking on which it began.

An even more conspicuous example is the world ages. When Bede entitles the Major Chronicle, *The Sixth Age*, is he making an historical claim? Put differently, when Bede cites a date "in the year of our Lord" thereby presupposing and invoking his theology of the world ages, is Bede still speaking historically? Bede would have certainly thought so. Given his insistence on providing precise dates and boundaries for each age, Bede would have likely taken it to be a *description* as well. Here, I wish to humbly depart from the saint and use Ankersmit's insight for clarification. A claim about being in the sixth age, like Bede understands himself to be writing within and about, is not *prima facie* an empirical claim subject to correspondence approaches to truth or falsity as Bede probably thought. What would it mean to falsify the world ages periodization that Bede and Augustine maintain? (Or, put in a more contemporary locution: What would it mean to falsify the periodization of Classical Period, Middle Ages, Modernity?). Even if Abraham or David was not a real person, one could still use the theological structure of time and the covenants to make sense of world history or simply rearrange the ages. The key here is that Abraham's existence does not constitute entirely the world ages theology. Furthermore, remember that the world ages are repetitions of the original seven days of creation. How can those days be falsified, especially in a reading like Augustine's? To be sure, truth and falsity are presumed insofar as certain empirical claims must be believed to affirm it (e.g., that there was a man named Jesus; he was the Messiah; he died and was resurrected, etc.). But the larger claim about the world ages presupposed in Bede's *Historia* is not at this "meta" level subject to the correspondence criterion in the *Ecclesiastical History* because it functions as a structuring principle and not as a straightforward historical claim. However, according to Ankersmit and the preceding argument, that does *not* make it unhistorical, since such claims are intrinsic to the historical task. Therefore, Bede is right to think that entitling his Major Chronicle *The Sixth Age* is an historical claim, but wrong to take it as a description because Bede did not distinguish between speaking and speaking about speaking.

If propositional truth and falsity are simply not at stake with regard to the question of whether it is a revolution, the world ages, or the figure in Codex Amiatinus, what kind of claims are they? Are they merely subjective assertions based on personal preferences? Are reading history through the world ages theological structure and calling the American war for independence from Britain a revolution simply arbitrary, subjective, and projectional claims? As Ankersmit notes, to be unable to see any other criteria beyond truth and falsity is something like a blind person saying there cannot be a table in the room because *he* cannot see it.[17] Ankersmit admits the search for these rational criteria, but not the correspondence truth criterion, is difficult, but the fact that historical writing carries on and furthers knowledge shows that it exists.[18] Ankersmit claims these are questions of "historical representation," not historical description (which is about correspondence and reference), and I will show the logic or "rationality" of such claims in what follows.

The "Logic" of Representation

Ankersmit subscribes to the substitution theory of representation, which claims that a representation of something "essentially is a substitute or replacement of something else that is absent."[19] Thus, the function of the discipline of history is to make present that which has faded into the absent past. Historical texts, therefore, serve as substitutes to the past, since the past is no longer present and readily available. Moreover, the representation aims at being "just as good as the original that it represents."[20] The difference between the represented and representation will still abide, though. Hence, an apparent tension or paradox occurs in representation between its similarity and difference to the represented. In this way, representation shares "logical affinities" with identity since both seek to overcome difference/distance in space and/or time. For example, a portrait of Tim Furry at the age of 25 still represents the same person I am now at age 32, despite the differences, and I would be recognizable by such a "dated" portrait. Furthermore, my wife could use such an old portrait to make me present, though of no concrete

---

17. Ankersmit, *Historical Representation*, 33–34.
18. Ibid., 35–36.
19. Ibid., 80.
20. Ibid., 81.

parental support sadly, when I am gone over a period of time. Representation performs an analogous task. Bede's reading of world history and the coming of Christianity to the British Isles seeks to make known and present the history of God's activity with his people. As Bede rightly recognized in his preface, his *Historia* would help provide examples for right and wrong Christian living for Northrumbians in his day, especially the King Ceolwulf.[21] Representation performs a similar task, according to Ankersmit, of preserving identity, while simultaneously acknowledging difference; this is the logic of substitution.

Representational logic also accounts for the ambiguity that historical investigation necessarily entails. Ankersmit argues that there are two types of things in the past: things that can be identified without their histories and those that require histories (or historical representation) for their identification and recognition.[22] Objects identifiable without histories are objects or events in the past that can be pointed to: e.g., Napoleon, St. Paul, the battle at Gettysburg, etc. Objects that need histories to be identified are more precarious. Without the actual recounting of the world ages by folks like Augustine, Isidore, and Bede, we would not know about them or be able to discuss and debate them. Also, in chapter 2, I relied on Thomas O'Loughlin's reading of the "Genesis tradition," another example of such an historical reality that needs its history to be identified. While individual thinkers and theologians can be identified within this tradition quite easily (like Bede) without writing a history about them, the Genesis tradition cannot be so identified because it requires the very history written about it to make it identifiable. As Ankersmit summarizes, "And we can therefore truly say of this latter category [things that require histories to be identified]. . . that they have no contours in the absence of the representation that has been proposed of them."[23] Ankersmit is saying that without the very histories and narrations of the world ages and the Genesis tradition, the world ages and the Genesis tradition would not be intelligible and therefore unidentifiable. The phrases "world ages" and "Genesis tradition" are not part of the past, since they are offered by historians after the fact. However, the language is still about the past and relates to objects in the past.

Ankersmit then draws this conclusion: "If there is no representation, in other words, then there is no represented as well."[24] These are "objects" that require histories to be written; in short, the historian's language about the

---

21. Bede, *EH*, 3.
22. Ankersmit, *Historical Representation*, 83.
23. Ibid.
24. Ibid.

past makes or constitutes the representational aspect of the past. However, he rightly distinguishes how this aspect of historical representation differs from historical description or more cognitively driven statements or propositions, which do, in fact, and rightly so, understand that objects exist independently of their descriptions. In other words, the question, "So was there really a Genesis tradition" is the wrong question for Ankersmit because the question wrongly presumes the Genesis tradition is an object in the past that we can readily find or identify apart from the actual writing and description of such a tradition. The question wrongly conflates and wrongly applies criteria from the two levels of historical writing to each other, specifically, criteria of description to representation.

Historical representation is not, however, utterly free of cognitive content and relativistic when it comes to the past. In other words, representation's only limit is decidedly not the historian's imagination in historical representation. Historical representation is always *about* the past; however, its relationship to reality is less determined than historical description, and this relationship cannot be precisely described in strict cognitive language or straightforward description. Since one cannot simply point to the Middle Ages, medieval exegesis, or the world ages (though Bede certainly attempts to make this possible), like one can to Martin Luther or St. Bede, the relationship is less determined because representation lacks a clear referent in the past. Lacking reference does not, however, mean the representation is not about the past. To continue using the sixth age example, "the sixth age" does not have a clear referent like Jesus of Nazareth does. Of course, the representation of the sixth age depends on descriptions of Jesus and his existence, but the sixth age is a claim *more than* about Jesus. It also entails claims about the Holy Spirit, the Church, and the sixth age's relationship to other ages past and future. While the sixth age necessarily includes descriptions and cognitive content, it cannot be completely reduced to its constituent descriptions without losing its own content as a representation. Though certain descriptions necessarily constitute a representation, the inability to reduce the representation to such descriptions without loss indicates its distinction and relationship to description. A claim about the sixth age necessarily includes cognitive content like Jesus' incarnation and resurrection, but it says more than simply Jesus was incarnated and resurrected because it describes an entire era that such events inaugurated. In short, any text that addresses or even relies on topics or eras like the Reformation, the Renaissance, the Middle Ages, medieval exegesis, the world ages, etc utilizes historical representation. It would be nearly impossible to write a history of people or events that lacked such representations. If all historical writing was simply historical description, then it would look like individual propositions strung together. In fact, histories are narrative in form and the whole, when finished, necessarily takes the shape of a representation, and the representation is not reducible to the cognitive historical descriptions necessarily involved as part of that representation.[25]

An illustration of a portrait may help further clarify my point. A portrait is a representation of a real person who sits while an artist paints her image. However, the painter does not first draw a photographic depiction of the person void of her personality. Instead the painter *simultaneously* paints the reality in front of them, the sitter, along with the person's personality. Given Quine's destruction of the analytic synthetic distinction, the same is true in historical writing; representation and description happen simultaneously. So, when history is written, historians do not say, "Now I am describing, and now I will begin representing." Consequently, Bede could easily conflate description and representation, since there is no separate methodological process that clearly distinguishes representation from description. We can only distinguish description from representation after the fact through abstraction. Though helpful, the abstraction must always be noted as an abstraction from the unity of the portrait or text.

Moreover, Ankersmit argues that representations, like a portrait, should be seen as proposals and not descriptions.[26] Proposals are suggestions or heuristics for understanding an historical event or person, and suggestions are not usually subject to propositional truth or falsity. It is true that we speak of portraits as true likenesses. However, likeness is not reducible to correspondence making correspondence unessential for a portrait. Take Picasso's portraits of his lovers and his self portraits as examples. Likeness is stretched beyond correspondence and strict reference, but it would still be legitimate to call them true or false likenesses without them corresponding exactly to the people they represent. Hence, there can be many true likenesses, portraits, and representations. I follow Ankersmit and opt for the language of proposal because of this multiplicity. While propositional truth and falsity may not be a rational criterion for proposals, we still engage in rational debate about which proposals we should enact and believe. For example, "Take the truck to the furniture store" is a quite straightforward and intelligible proposal about how one should act. But, it's neither true nor false. Notice, however, that one could still argue about its reasonability. One could object: "We're only going to look at furniture; we are not

25. I take this to be White's main point in his *magnum opus*, *Content of the Form*. Like Ankersmit, I depart from White's approach to representation insofar as he relies on literary theory in such a way that obscures the fact that representations are still about the past. See, for example, White, *Metahistory*; idem, *Figural Realism*.

26. Ankersmit, *Historical Representation*, 90.

going to buy anything today." This is a reasonable response showing that rational argument can occur around statements that can neither be true nor false. Now, the objection can be true or false based on if one actually ends up buying furniture, but this comes *after* the proposal. The grounds for determining what counts as reasonable precedes judgments of truth or falsity. In the truck example, the rational conversation and surrounding circumstances (e.g., perhaps an upcoming home renovation) regarding what one should do comes *prior* to judgments of truth and falsity about such a proposal. Analogously, consider again the US war for independence. How would appeal to the events of the revolution solve definitively which historians' description of the war as revolution (or not) is accurate, since their definitions of revolution are not entirely rooted in historical description? Such definitions certainly are related to history, since there are some shared criteria (e.g., battles, violence, change in authority, etc.) that are clearly historical events. However, one cannot settle the dispute on what counts as a revolution on historical grounds alone, but how one understands a revolution will determine the narration of historical events whose occurrence are not in question. As a result, Ankersmit concludes that representation logically precedes cognitively driven descriptions, since these aesthetic criteria (representation as proposal) come before rules are established to judge truth and falsity (like reference and correspondence).[27]

The difference between representation and description just elucidated leads to the third logical aspect: representations relate things to things, not words to things. The "whole" representation of the world ages, or more specifically the sixth age, must be treated as a thing or object, unlike a statement or proposition, because it has no clear referent, just like an object. Think of the portrait again: the portrait is a thing, like the person sitting for the portrait; it is not a sentence subject to rules of correspondence judging truth or falsity. It would be strange after all to hear someone call a portrait false (or true); good or bad, ugly or beautiful are ways we speak about portraits but true or false usually are not. Confusion easily arises since historical representation requires language and sentences that are subject to truth or falsity, yet the representation itself remains distinct from those claims. In other words, though constituted by language, representation is more like a non-linguistic portrait in how it functions. The ease of confusion from speaking to speaking about speaking sliding back and forth (description to representation) causes Ankersmit to go as far as to claim that this lack

---

27. Ibid., 96. Ankersmit has a newly published work on referential language in history: *Meaning, Truth, and Reference in Historical Representation*. I want to thank Ankersmit for providing me with a manuscript of this text prior to its publication; the text proved to be a wonderful help in understanding Ankersmit's overall argument and project.

of epistemological determinacy in representation is the very strength of history, despite those historians who ironically loathe their own discipline's apparent imprecision.[28]

The Representational Constitution of Figural Reading

I now want to shift attention to the relationship between representation and figural reading in St. Bede. Figural reading includes and surpasses simple historical description as Auerbach's work has so well demonstrated. "Figural interpretation establishes a connection between two events or persons, the first of which signifies not only itself but also the second, while the second encompasses or fulfills the first. The two poles of the figures are separate in time, but both, being real events or figures are within time, within the stream of historical life."[29] My interest is less in the type and anti-type parts of Auerbach's definition, though my focus in no way mitigates their role, and more in what must occur for such readings to even occur and be intelligible. I will show that events are read in light of something else and that something else is usually another category or event; Bede follows this use of *figura* frequently.

Since Bede tended to distinguish figural and literal/historical understanding, I will have to use his commentaries to cite examples of *figura*. Regarding the tree of life in Genesis 2, Bede says, "But this was done materially so that it would also be an allegorical figure of a sacrament, that is, a figure of God and of our Lord Jesus Christ . . ."[30] In other words, the tree of life signifies God's gift of Jesus Christ to humanity as the one who gives life and life abundantly. Later in Genesis, Bede suggests the creation of Eve from Adam's side is a figure of the redemption accomplished in Christ's crucifixion and return. "For it was fitting that the beginning of the human race, through the work of God, should proceed in such a way, since in prophetic figures it gave testimony of its redemption, which was going to come at the end of time by means of the same Creator."[31] The piercing of Christ's side at

---

28. Ankersmit, *Historical Representation*, 88. For example, historians who almost obsessively ask (or want to ask), "What is that?" when something like the Reformation, Renaissance, Enlightenment, Modernity, or the Liberal tradition is invoked; the "What is it?" question functions as an objection to any type of historical claim for which these terms could be used. Of course, as such, the question is a fair one, but usually its point is that it lacks cognitive, that is clear and precise, content and is therefore illegitimate as an historical claim. Here, Ankersmit reveals and clarifies the confusion arguing that it is, in fact, an historical claim, albeit not the same kind as a simple description.

29. Auerbach, "Figura," 53.

30. Bede, *On Genesis*, 112. "Sed hoc ita corpaliter factum est ut sacramenti quoque esset figura spiritalis, id est Dei et Domini nostri Iesu Christi" (*In genesim*, 47).

31. Ibid., 122. "Taliter enim decebat ut humani generis origo, Deo operante, procederet

the crucifixion was prefigured in the life-giving side of Adam. In these cases, Bede is reading Genesis in light of another event. He uses the life of Christ as a way to interpret these Genesis texts without simply leaving the text of Genesis behind; he takes a later historical event or epoch and reads the past in its terms (the creation of Eve in light of Christ and the sixth age).[32] Likewise, in *On Ezra and Nehemiah* and immediately after a brief treatment of the world ages highlighting the consecration of each age through sacrifice, Bede says, "All these events prefigured him who, in the sixth age, would come in the flesh and redeem the whole world by means of the sacrifice of his own flesh and blood."[33] Here, not only one event signifies a later event, but the consecration of all the preceding ages signifies Christ's death and consecration of the sixth age.

Just like the first five world ages and their consecration are interpreted in terms of Christ's crucifixion, since they point to it, a later event illuminates an earlier one making clear what those prior events were really about. In other words, Bede takes specific events and persons and places them into a larger or simply different context than their "original" historical setting. Bede's figural exegesis is a form of re-contextualizing. He puts historical events into a *different* context, often times the context of God's providential work in history delineated through the world ages; the Greater Chronicle displays this quite well. Or, in more traditional allegorical fashion, he will frequently take events and read them in the context of the Christian moral life.[34]

What I have said here does not negate Auerbach's famous definition already given. Instead, I have attempted to elucidate what makes such figural reading work or what it presumes, and that the language of figural can be extended to such usage. In short, I am arguing that it presumes a form of representation that Ankersmit has so well articulated. The traditional type and anti-type understanding can only work if something like representation as I have been articulating constitutes it. I could perform the same interpretive exercise on which I am about to embark on the other passages in *On*

---

quatenus redemption ipsius quae in fine erat seculi per eundem uentura conditorem concinentibus figuris testimonium daret" (*In genesim*, 57).

32. I could also cite just about any example in Bede's *Historia* here as well, since the whole work presupposes his world ages theology, specifically that Bede is writing in the sixth age.

33. Bede, *On Ezra and Nehemiah*, 54. "Quae cuncta in figuram praecesserunt eius qui in sexta aetate uenturus in carne et hostia eiusdem suae carnis ac sanguinis totum orbem erat redempturus" (*In Ezram et Neemiam*, 271–72).

34. Examples abound: In his later exegesis, see Bede, *On the Temple*—Book 1 especially offers many examples of moral allegorical reading in Bede. More specifically, Bede takes the door of portico of the temple to signify teachers who through their teaching help others enter the people of God; see *On the Temple*, 24.

Genesis and *On Ezra and Nehemiah* cited above, but this one from *On the Temple* should suffice to make clear what I am arguing.

Bede claims that the temple is a figure of Christ and the Church where Jesus and his called community fulfills the temple's prior signification. "[I]t is quite clear that the material temple was a figure of us all, that is, both of the Lord himself and his members which we are."[35] Not only is Bede using a type and anti-type relationship between the temple and Jesus, he is also recontextualizing the temple in terms of Christ and the Church; Christ and the Church becomes the normative background or context in which the temple now makes more or true sense. Bede did not articulate this process explicitly and neither did most other exegetes, but for Bede's exegetical conclusions to follow this recontextualization must take place.

Continuing with *De templo*, Bede concludes: "The point in Solomon's seeking help from Hiram in the work of the temple was that when the Lord came in the flesh and arranged to build a favourite home for himself, namely, the Church, he chose helpers for the work not from the Jews alone but also from the gentiles."[36] Not only is there signification from one historical event to another, but there is also a substantive and normative relationship that can only be accepted if one adheres to the broader theological claims about Jesus and his historical significance, specifically in this case that he founded the Church, which is the means by which the sixth age progresses by spreading the gospel. Without this broader representational background, Bede's reading of Solomon's and King Hiram's relationship makes little figural sense. Note here as well that such recontextualization does not, for Bede, imply a flight from a close reading of the temple in the OT because he is "seeking the spiritual mansion of God in the material structure" of the temple as described in 1 Kings 5.[37] Bede keeps close to the text and recontextualizes it in light of another historical event and that event's concomitant theological significance.[38]

---

35. Bede, *On the Temple*, 5. "constat utique quia figuram omnium nostrum et ipsius domini uidelicet et membrorum eius quae nos sumus templum illud materia tenuit" (*De templo*, 147).

36. Bede, *On the Temple*, 7. "Petit ergo Salomon in opera temple auxilium ab Hiram quia cum ueniens in carne dominus dilectam sibi domum uidelicet ecclesiam aedificare disponeret non de Iudaeis tantummodo uerum etiam de gentibus adiutores operis elegit" (*De templo*, 149).

37. Bede, *On the Temple*, 6. "Tractaturi igitur iuuante domino de aedificatione templo et in structura materiali spiritalem Dei mansionem quaesituri . . ." (*De templo*, 148).

38. In other places, Bede even forgoes the allegorical sense to draw straightforward conclusions from the literal or plain sense. See, for example, *On Ezra and Nehemiah*, 185, that I cited above where Bede opts for the literal over the allegorical.

The Inevitability of Figural History

Many contemporary historians and scholars, like Bede frequently did, want to distinguish sharply between historical/literal reading and figural/allegorical reading. However, if what I have been saying about representation is accurate, a clear distinction between them cannot easily be made. More specifically, if figural reading presumes representation, as I argued it does for Bede, that opens the possibility to argue that historical writing itself is intrinsically figural insofar as it is representational.

Historians work hard, and rightly so, to place events into their historical context and setting. I showed how historians continually tried harder and with more success to place Bede in his own Northumbrian context in chapter 1. However, such contextualization is not as easy or straightforward as it seems. Several historians simply presumed their own context as normative to judge Bede and his historical work. Seeking to avoid such caricatures, Charles Jones ended up using the category of Romance to help understand Bede. Even Jan Davidse, much like I am doing, used contemporary historical discussions to illuminate Bede.[39] My point here is the rather pedestrian one that contextualization provides intelligibility. However, there are numerous and legitimate historical contexts into which we can place any given person or event. Take Bede for example: a history could be written that understands him in the western Benedictine monastic tradition; likewise, he could be read in terms of the rise and decline of classical education in different geographical regions of the Roman Empire; yet again, he could be understood, as in Holder's essay, in relationship to the preceding Alexandrian exegetical tradition in western Christianity;[40] or, in DeGregorio's latest work, Bede and his exegesis could be seen in light of the reforms of the Northumbrian church of his day.[41] There is nothing wrong with putting Bede into any of these historical contexts and many have done so. However, there is no clear referent to the Alexandrian exegetical tradition. Even if one grants there to be multiple traditions, reference remains ambiguous at best. Moreover, an obvious referent is not forthcoming for DeGregorio's narrower contextualization of Bede and Northumbrian Church reform. Again, these representations are still about the past and depend on clear claims with referents subject to correspondence, but such larger contexts lack reference themselves. In short, there are simply different and legitimate historical contexts.

39. Davidse, "Sense of History in the Works of the Venerable Bede."
40. Holder, "Bede and the Tradition of Patristic Exegesis," 399–411.
41. DeGregorio, "*Nostrorum socordiam temporum*," 107–22; idem, "Bede's In *Ezram et Neemiam* and the Reform of the Northumbrian Church," 1–25.

Notice the methodological structure between such historical contextualization and Bede's figural reading that Auerbach's summary nicely captures. The historian attempts to render an event or person from the past in light of other categories or events not obviously present in the past being depicted. Bede reads deaths and sacrifices as consecrations of world ages in light of the sixth age and Christ; Jones reads Bede in reference to Romantic conceptions of history. Both historians understand a past event in terms of another non-empirical reality (in that past) in order to make it intelligible.[42] The major difference is that contemporary historians are less likely to re-contexualize the historical event in such explicit ways as Bede. To perform such an action risks falling prey to anachronism: to understand an historical person or event in terms of something out-of-place within its "original" temporal context. Lacking such methodological controls, Bede was free to re-contextualize, though he mostly did so only in his allegorical or figural readings. On this Bede does share an affinity with contemporary historians insofar as he thought that the historical task was mostly descriptive, hence his strict separation between the historical/literal and the figural sense. Despite such concerns about committing anachronism, however, contemporary historians inevitably practice it in order to make sense of the past and insofar as representation constitutes the practice of history. Contemporary historians use non-empirical categories, figures, analogies, tropes, or whatever is at hand to render the past intelligible. Such judgments are made about the appropriateness of such categories and are still about the past thereby making it part of the historical endeavor. I have simply pointed out how we must distinguish between description (speaking) and representation (speaking about speaking) in historical writing but that both are *necessary* for the writing of history.

Arthur Danto's account of narrative sentences deepens the similarity between figural exegesis and representation in historical work.[43] I will use narrative sentences as a particular kind of representation that I previously elaborated. More specifically, and in Danto's own words, narrative sentences are "sentences the truth of which entails that at least two time-separated events have happened."[44] For example, the sentence "Bede anticipated modern historical inquiry" presumes the truth of two events temporally distinct. This statement entails that Bede in the 8th century utilized historical methods and sensibilities that modern history also used. Likewise, "Washington became

42. As always, one cannot forget that these non-empirical realities still depend on claims about the past.

43. On narrative sentences, see Danto, *Narration and Knowledge*, 143–81, 293–97, 342–53.

44. Danto, *Narration and Knowledge*, 293.

the first president of the United States" entails that Washington became the first US president as well as that there were subsequent ones.[45] These sorts of sentences are undeniably historical and in the simple past tense grammatically speaking yet also presume other times and even the perspective of the present. Of course, few, if any, would (or should) object to these kinds of sentences being part of the historian's work of narrating the past because they simply are part and parcel of the historian's task and work.

Danto's narrative sentences capture well the proximity between narrations and objects, even though such sentences grammatically appear to be simply about the past. In other words, historians not only represent the past, that is use non-empirical language about the past, but they also, and more specifically, read events in light of other times and occasions. For example, Jones's characterization of Bede as Romantic, while clearly a representation, would also be a narrative sentence. Thus, historians come even closer to Auerbach's definition of *figura* insofar as an event of the past is read in light of another event. By linking and interpreting the past to other times and the present, narrative sentences also stitch together seemingly disparate temporal realities like the work of figural exegesis. The remaining significant difference is the kind of relationship these seemingly distinct times have with each other. Stricter uses of *figura* require the type and anti-type relationship, while historians usually do not explicitly advocate such normative relationships. Imbuing such meaning and significance does occur in the writing of history, however. A seemingly straightforward historical claim like, "Jon Hus anticipated the Reformation" gives significance to Hus's own apparent proto-Reformation actions and also can easily presume an evaluation of Catholicism at his time that not everyone would have shared.[46] Reading the past in light of the present or another event or time and giving them a particular significance as a result is one more similarity between contemporary historians and figural exegetes.

Next, I want to draw more conclusions vis-à-vis representation and Bede's *Historia* and exegesis. When Bede understands the time he narrates in his *Historia* as the sixth age, this is not simply a descriptive/cognitive claim. As a whole and in line with his theology of history, one should read the entire *Historia* as a representation of the sixth age as it occurs in Anglo-Saxon England, as Jan Davidse has argued.[47] This has several consequences. First,

---

45. This is Danto's own example; see *Narration and Knowledge*, 293.

46. The Hus example is from Danto, *Narration and Knowledge*, 293, but I am using it in a different way from Danto.

47. Davidse in "The Sense of History" argues this point, which I summarized in the last chapter. However, he did not discuss it in light of representation like I am, but his argument to read the *Historia* in terms of Bede's theology of history is the point I am making here.

the claim about the sixth age is not subject to claims of truth or falsity as correspondence. Again, this does not mean that historical descriptions have no role in the larger or meta-claim regarding the sixth age. If there was not a man named Jesus who lived, died, and was resurrected in the 1st century, then the sixth age, as Bede understood it, makes little sense. Second, since Bede presumes these truths, the claim of the sixth age functions *primarily* as a claim not about the world but about speaking and is, therefore, not subject to propositional truth or falsity so long as it is functioning in this way. As a result, and as a claim about speaking, the sixth age creates or constructs the possible truth claims that it governs. Similarly, when a contemporary historian chooses to have Descartes inaugurate the Enlightenment, this representation and narrative sentence, though dependent on descriptions regarding Descartes, then sets up the rest of the historical argument surrounding what the Enlightenment might mean and imply. *Therefore, when Bede names the time after Christ's incarnation and before his return the sixth age, it functions, philosophically speaking, in the same way as claims about the Reformation, Renaissance, Enlightenment, and revolutions.* Objections that Bede's language of the sixth age is unhistorical or theological (and therefore not historical) simply reveal an aesthetic (representation) bias that constitutes the practice of history and how it is conceived.

When contemporary historians look to Bede as something of an ancient colleague and laud his source documentation and other practices that anticipate contemporary standards in history, they fail to realize that what makes them the same is not these standards but a shared need to represent, and not simply describe, the past. Thus, when they show suspicion for Bede's more obviously theological moments in his historical writing, they fail to realize their very suspicion is what makes them and Bede historians, not contemporary historical standards. As discussed in chapter 1, when Charles Jones says Bede's history is done from a "Romance" perspective, no one would question he is still doing history, though Bede does not get the same courtesy when mentioning the world ages or the sixth age.[48] If what I am arguing is true, though, such a claim is just another form of historical representation as well as a narrative sentence. To be sure, contemporary historians are free to argue with Bede about his history and should. However, the common objection to Bede's work often comes *because* of his theological renderings or representation and presupposes that Bede lapses from historical speech to theology too frequently. As a result, moderns fault Bede for not

---

48. "Realism is a truthful depiction of nature, especially human nature; romanticism is an elevation beyond the range of the familiar into aspiration. Aspiration, elevation, exaltation, edification are all words used to describe the purpose of Romance," Jones, *Saints Lives and Chronicles in Early England*, 52.

being historical enough. Unfortunately, this objection misses its target, unless these historians want to argue they are not historians as well when they discuss the Renaissance, revolutions, a Romance perspective, Northumbian monasticism, or Alexandrian exegesis.

An historian could object that the Renaissance and Romanticism are completely unlike theological representations like the "sixth age" since theological representations include events like miracles and other events taken to be non-empirical. After all, the Renaissance names an empirical or historical movement frequently defined or explained by a new appreciation of the individual. However, with this definition there is no way to point to the Renaissance as if it were an object in the world like a person, building, or text. Of course the Renaissance depends on empirical claims, persons, and texts, but the specific word and its definition cannot be found in the past like those particular objects. Its only empirical existence resides in the historian's text as a representation about the past.[49] Yet such claims remain historical because such language is still about the past and inevitably tied to empirical and historical statements. In short, history is not reducible to empirical claims. In fact, this is the most important point I have been advocating with Ankersmit. Insistence on such reduction ironically makes contemporary historians more like Bede who also did not make the distinctions I am making. Again, representations depend on empirical claims but cannot be reduced to them.

What I have suggested at several previous places, I can now say with argumentative backing: What Bede and contemporary historians are arguing about is the very constitution of history as such and they are doing so *as* historians. Due to his understanding of how language describes history, Bede did not recognize it, but the claim of the sixth age, as a representation in the sense I have been describing via Ankersmit, can be seen both as history and as a kind of figural exegesis insofar as it narrates past events in light of another event in a different time much like contemporary historians do with narrative sentences. Hence, Bede, despite his desire to keep literal and allegorical speech and interpretation separate, was figurally exegeting history like historians today do, albeit with different representational content.

Bede and many contemporary historians share the belief that history should be descriptive; that it should offer true statements about the past. They are both right to understand the historical task in such a way. However, both neglect the constitutive role that representation plays in the writing of history. In attempting to steer clear of anachronistic readings,

---

49. Danto's work on narrative sentences makes this point quite well. See Danto, *Narration and Knowledge*, 143–82.

some later twentieth century historians noted that Bede's theological moments are simply part of his own historical perspective. They are right in this judgment. However, I have shown that the differences between Bede and our contemporary historical practices are not as stark as they might appear. Bede was not simply a good historian *then* as sympathetic readers of Bede who avoid anachronism would affirm. He can also be thought of as a good historian *now* given my argument about representation. Both Bede and contemporary historians rely on non-empirical representation to such an extent that I have claimed that all history can be said to be figural.

Allow me to clarify what I mean by claiming all history is figural. Briefly put, that all history is figural means that it relies upon non-empirical representation and narrative sentences because the very process of contextualization and historical narrative demands it, as I argued using Ankersmit, Danto, and Bede. I am not claiming that figural exegesis and historical writing are identical. I am only calling attention to the fact that both rely on non-empirical content and narrative sentences and, as a result, are analogous in enough ways that both can be called or at least *represented* as figural. Since Bede did not make such explicit figural connections in the *Historia*, I had to use his commentaries to explicate his understanding of *figura* and allegorical reading. For historical questions in Bede, I relied most heavily on the *Historia*, since it bears affinities with contemporary historical practice as many scholars have observed. History is not mere description; it depends on historical descriptions, but it needs representational content as well. Representations are about the past, but they lack clear reference and therefore cannot be subject to the correspondence criterion of truth and falsity. I have argued that Bede's own *Historia* and his figural exegesis function in just this fashion. Moreover, contemporary historians use narrative sentences that link and interpret past events in light of subsequent ones or the present much like Bede did in reading the temple in light of Christ and the Church. However, when contemporary historians object to Bede and his theological sensibilities in his historical writings, especially regarding religious instances like miracles, they fail to recognize that their differences are not simply historical—that they inhabit two difference times, a rather obvious recognition—but they are arguing over the constitution of history as it originates from representation. In other words, the content that historians use for representation matters because the selected content determines and shapes their historical narratives. However, the methods are quite similar making it possible to recognize Bede *and* ourselves as true historians.

To bring the argument full circle and back to chapter 1, an ironic conclusion results from my analysis. Historians, like Browne and Levison, who read Bede in light of modern methods, were both right and wrong. They were right, though not for the reasons they thought, to say that Bede was not an historian. They rightly discerned that they were actually arguing about the very constitution of history—that is, what counts as history. They were wrong to conclude that Bede was not an historian because they failed to recognize the representational aspect of all historical writing. Seeking to avoid anachronism, later historians were sympathetic to Bede and were right to see prior approaches that condemned Bede as flawed. However, they located the difference between Bede and themselves in the temporal gap between them. I have tried to suggest that the difference is not so much historical or temporal as it is in representational content. To be sure, such differences are related to our historical location, but we must be cautious to not reduce it to such a difference.

One final clarification needs to be made. When I say that Bede and contemporary historians share the need for representation in the writing of history, I do not mean to affirm that Bede and contemporary historians understand representation in an identical way. Contemporary historians would judge empirical evidence very differently from Bede, and I would not dispute that. However, if what I have argued is true, then the judgment that one is a better historian than the other can no longer be made on narrowly historical or empirical grounds because representation cannot be reduced to description. In short, the major difference between Bede and contemporary historians lies in the debate regarding what *counts* as historical. I am suggesting that what counts as historical is challenged in every writing of history insofar as all history writing is representational or figural. Each piece of history, while clearly about the past and dependent on such descriptive claims, also provides its own grounds for judging what counts as historical.

Take the language of a revolution once again; how one defines a revolution will determine how one evaluates and writes a history on the United States' war for independence. This does not necessarily put into dispute the events themselves but only how they are (re)presented. A Marxist and a capitalist historian could agree on every empirical detail of a battle or event and still represent them differently as part of a revolution or not. However, the language of revolution is just as much a part of the historical task as the empirical events themselves. Likewise, Bede and a contemporary historian could agree on many or all details in certain sections of his *Historia* and put them into a different overall context, like Bede's ideal for reform in his Northumbrian ecclesial context or the world ages. If representation and description are essential in the historian's task, then the very argument about what constitutes history as such is had in every historical essay and book, without explicit reference to such an argument. And, finally, Bede can argue with contemporary historians, *as* an historian himself.

Conclusion

Bede begins with Christ, his work, and the world ages, and then reads the OT in light of these, structuring his *Historia* accordingly. Historians who speak of the Renaissance, Reformation, or revolutions follow an analogous method as Christians like Bede, since such designations are after the fact representations and/or narrative sentences used to shed light on and interpret these prior events or persons. These designations, however, are usually not deemed unhistorical, like Bede's work has been. Again, such ways of reading are still about the past, though they lack a clear referent, like the world ages. However, such language is not part of the past itself being analyzed. Historians use such language because it "fits" with the past, despite not being present in it. Bede performs something similar, just in a more explicitly theological key. (However, the language of "The Reformation" conveys a theology as well but usually gets a free pass). The methodological structure of Bede and contemporary historians is analogous insofar as each takes a past event and reads it in light of other relevant and non-empirical language or events, including events or persons from a different time, that is narrative sentences. Bede and contemporary historians use similar reading techniques to investigate or exegete the past that includes representations that are about, yet not part of, the actual past under investigation.

I have suggested that what separates Bede from contemporary historians is not the temporal gap between us or even substantially different methods of historical investigation. Instead, I have insisted that the difference is one of representational content; in other words, what counts as history is what matters most and that such differences and debate happen all the time amongst historians. Therefore, we should not exclude Bede as an historian even when he is being explicitly theological in his history writing. By making this argument, I had to presume that Bede was not "back there" in the past, that he was in some way present with us.

Chapter 4 summarized recent research discussing how the concern to avoid anachronism arose out of a sense of loss and recognition that times are fundamentally separate from each other. Through the Ezra/Cassiodorus miniature in the Codex Amiatinus, I also showed that Bede did not believe the past to be "back there" and gone or absent from the present. Bede considered the great *patres* before him to be his contemporaries.

> The wheels placed underneath to support the laver of the temple raised the base from the ground when the blessed Pope Gregory recently in our own day ruled the Roman Church on the strength of the words of the Gospel; the same wheels fitted beneath God's chariot transported people long distances when the most venerable Fathers, Augustine [of Canterbury], Paulinus and the rest of their companions backed by the oracular sayings of the Gospel came to Britain at his command and a short while ago entrusted the word of God to believers.[50]

Here, Bede implies that Gregory is something of his contemporary (*nostris nuper temporibus beatus papa Gregorius*). Bede, of course, knows Gregory died over a century earlier, since his World Chronicle says that Pope Gregory "went to the Lord."[51] As Davidse summarizes, "To Bede, the Christian fathers belong to the past, but also to his present."[52] For these claims to be true, the past, present, and future require an openness or porosity to each other to be intelligible—an openness that Bede presumed and utilized.

I have been arguing that it would be arbitrary to call Bede's world ages or his theological moments in his *Historia* unhistorical insofar as Bede narrates such historical events in light of other representations that depend on historical reference, events like Christ's death and resurrection. It is my hope that I have made one of the last great *patres* present here by showing how Bede's work and those who have previously commented on it remain a present concern. While I have sketched his historical context when necessary, my goal was not simply to place him there in such a way that makes Bede's views benign because they belong to a past era. Instead, I have argued he demands and deserves a place at the table of modern history. I think such a perspective is faithful to Bede, who lacked a sense of anachronism, yet also deeply contemporary, since I make it recognizing the difference between representation and description in order show Bede's relevance as an historian for contemporary historical and theological discussions.

50. Bede, *On the Temple*, 98. "Rotae basem subpositae ad portandum luterem temple a terra sustollebant cum nostris nuper temporibus beatus papa Gregorius euangelicis roboratus eloquiis Romanam rexit ecclesiam; rotae eaedem currus Dei subnexae longe gestabant cum reuerendissimi patres Augustinus Paulinus et ceteri socii eorum eisdem euangelicis confirmati oraculis iubente illo uenere Brittanniam et uerbam Dei incredulis dudum commisere gentibus" (*De templo*, 218).

51. Bede, *On the Reckoning of Time*, 227. "Migrauit ad dominum" (*De temporum ratione libre*, 523). I do not think Bede is referring to sharing the sixth age with Gregory because he uses the language of *tempus* and not *aetas*. For examples of how he uses these words differently, see his *De temporum ratione libre* where *aetas* is primarily used to refer to the world ages.

52. Davidse, "The Sense of History in the Works of the Venerable Bede," 656.

Conclusion

Argument Summary

FOR THE SAKE OF clarification, and since my argument has ventured across disciplines and time periods, I want to reiterate and summarize my argument and what it has accomplished. Chapter 1 set the stage in two ways for my argument. First, by tracing the fault lines in contemporary Bedan scholarship regarding his *Ecclesiastical History* I put my own argument within a specific contemporary conversation. Second, I teased out implicit historiographical, philosophical, and theological issues within that scholarly conversation germane to my point regarding the ability to understand Bede's sense of history in light of the differences between modern approaches (e.g. anachronism) and Bede himself. Moreover, in following the recent trajectory represented by scholars like Scott DeGregorio, I agree that Bede's *Ecclesiastical History* can only be understood in light of his exegesis, which led into chapter 2.

Chapter 2 argued that the relationship between Bede's exegesis and *Historia* is theologically ambiguous. By investigating *De templo* and the *Historia*, which Bede was simultaneously writing, I show the differences between Bede's practice of exegesis and history. Moreover, the relationship between these texts is external. That is, while there are thematic similarities, as Mayr-Harting rightly observed, exegesis of any variety never really animates Bede's account in the *Historia* in a significant or substantial manner. Of course, this is not to say that the *Historia* is not theologically motivated or even theological through and through; without question it is and I have not suggested otherwise. My point here is rather focused: that *historia* and allegorical exegesis are ambivalently separated for Bede, and I use his commentary on Genesis to continue this argument in chapter 3. By comparing Bede's and Augustine's commentaries on Genesis, chapter 3 shows how Bede differed in important ways when it came the literal/historical sense of Scripture. Bede did not see the allegorical as internal to the historical sense in the way that Augustine did, and, moreover, in most cases, Bede takes the historical sense to be descriptive. In other words, Bede read the literal sense of Genesis 1 as if he were standing by reporting on events as they transpired. Augustine's literal reading, however, did not think the opening verses of Genesis 1 had a physical referent; he also was willing to figurally interpret history while Bede was not. As a result, I conclude that, in contradistinction from Bede, for Augustine the allegorical internally constitutes the literal sense of Scripture. This conclusion is supported by how the understanding of revelation changed from Augustine to Bede as I used the work of O'Loughlin to demonstrate.

Chapters 4 and 5 sought to answer questions raised in the opening chapters by bringing Bede into conversation with contemporary historical theory. I contrasted the difference between modern notions of the past, its status, and Bede's understanding of history where the past was not separated from the present allowing for anachronism in historical writing. This raises the question: Can Bede be understood on his own terms if he is treated as an object "back there" in the past and distant from of our contemporary conversation regarding history and exegesis? I seek to answer this question in the affirmative through my use of Ankersmit and his constructive appropriation of the representation in historical writing. It is worth stating again that representational language does not float free from description and historical reality; representation draws attention to the fact that language can never be simply descriptive, while still being accountable to such empirical realities. I argued that representational language, as distinct from descriptive language, is necessary and internal to the writing of history as such. As a result, depending on how one represents Bede, he can be our interlocutor on historical matters, which is precisely what I sought to do using contemporary historical theory. Furthermore, the fact that historical writing requires representation also impacts how one understands Christian allegorical exegesis. I go so far to suggest that all history writing is figural or allegorical insofar as it is representational.

Conclusions

In the introduction and throughout this work, I have argued that philosophical and "speculative" issues impact the writing of history and what counts as history. After the more detailed study, I am now able to speak more directly to how and why this is the case, specifically for Bede and Augustine. There are two primary areas I want to review and from which I will draw conclusions that will open up new trajectories in the project I have begun here. The first is conceptions of the God-World relationship, that is nature and grace, and the second is the representational constitution of historical writing.

Nature and Grace

My comparison of Bede and Augustine implicitly showed that questions of nature and grace impact exegesis and the writing of history, which I now want to spend more time specifically explicating. Bede's own views on nature and grace are ambiguous as I demonstrated, especially in this commentary on Genesis 1. He adheres to classic Augustinian doctrinal positions regarding God's nature (God is spirit and omnipotent) and *creatio ex nihilo*, but he simultaneously reads Genesis 1 in profoundly different ways than the bishop of Hippo. In light of his reading of Genesis 1, his affirmation of these doctrinal claims remains ambivalent or least difficult to reconcile with his own specific interpretations. Since Bede read Genesis 1 literally as if he were a bystander watching God create, while also affirming that the days were twenty-four-hour days and providing specific dates for creation, God's relationship to the world takes on a precarious form. In order to better understand how Bede related the literal and figural senses, chapter three noted that Bede's bystander interpretation requires him to take the position that the days are twenty-four hours long and that Bede's penchant is for the literal sense to have physical referents; in the language of chapter five, Bede believes that the literal sense should *describe* events with the exception of language about God (e.g., God's hand, eyes, etc.).

The unusual position this places Bede in theologically vis-à-vis how God relates to the world is significant, if not immediately obvious. Bede does acknowledge the fact that humans' composite speech cannot be ignored in such theological matters, though one is left asking to what extent he takes his own advice at times. When commenting on the simultaneous creation of heaven and earth he notes that human language cannot describe that simultaneity.[1] However, Bede continues to use temporal language, even if not literally, to discuss this creation. He says that God existed eternally before time, without qualification or caveat, and talks about the "swiftness" of God's action in creating both heaven and earth simultaneously.[2] I hesitate to make too much of such language since humans have no other words to use but temporally located ones. That said, Bede does not think it necessary to qualify such uses of language in the way that Augustine repeatedly did. Once Bede has committed himself to such a literal reading, he has opened

---

1. Bede, *On Genesis*, 68.
2. Ibid.

himself up to these kinds of questions: Where did the light come from for evening and morning before the sun was created? What does it mean for the days to be twenty-four hours long before there was a sun? In what way did God say, "Let there be light?"

Bede seems aware of these kinds of questions in his commentary as he makes attempts at addressing them. For example, Bede says, "And there was evening, with the light gradually setting after the completed period of the length of the day and passing beneath the lower parts of the world, which now regularly happens at night with the familiar circuit of the sun."[3] Attempting to take this verse as some kind of physical description he likens this light to how the sun now functions. In fact, "... it is also preferred to say that there was evening and morning rather than night and day, in order to reveal that what was then done by the circuit of that first and most excellent light is now known to be performed day and night by the circuit of the sun."[4] Thus, the light made on the first day has the same literal function as the sun. It does not appear that Bede thought this light might not be a physical light at all in the way that Augustine suggested.[5] On the other hand, Bede is clear that God did not literally speak any words when he created, since this would be unfitting for God's simple mode of intellection.[6] Regarding the speech of God, Bede does say this is a reference to the only-begotten Son, and he appeals to John 1. Interestingly, Augustine uses John 1 to argue that "in the beginning" also refers to the Word, while Bede does not. Bede, instead, uses the occasion of his commenting on "in the beginning" to depart from Augustine insinuating Augustine's reading is not literal at all but might leave the history behind. Bede continues to pursue the most descriptive/literal reading possible by linking God speaking to the Word whereas "beginning" is a much less direct association.

By reading the creation account in this descriptive way, Bede muddles the how of creation with the why. The late Dominican Herbert McCabe articulates the importance of this distinction clearly and succinctly in relation to issues of nature and grace.[7] For McCabe the important question about creation is: Why is there anything at all instead of nothing?[8] Everything that is is bounded by nothing insofar as God creates *ex nihilo*. "There is

---

3. Bede, *On Genesis*, 75.
4. Ibid.
5. For Augustine's non-physical reading of light in Gen 1, see *On Genesis*, 1.5–6; *The Literal Meaning of Genesis*, 1.7–8, 17.
6. Bede, *On Genesis*, 73–75.
7. I am using McCabe, *God Matters*.
8. See McCabe, *God Matters*, 2–5.

indeed a difficulty about having a concept of 'everything,' for we ordinarily conceive of something with, so to say, a boundary around it: this is a sheep and not a giraffe. But *everything* is bounded by *nothing* . . . To put what is the same point another way: we can have no concept of nothing, absolutely speaking."[9] And later,

> It is clear that we reach out to, but do not reach, an answer to our ultimate question, how come anything instead of nothing? But we are able to exclude some answers. If God is whatever answers our question, how come everything? then evidently he is not to be included amongst everything. God cannot be a thing, an existent among others. It is not possible that God and the universe should add up to make two. Again, if we are to speak of God as causing the existence of everything, it is clear that we must not mean that he makes the universe out of anything. Whatever creation means it is not a process of making.[10]

I am suggesting that Bede understands well everything except the last sentence precisely because he wants to make Genesis 1 about the how and process of creation.[11]

McCabe rightly notes that how one conceives of creation directly impinges upon how one understands God's action in the world. God does not interfere with the creation that is bounded by nothing; in other words, God is not externally related to his creation in such a way that he meddles or interferes with it.[12] Instead, God "must be in everything that happens and everything that exists in the universe . . . Every action in the world is an action of God; not because it is not an action of a creature but because it is by God's action that the creature is *itself* and has its *own* activity."[13] As a result, God does not need to give his creation additional revelatory significance; it possesses it simply in virtue of its being/existence. In other words, all creation points to God and to Jesus Christ. To be sure, the incarnation and our salvation are gratuitous gifts, but creation itself must be consonant with such a gift otherwise Jesus would be a surd.[14]

9. McCabe, *God Matters*, 5, italics in original.

10. Ibid., 6.

11. For a contemporary and astute account that takes the how/why distinction seriously in light of science and the debate between atheists and creationists, see Cunningham, *Darwin's Pious Idea*.

12. McCabe, *God Matters*, 6.

13. Ibid., 6–7; italics in original. For more on the non-competitive relationship between God and free rational creatures see, *God Matters*, 10–24.

14. While my position is not identical to de Lubac's, his account in *Mystery of the Supernatural* is fairly close.

I noted in chapter three that Bede thought God needed to make creation and events revelatory or theological figures properly speaking, and I have just used McCabe to outline why that should not be the case theologically. Moreover, Bede had a narrower view of revelation than Augustine that Thomas O'Loughlin traced through what he calls the Genesis tradition. When all of these points and issues surrounding nature and grace are combined, one can see how Bede would by and large refuse to exegete history in order to give preeminence to Scripture and how it impacted Bede's practice of history insofar as history became a place of few figures. There were some, of course, but these were God giving them that special, revelatory status. Bede, when doing history, was not looking for theological figures like could be found in Scripture. Moreover, he did not use Scripture as a revelatory reference point to find historical figures. Biblical exemplars were not found in history again; that is, saints, bishops, and other Christians in Anglo-Saxon church were not types of biblical figures, which Bede could have affirmed while *still* giving Scripture its rightful place of preeminence.

Again, I want to reiterate that Bede's *Historia* is a piece of theology through and through; I do not think anyone would dispute that. My investigation here has sought to see what *kind* of theology it is—what sorts of theological claims and presumptions animate it. I am arguing that Bede's understanding of nature and grace was one reason why he did history differently than someone like Augustine. Contemporary historians might object that *any* theology of nature and grace would be inappropriate to impact the writing of history. It seems to me that that very position is already taking sides in a discussion about nature and grace, and even in a more radical (and secular) direction than Bede. I will show why that is the case now.[15]

The Representation of Bede and Historical Writing

In order to show how theological and philosophical concerns and positions impact the writing of history, I will bring together chapters one and five in a clearer fashion. In short, I will demonstrate that historians throughout the twentieth century, who worked on Bede, were presuming, as we all are, certain philosophical and theological positions in their representations of Bede. Representations are more than descriptions, yet depend on them. In other words, when I interrogate scholars' representations of Bede, I am more concerned with how Bede gets framed by such empirically ambiguous content as representation than I am with historical matters of fact. As I

---

15. I am not the first person to argue such a claim. Milbank famously made a similar argument, albeit about social theory and not historical theology. See his *Theology and Social Theory*.

argued in chapter five, descriptions are essential to the historian's task, but history cannot be reduced to them.

I will begin by revisiting Colgrave's analysis of Bede's *Historia* in relation to the Christian hagiographical tradition.[16] To summarize my evaluation, I noted that Colgrave does a better job than some of his predecessors but still falls short because he wants to distinguish three Bedes (historian, theologian, and hagiographer) and reads Bede as a precursor to modern historical standards. I need not recount all of Colgrave's words here again, but I will offer one quote and place that within Colgrave's larger representation. Colgrave depicts Bede's narration of King Edwin's conversion in book two of the *Historia* as such: "All this seems natural and has the appearance of strict history. But meanwhile Bede interpolates somewhat awkwardly a long account of a vision which Edwin had had when he was in exile... and in great danger."[17] Colgrave provides no reason for why this "interpolation" is "awkward," but he seems to think it is obviously the case.

Whatever Colgrave precisely means by "strict history," it is clear that hagiography and theology are not part and parcel of its domain, and that it is preferable, in Colgrave's mind, to Bede's combination of these modes of thought. Hence, Bede must be purified of such non-historical components in order to locate the true history within his *Historia*. Once this is done, Bede can be said to be "far in advance" of his contemporaries regarding historical inquiry.[18] In addition to being sharply distinguished from hagiography and theology, strict history also appears to be something of an empiricist enterprise given the distinctions Colgrave thinks necessary to make at the end of his essay.

> We live in a time when the rapid advance in knowledge, both of the external world and of the human mind, has overwhelmed the self-confident materialism of the recent past... We may not regard the underlying facts in precisely the same light as did Bede and his contemporaries; but we are bound to treat with reverent sympathy the forms in which they embodied those facts and thus projected their own faith and hope upon the external world.[19]

The language of external world and projection reveals Colgrave's philosophical and theological representational frame. Even though he rejects the "materialism of the recent past," faith is still something inside the subject

16. Colgrave, "Bede's Miracle Stories," 201–29.
17. Ibid., 216.
18. Ibid., 228–29.
19. Ibid., 229.

and is projected out onto the external world. Here, Colgrave has taken a stance on questions of nature and grace whether he acknowledges it or not: God seemingly works inside humans and not in the external world thereby creating a situation where God is absent from the external created realm. Two germane results follow this position. First, God relates to the world externally as the human subject relates to the external world. This makes God ontologically compete with his creation vying for space and action in the world like humans do. Second, divine action is understood to be outside the purview of the discipline of history. In other words, historians *qua* historians are not able by the definition of "strict history" to include miracles or the like in their work as being miracles or actions of God. They can discuss them under a putatively atheological descriptive category like hagiography[20] and/or as an artifact of the past—what Bede or someone else believed in their own unique time and historical context, but that is all.

As mentioned in chapter one, several scholars sought to address Bede's treatment by Colgrave and others, like Charles Jones. Specifically, Benedicta Ward defends Bede by rightly calling attention to what Bede found important in miracles.[21] Noting that Bede chose to use the word *signa* for miraculous events, instead of *miracula*, Ward argues that what mattered to Bede was what the event signified.[22] In other words, Bede was primarily interested in what the miracle was saying or pointing to. "It was what was signified that mattered; the wonder itself was secondary."[23] Furthermore, "There are few if any instances in Bede's works where he tells a story simply for the sake of causing wonder: the wonder is always subservient to the main issue, which is salvation."[24] Ward uses several examples from Bede to demonstrate her point; one will suffice here. In book II of the *Historia*, Bede recounts Bishop Laurence's dream where the bishop was being admonished and whipped by St. Peter. Ward interprets the story as such: "It is the chief of the Apostles who chides Laurence, asserting his own responsibility for the Church in Britain and the responsibility of Laurence as his representative in the line of the apostles. Bede's theme here is authority in the Christian Church . . ."[25]

---

20. I say atheological category because "hagiography" was not a term used by ancient and medieval Christians to describe what they were doing. That is, this term is a later "description" of a genre used to make sense of certain texts and persons. Interestingly, the start of critical study of saints' lives began with the Jesuit Bollandists in the 17th century.

21. Ward, "Miracles and History."
22. Ibid., 70–72.
23. Ibid., 71–72.
24. Ibid., 72.
25. Ibid., 74.

In short, Bede shared this miraculous vision not simply to put wonder on display but to demonstrate God's care for the fledgling faith of the British Church and the importance of authority exercised in humility that models Christ crucified.[26] Bede was not concerned about the how or mechanics of miracles, like we moderns are. Thus, to read Bede's miracles stories and seek answers to questions of how is to place an anachronistic frame on Bede's work and history. While Ward never uses the word anachronistic in her defense of Bede, her argument is clearly against Colgrave's criticism that Bede's history contains "wonder tales" where the focus is on the wonder and how of the act.[27] Her overall argument that appeals to understanding Bede in his own setting according to conceptions of nature in the 7th and 8th centuries, along with Bede's own use of miracles as signs, displays her implicit thought regarding Colgrave's anachronistic take on the venerable doctor of the Church.

Though I applaud Ward's defense and think she is right about Bede and his use of miracle stories, I want to point out what has and has not been accomplished in her argument. In fact, an interesting irony arises, which I take to be rooted in her use of anachronism to accomplish her task of defending the late saint.

As my summary already alluded to, Ward is clear that Bede used the miracle stories and material for his own theological purposes in the *Historia*. "Bede is using his miracle material from the inside, and he shapes it according to his purposes."[28] In other words, he uses each story not simply to recount some wondrous event but to make a point to the reader about what God is doing in the world, specifically in the English Church. For example and as mentioned above, Bede uses Laurence's dream to show that God cared for the young English church and that her leaders were of the apostles' ilk. Bede is using miracle stories for his own contemporary theological and ecclesial purposes which coincides with his expressed moral purpose of history in the preface of the *Historia*: "Should history tell of good men and their good estate, the thoughtful listener is spurred on to imitate the good; should it record the evil ends of wicked men, no less effectually the devout and earnest listener or reader is kindled to eschew what is harmful and perverse, and himself with greater care pursue those things which he has learned to be good and pleasing the sight of God."[29] In sum, Ward understands and argues that Bede used reliable sources and information, given his

26. Ibid., 74–75.
27. Ibid., 70.
28. Ibid., 76.
29. Bede, *EH*, preface.

own setting, and used them for his own theological and moral purposes; she understood that Bede wrote history for a contemporary purpose, to have an impact on his own people and readers. The contemporary purpose to Bede's history writing is exactly where the aforementioned irony arises in Ward's defense of Bede.

Bede used past events, like miracles, to make moral and theological points in his own contemporary setting. In other words, the past became part of the present and impacted it directly through Bede's work. However, this is precisely what does not happen in Ward's brief essay. Ward makes her point by noting the separation or difference between modern or contemporary fascinations regarding miracles (the how) and Bede's early medieval/late patristic perspective where the world "was shot through with divinity."[30] In other words, to neglect this important theological point risks anachronistic readings of Bede. Quite clearly, this is an accurate description. However, it does not seek to make Bede present in the same way that Bede seeks to make the events and persons present in his historical writings to impinge upon the present day. In other words, Ward has preserved a more accurate reading of Bede by keeping him in the past, "back there." She does not argue that Bede is right or that Bede's approach to miracles is superior or more persuasive than a modern one. At an even lower level, given the difference she acknowledges and utilizes to make her argument, Bede cannot even be seen as a live option to today. That is, while she does not make an explicit argument for the superiority of Bede's view, neither does she present Bede as a person with whom we could responsibly agree because the time periods are so different. Why?

It is, of course, somewhat speculative to say why, at least with any high level of confidence, but the importance that the anachronistic fallacy plays in her critique of others likely makes her hedge in bringing Bede to bear on contemporary historiography and philosophy. Since Ward criticizes others for bringing contemporary standards to Bede, she is careful not to bring Bede's old ways of thought to bear on the very different present. While such a construal of difference helps defend Bede, it does little to no theological work that Bede himself thought history included, which Ward even recognizes in her analysis of miracles. As a result, Ward ends up defending Bede through a practice of history that is foreign to Bede himself. Hence, the irony of anachronism in contemporary historical thought when it addresses figures, events, and thought from traditions that precede its rise to prominence in the discipline of history during the Renaissance. In sum, anachronism frequently functions as a representational frame in the writing

---

30. Ward, "Miracles and History," 71.

of history that seeks to keep the past and present separated. And, as long as it remains unchallenged, anachronism's use in modern approaches to history will continue to appear superior to its predecessors by default. In this subtle way, Ward's defense of Bede, while astute and useful, does not address the fundamental philosophical and theological differences between Bede's practice of history and more modern varieties. In the end, Ward's historical approach to Bede risks seeing theology as an "add on" to history which Bede would not acknowledge. Thus, theologies of nature and grace also impinge on historical accounts that use anachronism.

I have sought to address the lacuna in representations of Bede by seeking to explicate the more fundamental philosophical and theological differences between Bede and more modern approaches to history. Bede, in a sense, and as recognized by many twentieth century historians, both anticipates more modern historical inquiry while also holding onto his own deeply theological views of history, which modern historians want to jettison. In other words, Bede is something of an ambiguous figure for historians. He is appealed to by modern historians as a giant of his time insofar as he resembles their own presumptions. However, he makes many of them uncomfortable with his clear theological purposes in his historical task. I have sought to show that these theological (and philosophical) assumptions, despite Bede's own theological ambiguity, cannot be jettisoned without changing the very nature of the historical task.

More specifically, I have argued that the relationship between Bede's *Historia* and exegesis is theologically precarious in such a way that Bede does not follow through with theological consistency, as Augustine does, when approaching the historical task insofar as Augustine allows himself to figurally exegete history while Bede does not. Thus, Bede will be seen more sympathetically by historians as an historian than Augustine by more modern accounts. Finally, I have sought to make the case that figural history is inevitable in such a way that the practice of history by the folks like Augustine and Bede can be seen in a more persuasive way than previously thought. That is, they and their understandings and practices of history can be live options for us and not simply relics of the past and objects of historical inquiry.

Bibliography

Ankersmit, Frank. *Historical Representation*. Stanford: Stanford University Press, 2001.
———. *Meaning, Truth, and Reference in Historical Representation*. Ithaca, NY: Cornell University Press, 2012.
———. *Sublime Historical Experience*. Stanford: Stanford University Press, 2005.
Armstrong, A. H., and R. A. Markus. *Christian Faith and Greek Philosophy*. New York: Sheed & Ward, 1960.
Arnold, Duane, and Pamela Bright, editors. "De doctrina Christiana." In *A Classic of Western Culture*. Notre Dame: University of Notre Dame Press, 1995.
Auerbach, Erich. "Figura." In *Scenes from the Drama of European Literature: Six Essays*, 49–56. New York: Meridian, 1959.
Augustine. *The City of God against the Pagans*. Translated by R. W. Dyson. Cambridge Texts in the History of Political Thought. Cambridge: Cambridge University Press, 1998.
———. *Confessions*. Translated by H. Chadwick. Oxford World's Classics. Oxford: Oxford University Press, 1991.
———. *Confessionum Libri XIII*. Edited by L. Verheijen. CCSL 27. Turnhout: Brepols, 1981.
———. *De ciuitate Dei: English and Latin (The City of God against the Pagans)*. Loeb Classical Library L411–17. Cambridge: Harvard University Press, 1963.
———. *De consensu evangelistarum*. Edited by F. Weihrich. CSEL 43. 1904. Reprint, New York: Johnson, 1994.
———. *De doctrina Christiana*. Edited by W. M. Green. CSEL 8. Vienna: Hoelder-Pickler-Tempsky, 1963.
———. *De doctrina Christiana*. Edited by J. Martin. CCSL 32. Turnhout: Brepols, 1962.
———. *De genesi ad litteram*. Edited by J. Zycha. CSEL 28. 1894. Reprint, New York: Johnson, 1994.
———. *De genesi ad litteram inperfectus liber*. Edited by J. Zycha. CSEL 28. 1894. Reprint, New York: Johnson, 1994.
———. *De genesi contra manichaeos*. Edited by D. Weber, 1998. CSEL 91. Vienna: Österreichische Akademie der Wissenschaften.
———. *De libero arbitrio*. Edited by W. M. Green. CSEL 74. Vienna: Hoelder-Pichler-Tempsky, 1956. Reprint, New York: Johnson, 1994.
———. *De trinitate*. Edited by W. J. Mountain and F. Glorie. CCSL 50. Turnhout: Brepols, 1968.

———. *Literal Meaning of Genesis*. Translated by Edmund Hill. In *On Genesis*, edited by Boniface Ramsey and translated by Edmund Hill. Hyde Park, NY: New City, 2006.

———. *On Christian Teaching*. Translated by R. P. H. Green. Oxford World's Classics. Oxford: Oxford University Press, 1997.

———. *On Genesis: A Refutation of the Manichees*. Edited by Boniface Ramsey. Translated by Edmund Hill. The Works of St. Augustine 1/13. Hyde Park, NY: New City, 2006.

———. *On the Catechizing of the Uninstructed*. Translated by S. D. F. Salmond. Christian Classics Ethereal Library. Online: http://www.ccel.org/ccel/schaff/npnf103.iv.iii.html.

———. *The Trinity*. 4th ed. Translated by Edmund Hill. The Works of St. Augsutine 1/5. Hyde Park, NY: New City, 1991.

———. *Unfinished Literal Commentary on Genesis*. In *On Genesis*, edited by Boniface Ramsey and translated by Edmund Hill. Hyde Park, NY: New City, 2006.

———. *The Works of St. Augustine: A Translation for the 21st Century*. Edited by Boniface Ramsey. 20 vols. Hyde Park, NY: New City Press, 1990–.

Ayres, Lewis. *Nicea and Its Legacy: An Approach to Fourth-Century Trinitarian Theology*. Oxford: Oxford University Press, 2004.

Bede. *Commentary on the Acts of the Apostles*. Translated by L. T. Martin. Kalamazoo: Cistercian, 1989.

———. *De natura rerum libra*. Edited by C. Jones et al. CCSL 123A. Turnhout: Brepols, 1975.

———. *De schematibus et tropis*. Translated by Calvin Kendall. Saarbrücken: AQ-Verlag, 1991.

———. *De tabernaclo*. Edited by D. Hurst. CCSL 119A. Turnhout: Brepols, 1969.

———. *De templo*. Edited by D. Hurst. CCSL 119A. Turnhout: Brepols, 1969.

———. *De temporibus liber*. Edited by C. Jones. CCSL 123C. Turnhout: Brepols, 1980.

———. *De temporum ratione liber*. Edited by C. Jones. CCSL 123B. Turnhout: Brepols, 1977.

———. *The Ecclesiastical History of the English People*. Translated by Bertram Colgrave. In *The Ecclesiastical History of the English People; The Greater Chronicle; Bede's Letter to Egbert*, edited by Judith McClure and Roger Collins. Oxford World's Classics. Oxford: University of Oxford Press, 1999.

———. *Expositio Actuum Apostolorum*. Edited by M. Laistner. CCSL 121. Turnhout: Brepols, 1960.

———. *The Greater Chronicle*. Translated by Judith McClure and Roger Collins. In *The Ecclesiastical History of the English People; The Greater Chronicle; Bede's Letter to Egbert*, edited by Judith McClure and Roger Collins. Oxford World's Classics. Oxford: University of Oxford Press, 1999.

———. *Histoire Ecclésiastique du Peuple Anglais*. SC 489–91. Paris: Cerf, 2005.

———. *In Cantica Canticorum*. Edited by D. Hurst. CCSL 122. Turnhout: Brepols, 1983.

———. *In Ezram et Neemiam*. Edited by D. Hurst. CCSL 119A. Turnhout: Brepols, 1969.

———. *In genesim*. Edited by C. Jones. CCSL 118A. Turnhout: Brepols, 1967.

———. *In Lucam*. Edited by D. Hurst. CCSL 120. Turnhout: Brepols, 2001.

———. *In primam partem Samuhelis*. Edited by D. Hurst, CCSL 119. Turnhout: Brepols, 1962.
———. *On Ezra and Nehemiah*. Translated by Scott DeGregorio. Liverpool: Liverpool University Press, 2006.
———. *On Genesis*. Translated by C. Kendall. Liverpool: Liverpool University Press, 2008.
———. *Letter to Egbert*. Translated by Carolus Plummer. In *The Ecclesiastical History of the English People; The Greater Chronicle; Bede's Letter to Egbert*, edited by Judith McClure and Roger Collins. Oxford World's Classics. Oxford: Oxford University Press, 1999.
———. *The Life and Miracles of St. Cuthbert, Bishop of Lindesfarne (721)*. Internet Medieval Sourcebook. Online: http://www.fordham.edu/halsall/basis/bede-cuthbert.asp.
———. *On the Nature of Things and On Times*. Translated by Calvin Kendall and Faith Wallis. Liverpool: Liverpool University Press, 2011.
———. *On the Reckoning of Time*. Translated by Faith Wallis. Liverpool: Liverpool University Press, 1999.
———. *On the Song of Songs*. Translated by A. Holder. New York: Paulist, 2011.
———. *On the Tabernacle*. Translated by Arthur Holder. Liverpool: Liverpool University Press, 1994.
———. *On the Temple*. Translated by S. Connolly with an Introduction by Jennifer O'Reilly. Liverpool: Liverpool University Press, 1995.
———. *Opera Historica*. Translated by C. Plummer. In *Venerabilis Baedae Historiam Ecclesiasticam Gentis Anglorum: Bede's Ecclesiastical History of England*, edited by Carolus Plummer. Oxford: E typographeo Clarendoniano, 1896.
Blair, Peter H. "The Historical Writings of Bede." In *La Storiografia Altomedievale 10–16 April 1969*, 197–221. Settimane di Studio del Centro Italiano di Studi sull'Alto Medioevo 17. Spoleto: Presso la sede del Centro, 1970.
———. *Northumbria in the Days of Bede*. London: Gollancz, 1976.
———. *The World of Bede*. Cambridge: Cambridge University Press, 1990.
Bonner, Gerald. "Bede and Medieval Civilization." *Anglo-Saxon England* 2 (1973) 71–90.
———, editor. *Famulus Christi: Essays in Commemoration of the Thirteenth Centenary of the Birth of the Venerable Bede*. London: SPCK, 1976.
Brandt, W. J. *The Shape of Medieval History: Studies in Modes of Perception*. New Haven: Yale University Press, 1966.
Breisach, Ernst. *Historiography: Ancient, Medieval, Modern*. Chicago: University of Chicago Press, 1994.
Bright, Pamela. *The Book of Rules of Tyconius: Its Purpose and Inner Logic*. Notre Dame, IN: University of Notre Dame Press, 1988.
Browne, George F. *The Venerable Bede: His Life and Writings*. New York: Macmillan, 1919.
Brown, George H. *Bede, the Venerable*. Boston: Twayne, 1987.
———. *A Companion to Bede*. Woodbridge: Boydell, 2009.
———. "Quotations from Isidore in Bede's Commentary on Genesis 4:25–26." *Notes and Queries* 56 (2009) 163–65.
Bruce-Mitford, R. L. S. *The Art of the Codex Amiatinus: Jarrow Lecture 1967*. Jarrow: Jarrow Parish, St. Paul's House, 1969.

Burke, Peter. *The Renaissance Sense of the Past*. New York: St. Martin's, 1970.
Campbell, James. "Bede." In *Latin Historians*, edited by T. A. Dorey, 159–90. New York: Basic Books, 1966.
———. *Essays in Anglo-Saxon History*. London: Continuum, 1986.
Capelle, D. Bernard. "Le rôle théologique de Bède le Vénérable." *Studia Anselmiana* 6 (1936) 1–40.
Carroll, M. T. A. *The Venerable Bede: His Spiritual Teachings*. Washington, DC: Catholic University Press, 1946.
Carruthers, Mary. *The Book of Memory: A Study of Memory in Medieval Culture*. Cambridge: Cambridge University Press, 1992.
Caspary, Gerard E. *Politics and Exegesis: Origen and the Two Swords*. Berkeley: University of California Press, 1979.
Cassiodorus. *Institutions of Divine and Secular Reasoning*. Translated by J. M. Halport. Chicago: University of Chicago Press, 2004.
Chadwick, Henry. *Early Christian Thought and the Classical Tradition: Studies in Justin, Clement, and Origen*. Oxford: Oxford University Press, 1966.
Childs, Brevard S. *Biblical Theology in Crisis*. Philadelphia: Westminster, 1970.
Clark, Francis. *The "Gregorian" Dialogues and the Origins of Benedictine Monasticism*. Leiden: Brill, 2003.
Clark, James. *The Benedictines of the Middle Ages*. Woodbridge, UK: Boydell, 2011.
Colgrave, Bertram. "Bede's Miracle Stories." In *Bede: His Life, Times, and Writings*, edited by A. H. Thompson, 201–29. Oxford: Clarendon, 1935.
Colgrave, Bertram, and R. A. B. Mynors, editors. *The Ecclesiastical History of the English People*. Oxford: Clarendon, 1969.
Collingwood, R. G. *The Idea of History*. Rev. ed. Oxford: Oxford University Press, 1994.
Connolly, Seán. *Bede: On the Temple*. Liverpool: Liverpool University Press, 1995.
Cunningham, Conor. *Darwin's Pious Idea: Why the Ultra-Darwinists and Creationists Both Get It Wrong*. Grand Rapids: Eerdmans, 2010.
da Fabriano, Gilio. *The Errors of Painters*. 1564.
Daly, C. T., J. Doody, and K. Paffenroth, editors. *Augustine and History*. Lanham, MD: Lexington, 2008.
Daniélou, Jean. *Gospel Message and Hellenistic Culture*. Translated by J. A. Baker. Philadelphia: Westminster, 1973.
Danto, Arthur. *Narration and Knowledge: Including the Integral Text of Analytical Philosophy of History*. Columbia Classics in Philosophy. New York: Columbia University Press, 1985.
Davidse, Jan. "On Bede as Christian Historian." In *Beda Vernerabilis: Historian, Monk, and Northumbrian*, edited by L. A. J. R. Houwen and A. A. MacDonald, 1–15. Groningen: Forsten, 1996.
———. "The Sense of History in the Works of the Venerable Bede." *Studi Medievali* 23 (1982) 647–95.
Dawson, John D. *Allegorical Readers and Cultural Revision in Ancient Alexandria*. Berkeley: University of California Press, 1992.
———. *Christian Figural Reading and the Fashioning of Identity*. Berkeley: University of California Press, 2002.
Dalye, Lowrie. *Benedictine Monasticism: Its Formation and Development through the Twelfth Century*. New York: Sheed & Ward, 1965.

DeGregorio, Scott. "Bede, the Monk, as Exegete: Evidence from the Commentary on Ezra-Nehemiah." *Revue Bénédictine* 115 (2005) 1–25, 343–69.

———. "Bede's *In Ezram et Neemiam* and the Reform of the Northrumbrian Church." *Speculum* 79 (2004) 1–25.

———. "*Nostrorum socordiam temporum*: The Reforming Impulse of Bede's Later Exegesis." *Early Medieval Europe* 11 (2002) 107–22.

DeGregorio, Scott, editor. *Innovation and Tradition in the Writings of the Venerable Bede*. Morgantown, WV: West Virginia University Press, 2006.

de Lubac, Henri. *Exégèse medieval: les quatre sens de l'Ecriture*. 3 vols. Paris: Desclée de Brouwer, 1993. In English, *Medieval Exegesis: The Four Senses of Scripture*. 4 vols. Grand Rapids: Eerdmans, 1998–.

———. *History and Spirit: The Understanding of Scripture according to Origen*. Translated by Anne E. Nash. San Francisco: Ignatius, 2007.

———. *The Mystery of the Supernatural*. Translated by Rosemary Sheed. New York: Crossroad, 1998.

Dempsey, Charles. "Response: *Historia* and Anachronism in Renaissance Art." *The Art Bulletin* 87 (2005) 416–21.

DiTommaso, Lorenzo, and Lucian Turcescu, editors. *The Reception and Interpretation of the Bible in Late Antiquity*. Leiden: Brill, 2008.

Dupré, Louis. *Passage to Modernity: An Essay in the Hermeneutics of Nature and Culture*. New Haven: Yale University Press, 1993.

Eckenrode, T. R. "The Venerable Bede and the Pastoral Affirmation of the Christian Message in Anglo-Saxon England." *The Downside Review* 99 (1981) 258–78.

Evans, J. M. *Paradise Lost and the Genesis Tradition*. New York: Oxford University Press, 1968.

Fairless, Peter. *Northumbria's Golden Age: The Kingdom of Northumbria, AD 547–735*. York: Sessions, 1994.

Farrell, R. T., editor. *Bede and Anglo-Saxon England: Papers in Honour of the 1300th Anniversary of the Birth of Bede*. Oxford: British Archaeological Reports, 1978.

Fasolt, Constantin. *The Limits of History*. Chicago: University of Chicago Press, 2003.

Fischer, David H. *Historians' Fallacies: Toward a Logic of Historical Thought*. New York: Harper & Row, 1970.

Foot, Sarah. *Monastic Life in Anglo-Saxon England, c. 600–900*. New York: Cambridge University Press, 2006.

Fowl, Stephen. *Engaging Scripture: A Model for Theological Interpretation*. Oxford: Blackwell, 1998.

Frei, Hans. *The Eclipse of Biblical Narrative: A Study in Eighteenth and Nineteenth Century Hermeneutics*. New Haven: Yale University Press, 1974.

———. "The 'Literal' Reading of Biblical Narrative in the Christian Tradition." In *The Bible and the Narrative Tradition*, edited by Frank McConnell, 40, 64–81. New York: Oxford University Press, 1986.

Gadamer, Hans-Georg. *Truth and Method*. Translated by Joel Weinsheimer and Donald Marshall. 2nd ed. New York: Continuum, 1993.

———. "The Universality of the Hermenentical Problem." In *Philosophical Hermeneutics*, translated and edited by David Linge, 3–17. Berkeley: University of California Press, 1976.

Gillespie, Michael A. *The Theological Origins of Modernity*. Chicago: University of Chicago Press, 2008.

Glare, P. G. W., editor. *Oxford Latin Dictionary*. Oxford: Clarendon, 1982.
Goffart, Walter. "Bede's *Uera lex historiae* Explained." *Anglo-Saxon England* 34 (2005) 111–16.
———. *The Narrators of Barbarian History (A.D. 550–800): Jordanes, Gregory of Tours, Bede, and Paul the Deacon*. Princeton: Princeton University Press, 1988.
Gransden, Antonia. "Bede's Reputation as an Historian in Medieval England." *Journal of Ecclesiastical History* 32 (1981) 397–425.
Green, Joel B., and Max Turner, editors. *Between Two Horizons: Spanning New Testament Studies and Systematic Theology*. Grand Rapids: Eerdmans, 2000.
Grégoire le Grand. *Commentaire sur le premier livre des Rois*. Edited by Pierre de Cava, Adalbert de Vogüé, and Christophe Vuillaume. SC 449. Paris: Cerf, 1989–.
———. *Dialogues*. Edited by Adalbert de Vogüé. SC 251. Paris: Cerf, 1978–.
Gunn, Vicky. *Bede's* Historiae: *Genre, Rhetoric and the Construction of the Anglo-Saxon Church*. Woodbridge, UK: Boydell, 2009.
Haddock, B. A. *An Introduction to Historical Thought*. London: Edward Arnold, 1980.
Hanning, Robert. *The Vision of History in Early Britain: From Gildas to Geoffrey of Monmouth*. New York: Columbia University Press, 1966.
Hart, David Bentley. *The Beauty of the Infinite: The Aesthetics of Christian Truth*. Grand Rapids: Eerdmans, 2003.
Hays, Richard. *The Conversion of the Imagination: Paul as Interpreter of Israel's Scripture*. Grand Rapids: Eerdmans, 2005.
———. *Echoes of Scripture in the Letters of Paul*. New Haven: Yale University Press, 1993.
Higham, N. J. *An English Empire: Bede and the Early Anglo-Saxon Kings*. Manchester: Manchester University Press, 1995.
Holder, Arthur. "Allegory and History in Bede's Interpretation of Sacred Architecture." *The American Benedictine Review* 40 (1989) 115–31.
———. "Bede and the Tradition of Patristic Exegesis." *Anglican Theological Review* 72 (1990) 399–411.
Hooker, Richard. *Of the Laws of Ecclesiastical Polity*. 2 vols. Cambridge: Cambridge University Press, 1977.
Howorth, H. H. "The Influence of St. Jerome on the Canon of the Western Church." *Journal of Theological Studies* 10 (1909) 481–96; 11 (1910) 321–47; 13 (1911) 1–18.
Isidore. *Etymologiae*. Edited by W. M. Lindsay. Oxford, Oxford University Press, 1911.
Jackson, B. D. "The Theory of Signs in St. Augustine's *De doctrina Christiana*." *Revue d'Etudes Augustiniennes et Patristiques* 15 (1969) 9–49.
Jenkins, C. "Bede as Exegete and Theologian." In *Bede: His Life, Times, and Writings: Essays in Commemoration of the Twelfth Centenary of His Death*, edited by A. H. Thompson, 152–200. Oxford: Clarendon, 1935.
Johnson, Mark. "Another Look at the Plurality of the Literal Sense." *Medieval Philosophy and Theology* 2 (1992) 117–41.
Jones, Charles W. *Saints' Lives and Chronicles in Early England*. Ithaca, NY: Cornell University Press, 1947.
———. "Some Introductory Remarks on Bede's Commentary on Genesis." *Sacris Eruditi* 19 (1969–70) 115–98.
Kabede, Messay. "Religion and Revolution: Tocqueville's Insight into the Revolutionary Spirit." *Suvidya Journal of Philosophy and Religion* 3 (2009) 63–85.

Kaczynski, Bernice. "The Authority of the Fathers: Patristic Texts in Early Medieval Libraries and Scriptoria." *Journal of Medieval Latin* 16 (2006) 1–27.
Kannengiesser, Charles, editor. *Handbook of Patristic Exegesis*. 2 vols. Leiden: Brill, 2004.
Kemp, Anthony. *The Estrangement of the Past: A Study in the Origins of Modern Historical Consciousness*. New York: Oxford University Press, 1991.
Kendall, Calvin. "Bede's *Historia Ecclesiastica*: The Rhetoric of Faith." In *Medieval Eloquence: Studies in the Theory and Practice of Medieval Rhetoric*, edited by J. Murphy, 145–72. Berkeley: University of California Press, 1978.
———."The Responsibility of *Auctoritas*: Method and Meaning in Bede's Commentary on Genesis." In *Innovation and Tradition in the Writings of the Venerable Bede*, edited by Scott DeGregorio, 106–19. Morgantown, WV: University of West Virginia Press, 2006.
Knowles, David. *The Heads of Religious Houses, England and Wales, 940–1216*. Cambridge: Cambridge University Press, 1972.
———. *Medieval Religious Houses, England and Wales*. London: Longman, 1971.
———. *The Monastic Order in England: A History of Its Development from the Times of St. Dunstan to the Fourth Lateran Council, 940–1216*. Cambridge: Cambridge University Press, 1966.
Laistner, M. L. W. "The Library of the Venerable Bede." In *Bede: His Life, Times, and Writings: Essays in Commemoration of the Twelfth Centenary of His Death*, edited by A. H. Thompson, 237–66. Oxford: Oxford University Press, 1969.
Leclerq, Jean. *The Love of Learning and the Desire for God: A Study in Monastic Culture*. Translated by C. Misrahi. New York: Fordham University Press, 1982.
Levison, Wilhelm. "Bede as Historian." In *Bede: His Life, Times, and Writings: Essays in Commemoration of the Twelfth Centenary of His Death*, edited by A. H. Thompson, 111–51. Oxford: Clarendon, 1935.
Manuel, Frank. "The Use and Abuse of Psychology in History." In *Historical Studies Today*, edited by Felix Gilbert and Stephen Graubard, 211–37. New York: Norton, 1972.
Markus, R. A. *Saeculum: History and Society in the Theology of St. Augustine*. Cambridge: Cambridge University Press, 1970.
———. "Signs, Communication, and Communities in Augustine's *De doctrina Christiana*." In *De doctrina Christiana: A Western Classic*, edited by Duane Arnold and Pamela Bright, 97–108. Notre Dame: University of Notre Dame Press, 1995.
Marrou, Henri. *A History of Education in Antiquity*. Translated by George Lamb. New York: Sheed & Ward, 1956.
Marsden, Richard. "*Manus Bedae*: Bede's Contribution to Ceolfrith's Bibles." *Anglo-Saxon England* 27 (1998) 65–85.
Maximus the Confessor. *Mystagogia*. Edited by Christian Boudignon. Corpus Christianorum, Series Graeca 69. Brepols: Turnhout, 2011.
Mayr-Harting, Henry M. R. E. *The Venerable Bede, the Rule of St. Benedict, and Social Class*. Jarrow Lecture 1976. Jarrow: Rector of Jarrow, 1976.
McAuliffe, Jane, Barry Walfish, and Joseph Goering, editors. *With Reverence for the Word: Medieval Scriptural Exegesis in Judaism, Christianity, and Islam*. Oxford: Oxford University Press, 2010.
McCabe, Herbert. *God Matters*. New York: Mowbray, 2005.

McClure, Judith. "Bede's Notes on Genesis and the Training of the Anglo-Saxon Clergy." In *The Bible in the Medieval World: Essays in Memory of Beryl Smalley*, edited by Katherine Walsh and Diana Wood, 24–29. Oxford: Blackwell, 1985.

McClure, Judith, and Roger Collins, editors. *The Ecclesiastical History of the English People; The Greater Chronicle; Bede's Letter to Egbert*. Oxford: Oxford University Press, 1999.

Meyvaert, Paul. *Bede and Gregory the Great*. Jarrow Lecture 1964. Jarrow: Rector of Jarrow, 1964.

———. "Bede and the Church Paintings of Wearmouth-Jarrow." *Anglo-Saxon England* 8 (1979) 63–77.

———. "Bede, Cassiodorus, and the Codex Amaitinus." *Speculum* 71 (1996) 827–83.

———. "Bede the Scholar." In *Famulus Christi: Essays in Commemoration of the Thirteenth Centenary of the Birth of the Venerable Bede*, edited by Gerald Bonner, 41, 51–55. London: SPCK, 1976.

———. "The Date of Bede's *In Ezram* and His Image of Ezra in the Codex Amiatinus." *Speculum* 80 (2005) 1087–1133.

Milbank, John. *Theology and Social Theory: Beyond Secular Reason*. Oxford: Blackwell, 1990.

———. *The Word Made Strange: Theology, Language, Culture*. Oxford: Blackwell, 1997.

Milbank, John, C. Pickstock, and G. Ward, editors. *Radical Orthodoxy: A New Theology*. London: Routledge, 1999.

Minear, Paul. *The Bible and the Historian: Breaking the Silence about God in Biblical Studies*. Nashville: Abingdon, 2003.

Mommsen, Theodore. "Petrarch's Conception of the Dark Ages." *Speculum* 17 (1942) 226–42.

Nagel, Alexander, and Christopher Wood. *Anachronic Renaissance*. New York: Zone Books, 2010.

———. "Toward a New Model of Renaissance Anachronism." *The Art Bulletin* 87 (2005) 403–15.

Nees, Lawrence. *Early Medieval Art*. Oxford: Oxford University Press, 2002.

O'Daly, Gerard. *Augustine's City of God: A Reader's Guide*. New York: Oxford University Press, 2004.

O'Keefe, John, and R. R. Reno, editors. *Sanctified Vision: An Introduction to Early Christian Interpretation of the Bible*. Baltimore: Johns Hopkins University Press, 2005.

O'Loughlin, Thomas. *Teachers and Code-Breakers: The Latin Genesis Tradition, 430–800*. Turnhout: Brepols, 1999.

Petrarch. *Letters*. Translated by James Robinson and Henry Winchester. New York: Putnam, 1909.

Pickstock, Catherine. *After Writing: On the Liturgical Consummation of Philosophy*. Oxford: Blackwell, 1998.

Plummer, Carolus, editor. *Venerabilis Baedae Historiam Ecclesiasticam Gentis Anglorum: Bede's Ecclesiastical History of England*. 2 vols. Oxford: E typographeo Clarendoniano, 1896.

Quine, W. V. O. "Two Dogmas of Empiricism." *The Philosophical Review* 60 (1951) 20–43.

Radner, Ephraim. *A Brutal Unity: The Spirtual Politics of the Christian Church*. Waco, TX: Baylor University Press, 2012.

———. *The End of the Church: A Pneumatology of Christian Division in the West.* Grand Rapids: Eerdmans, 1998.

———. *Hope Among the Fragments: The Broken Church and Its Engagement with Scripture.* Grand Rapids: Brazos, 2004.

———. *Leviticus.* Grand Rapids: Brazos, 2008.

Ray, Roger D. "Bede, the Exegete, as Historian." In *Famulus Christi: Essays in Commemoration of the Thirteenth Centenary of the Birth of the Venerable Bede,* edited by Gerald Bonner, 125–40. London: SPCK, 1976.

———. "Bede's *Uera Lex Historiae.*" *Speculum* 55 (1980) 1–21.

———. "What Do We Know about Bede's Commentaries?" *Recherches de théologie ancienne et medieval* 49 (1982) 5–20.

Rector, H. J. "The Influence of St. Augustine's Philosophy of History on the Venerable Bede in the Ecclesiastical History of the English People." PhD diss., Duke University, 1975.

Reventlow, Henning G. *History of Biblical Interpretation.* Vol. 1, *From the Old Testament to Origen.* Translated by L. G. Perdue. Atlanta: SBL, 2009.

———. *History of Biblical Interpretation.* Vol. 2, *From Late Antiquity to the End of the Middle Ages.* Translated by J. O. Duke. Atlanta: SBL, 2009.

———. *History of Biblical Interpretation.* Vol. 3, *Renaissance, Reformation, Humanism.* Translated by J. O. Duke. Atlanta: SBL, 2009.

Ricoeur, Paul. *Memory, History, Forgetting.* Translated by K. Blamey and D. Pellauer. Chicago: University of Chicago Press, 2004.

Ritter, Harry. "Anachronism." In *Dictionary of Concepts in History,* edited by Harry Ritter, 9–13. New York: Greenwood, 1986.

Robinson, Bernard. "The Venerable Bede as Exegete." *The Downside Review* 112 (1994) 201–26.

Rogers, Eugene. "How the Virtues of an Interpreter Presuppose and Perfect Hermeneutics: The Case of Thomas Aquinas." *Journal of Religion* 76 (1996) 64–81.

Rorty, Richard. *Philosophy and the Mirror of Nature.* Princeton: Princeton University Press, 1981.

Schneiders, Sandra. "Faith, Hermeneutics, and the Literal Sense of Scripture." *Theological Studies* 39 (1978) 719–36.

Sellers, Wilfrid. "Empiricism and the Philosophy of Mind." *Minnesota Studies in the Philosophy of Science, Vol. I: The Foundations of Science and the Concepts of Psychology and Psychoanalysis,* edited by Herbert Feigl and Michael Scriven, 253–329. Minneapolis: University of Minnesota Press, 1956.

Shoedel, William R., and Robert L. Wilkin, editors. *Early Christian Literature and the Classical Intellectual Tradition: In Honorem Robert Grant.* Paris: Beauchesne, 1979.

Simonetti, Manlio. *Biblical Interpretation in the Early Church: An Historical Introduction to Patristic Exegesis.* New York: T. & T. Clark, 1994.

Smalley, Beryl. *Historians in the Middle Ages.* London: Thames & Hudson, 1974.

———. *The Study of the Bible in the Middle Ages.* Oxford: Oxford University Press, 1952.

Spijker, Ineke van't, editor. *The Multiple Meanings of Scripture: The Role of Exegesis in Early Christian and Medieval Culture.* Leiden: Brill, 2009.

Suger, Abbot. *De Consecratione.* Translated by E. Panofsky as *Abbot Suger on the Abbey Church of St. Denis and Its Art Treasures.* Princeton: Princeton University Press, 1946.

Tanner, Kathryn. "Theology and the Plain Sense." In *Scriptural Authority and Narrative Interpretation*, edited by Garrett Green, 59–78. Philadelphia: Fortress, 1987.

Teske, Roland. *Augustine of Hippo: Philosopher, Exegete, and Theologian*. Milwaukee: Marquette University Press, 2009.

Thacker, Alan. "Bede's Ideal of Reform." In *Ideal and Reality in Frankish and Anglo-Saxon Society*, edited by Patrick Wormald et al., 149. Oxford: Blackwell, 1983.

Thompson, A. H., editor. *Bede: His Life, Times, and Writings: Essays in Commemoration of the Twelfth Centenary of His Death*. Oxford: Clarendon, 1935.

———. *The World of Bede*. Cambridge: Cambridge University Press, 1990.

Trinkaus, Charles. *The Poet as Philosopher: Petrarch and the Formation of Renaissance Consciousness*. New Haven: Yale University Press, 1979.

Turner, Denys. "Allegory in Christian Late Antiquity." In *The Cambridge Companion to Allegory*, edited by Rita Copeland and Peter Struck. Cambridge: Cambridge University Press, 2010.

———. *Eros and Allegory: Medieval Exegesis of the Song of Songs*. Kalamazoo, MI: Cistercian, 1995.

Tyconius. *The Book of Rules*. Translated by William Babcock. Atlanta: SBL, 1989.

Vessey, M., et al., editors. *History, the Apocalypse, and the Secular Imagination: New Essays on Augustine's City of God*. Bowling Green, OH: Philosophy Documentation Center, 1999.

Wallace-Hadrill, J. M. "Bede and Plummer." In *Famulus Christi: Essays in Commemoration of the Thirteenth Centenary of the Birth of the Venerable Bede*, edited by Gerald Bonner, 366–85. London: SPCK, 1976.

Ward, Benedicta. "Miracles and History: A Reconsideration of the Miracle Stories Used by Bede." In *Famulus Christi: Essays in Commemoration of the Thirteenth Centenary of the Birth of the Venerable Bede*, edited by Gerald Bonner, 70–76. London: SPCK, 1976.

———. *The Venerable Bede*. London: Continuum, 1990.

Watson, Francis. *Text, Church, and World: Biblical Interpretation in Theological Perspective*. Edinburgh: T. & T. Clark, 1994.

Weltin, E. G. *Athens and Jerusalem: An Interpretive Essay on Christianity and Classical Culture*. Atlanta: Scholars, 1987.

White, Hayden. *The Content of the Form: Narrative Discourse and Historical Representation*. Baltimore: Johns Hopkins University Press, 1987.

———. *Figural Realism: Studies in the Mimesis Effect*. Baltimore: John Hopkins University Press, 1999.

———. *Metahistory: The Historical Imagination in Nineteenth-Century Europe*. Baltimore: Johns Hopkins University Press, 1975.

Whitman, Jon. *Allegory: The Dynamics of an Ancient and Medieval Technique*. Cambridge, MA: Harvard University Press, 1987.

Wilken, Robert Louis. "In Defense of Allegory." In *Theology and Scriptural Imagination*, edited by L. Gregory Jones and James J. Buckley, 35–50. Oxford: Blackwell, 1998.

Wittgenstein, Ludwig. *On Certainty*. Translated by G. E. M. Anscombe. Oxford: Blackwell, 1991.

———. *Philosophical Investigations*. Translated by G. E. M. Anscombe. Englewood Cliffs, NJ: Prentice-Hall, 1958.

Wormald, Patrick, with Donald Bullough and Roger Collins, editors. *Ideal and Reality in Frankish and Anglo-Saxon Society: Studies Presented to J. M. Wallace-Hadrill.* Oxford: Blackwell, 1983.

Young, Frances. *Biblical Exegesis and the Formation of Christian Culture.* Cambridge: Cambridge University Press, 1997.

Index

Abelard, 31
allegoria factis, 63
allegorical exegesis, 8, 13–16, 45–7
Ambrosius, 65
anachronism, 10–11, 93–96, 98, 108–10
anachronism in art, 96
anachronistic fallacies, 94
Anglo-Saxon monasticism, 5
Ankersmit, Frank, 43
    historical representation, substitution theory of, 118–23
    history writing in relationship to the philosophy of language, 114–18
    representational logic, 119
Anselm of Canterbury, 31
Aquinas, 8
Auerbach, Erich, 6–7, 56, 124
Augustine
    Bede, influence on, 69–70
    creation, differences with Bede, 71
    and the Genesis tradition, 65, 66; literal commentaries on creation, 70–74, 87–91
    philosophy of history, 102
    sense of signs in historical events, 103–5
    on the world ages, 78–83
Ayers, Lewis, 8–9

Basil, 65, 77
Bede
    allegorical approach in *De tabernaculo,* 45
    allegorical approach to Scripture, 13–16, 45–47
    allegorical interpretation of creation, 75–78
    anachronism in art, 98–101
    anachronisms, function of, 108–11
    Augustine, influence of, 69–70
    conception of the past *vs.* modern understandings of anachronism, 110–11
    creation, differences with Augustine, 71
    the eight world ages, 106–7
    as exegete of Scripture, 45
    figural connection between Old Testament and *Historia* kings and leaders, 55
    figural exegesis, 46, 124, 130
    Genesis, commentary on, 10, 47, 64–91
    hagiographer and historian, 24, 26
    history concerned with particular and universal simultaneously, 51
    life, summary of, 4–5, 15, 44
    literal and allegorical disparities, 112–13
    miracle stories in *Historia,* 15–17, 21–24, 31–32, 42, 142–45
    relationship between *De templo* and the *Historia,* 10
    relationship between figural exegesis of the temple and the *Historia,* 50–55
    relationship of exegetical and historical works, 2–3

159

Allegorizing History

uera lex historiae, 26–28, 33–36
use of *hyperbaton* in *Historia*, 36
use of Scripture and history, 55–63
works, focus of, 6
on the world ages, 83–87
Book of Rules, The (Tyconius), 46
Bosham, Herbert, 31
Browne, George F., 17–18, 42
Bruce-Mitford, R. L. S., 100
Burke, Peter, 94–95

Cassiodorus, 65
Christian exegesis, 1–2
Chronicon (Eusebius), 34
City of God (Augustine), 62
Colgrave, Bertram, 19, 30
    analysis of *Historia* in relation to the Christian hagiographical tradition, 141–2
    Bede's miracle stories in *Historia*, commentary on, 21–24, 42
Collingwood, R. G., 1
creation, 71, 138–40
Cuthbert, 15

Danto, Arthur, 127–28
Davidse, Jan, 9, 11
    theological framing of Bede's history, 38–42, 43, 50–51
    use of contemporary historical discussions to understand Bede, 126
Dawson, David, 7
De ciuitate Dei (Augustine), 80
De doctrina Christiana (Augustine), 103–5
De genesi ad litteram (Augustine), 70
De genesi contra manichaeos (Augustine), 70
de Lubac, Henri, 8, 46
De schematibus et tropis (Bede), 33, 36
De tabernaculo (Bede), 35, 45
De templo (Bede), 56–59, 68
    Bede's commentary on 2 Chronicles 4:8, 48–9
    Bede's use of the adverb *ita*, 60–63
    relationship to *Historia*, 47–55
DeGregorio, Scott

Bede's writing of *Historia* as a form of moral advocacy and reform for the Northumbrian church, 49
the Ezra-Cassiodorus miniature, 101

Ecclesiastical History of the English People (Bede). *See also Historia*:
    Bede, summary of life, 4–5, 44
    Carolus Plummer's commentary (1896), 13–17
    historiography of recent scholarship, 9, 17–43, 135–6
Errors of Painters, The (da Fabriano), 96
Etymologiae (Isidore), 67
Eucherius, 65
Eusebius, 28
Evagrius of Antioch, 22
exegesis, allegorical. *See* allegorical exegesis
exegesis, Christian. *See* Christian exegesis
exegesis, figural. *See* figural exegesis
Ezra-Cassiodorus miniature, 99, 110, 133
    anachronism in art, 98–101

Famulus Christi, 29–30
Fasolt, Constantin
    anachronism in the writing of history as "sinful," 93
    history, definition of, 6
figural exegesis, 127–28
figural history, inevitability of, 126–33, 145
figural interpretation, 6–7, 56, 124
Fischer, David, 94
Foot, Sarah, 5

Gadamer, Hans-Georg, 1, 111
Genesis tradition, 65–67
    commentators, 65
    features of, 65–67
God-World relationship. *See* nature and grace
Goffart, Walter, 49

Index

Hanning, Robert, 33
Historia
    Bede's figural exegesis of the temple, relationship of, 50–55
    Carolus Plummer commentary, 9, 13–17
    Charles Jones commentary, 24–29
    George F. Browne commentary, 17–18
    as a piece of theological history, 62
    relationship to *De templo*, 47–55, 135
    scholarship in the twentieth century, 17–43
    Wilhelm Levison commentary, 18–21, 24, 42
Historia ecclesiastica gentis Anglorum (Bede), 68. See also *Ecclesiastical History of the English People* (Bede); *Historia*
historia ipsa, 41, 50–51
historical representation
    Bede's *Historia* and exegesis, 128–33
    contextualization and Bede's figural reading, 126–27
    logic of substitution, 119
    as proposal, 121–22
    relationship to Bede's figural reading, 123–25
    substitution theory of, 118–23
Historical Representation (Ankersmit), 114
historical task, objectivist or historicist approach to, 40
history
    defined by Constantin Fasolt, 6
    issues impacting the writing of, 136–45
history, sense of
    addressed by Peter Burke, 94–5
    sense of anachronism, 95–98
History of the Abbots
    commentary by George F. Browne, 17
Holder, Arthur, 45, 86–87
Hugh of Cluny, 31

hyperbaton, 36

In Ezram et Neeiam, 68
In genesim, 39, 64, 68, 83–87
Institutions (Cassiodorus), 100
Isidore of Seville, 65
ita. See *De templo*
Jenkins, Claude, 18, 21
Jerome, 34–5
Jones, Charles, 30, 34
    Bede's *Historia*, commentary on, 25–29, 42
    dating of *In genesim*, 68
    In genesim, description of Bede's commentary, 64
    historia, Bede's meaning of, 24
    History of the Abbots and *Life of St. Cuthbert*, comparison of, 26
    using the category of Romance to understand Bede, 126, 129

Kendall, Calvin, 77
    Bede's rhetorical posture and writing in *Historia*, 36–37, 43
    Bede's use of the language of *mysterium, allegoria, arcanum,* and *sacramentum*, 46
    dating of *In genesim*, 68
King Oswiu
    Synod at Whitby, 52–53

Letter to Egbert (Bede)
    George F. Browne commentary, 17
    perceived decline of the Church in northern Britain, 49
Levison, Wilhelm, 18–21, 24, 42
Life of St. Antony (Athanasius), 22
Life of St. Cuthbert (Bede), 17
Life of St. Wildrid (Eddius), 26
literal sense, 8–9

Manuel, Frank, 93
Mayr-Harting, Henry, 47
McCabe, Herbert, 138–40
Meyvaert, Paul, 30–31, 42

Nagel, Alexander, 108–10
narrative sentences defined, 127–28

161

Allegorizing History

nature and grace, theologies of, 11
  Bede's views on, 137–40
  difference in understanding between Bede and Augustine, 71, 140

O'Loughlin, Thomas
  the Genesis tradition, 65–66, 119, 140
On Christian Teaching (Augustine), 34, 102
On Genesis
  A Refutation of the Manichees (Augustine), 80
Origen, 7

Pelagian heresy, 22
Perpetual Virginity of Blessed Mary (Jerome), 27
Petrarca, Francesco. *See* Petrarch
Petrarch, 10, 97
Plummer, Carolus
  Bede's *Ecclesiastical History* (1896 edition), commentary on, 13–17, 24
  Bede's *Ecclesiastical History* (1896 edition), introduction to, 9, 42
  dating of *In genesim*, 68
  defense of Bede's figural exegesis, 93

Quine, W. V. O., 8, 115, 121

Ray, Roger
  comparison between Bede's exegesis and history, 33–36, 42
  revision of Colgrave's translation, 35
Ritter, Harry, 94, 98
Rogers, Eugene, 8

Salisbury, John, 31
Scripture
  1 Corinthians 5, 55, 56
  1 Corinthians 10, 39
  1 Kings 6, 53

2 Chronicles 4:8, Bede's commentary in *De templo,* 48–49
  Bede as exegete of, 45
  Bede's allegorical approach to, 13–16, 45–47
  Bede's use of biblical figures and their relationship to other historical events, 55–63
  Galatians 4, 46
  Genesis, Bede's commentary on, 47
  Genesis 1, Bede's literal exegesis, 10
  Numbers 21, 51
Sellars, Wilfrid, 8
signs, aspects of, 103–5
St. Bede. *See* Bede
Synod of Whitby (664 AD), 52–53

Teachers and Code-Breakers: The Latin Genesis Tradition 430-800 (O'Loughlin), 65
temple
  as a figure of Christ and the Church, 56
truths
  synthetic and analytic, 115–18, 121

uera lex historiae
  Cicero's classic definition of, 34
  in *Historia,* 28, 33–36
  Jerome's understanding of, 34–35

Valla, Lorenzo, 97
Venerable Bede: His Life and Writings, The (Browne), 17
Vision of St. Augustine, The (Carpaccio), 96

Ward, Benedicta
  Bede's use of miracle stories, 142–45
  defense of Bede's historical work, 31–32, 42
White, Hayden, 1
Wittgenstein, Ludwig, 4, 8
Wood, Christopher, 108–10
world ages
  difference in writing between Augustine and Bede, 85

www.ingramcontent.com/pod-product-compliance
Lightning Source LLC
Chambersburg PA
CBHW050816160426
43192CB00010B/1789